GEORG BÜCHNER

GEORG BÜCHNER

and the Birth of the Modern Drama

David G. Richards

State University of New York Press
Albany   1977

Georg Büchner
First Edition
Published by State University of New York Press
99 Washington Avenue, Albany, New York 12246
©1977 State University of New York
All rights reserved.

Composed by
Typography Services
Loudonville, New York 12211

Printed and made in the United States of America

Library of Congress Cataloging in Publication Data

Richards, David Gleyre, 1935-
Georg Büchner.
Bibliography: p.
Includes index.
1. Büchner, Georg, 1813-1837—Criticism and
interpretation.
PT1828.B6R5   831'.7   76-902
ISBN 0-87395-332-0
ISBN 0-87395-333-4 microfiche

To Peter Heller

CONTENTS

PREFACE

Büchner is one of those few seminal figures whose works constitute a turning point in the development of art: his three plays anticipate and have influenced almost every form of theater our century has created: "The psychological, the social-critical, the realistic, the naturalistic, the expressive, the surreal, the epic, the lyrical, and the 'gestic' (Beckett, Ionesco, Adamov) theater can refer to Georg Büchner as a source, and they do refer to him."[1] *Woyzeck* is one of the few plays Artaud wanted to stage as part of his program for a "Theater of Cruelty," a theater whose unique language is "half-way between gesture and thought."[2] The Documentary Theater of Peter Weiss, Rolf Hochhuth, and Heinar Kipphardt also has its source in Büchner's works, both directly and indirectly through Brecht. In some respects he shared the state of mind recognized by the representatives of Dada as the essence of their movement, and he also developed a technique of representation which anticipates Dada and Cubist collages in its striking, sometimes shocking, juxtapositions of contrasting elements and its use of fragmented, multi-faceted perspectives. Like Cézanne and Van Gogh in painting, Rimbaud in poetry, or Schönberg and Ives in music, Büchner broke with the past to discover new modes of perception, experience, and consciousness and to create the artistic means for expressing them. Each of his works represents a new departure and contains unique possibilities for further development.[3]

Although Büchner has now become recognized as the first modern playwright and has been the subject of numerous books and articles—more than 600 to date—relatively little has been written about him in English. In the hope that the present study, the most comprehensive yet to appear in English, will be useful for the general reader as well as for the specialist, I have translated all quotations from Büchner and from foreign scholarship. (If I have been guilty of any distortions or misrepresentations in these translations, it is entirely unintentional and with my apologies.) I think it is safe to assume that readers who prefer to consult the original texts will have ready access to Lehmann's or another edition of Büchner's works and to many, if not most, of the books and articles quoted.

The chapters of this study supplement each other, yet each one may stand alone. The introductory chapter provides a brief biography, including translations of key passages from Büchner's letters and other writings and from documents relating to Büchner. Most of this material has not yet been published in English. This chapter is meant to introduce Büchner to those not yet familiar with the details of his fascinating life, but also to correct some of the factual errors contained in some of the essays on Büchner published in this country. Readers already familiar with the major accounts of Büchner's life may wish to read only the part of this chapter that deals with his usually neglected, but revealing school essays (pp. 2-6). The contrast between these and his often quoted letter on determinism reveals a crisis of idealistic belief similar in nature and in its consequences to Heinrich von Kleist's "Kant-crisis."

Danton's Death is probably the most extraordinary first play ever written. Owing to its richness and complexity, it fairly demands a full-length study of its own. Since a one-sided, narrowly reductionistic approach cannot possibly do justice to this play, I have chosen to discuss a variety of topics and stylistic elements. If my essay proceeds by expansion and accretion rather than in a linear, expository manner, it can claim a certain affinity with its subject matter.

The chapter on *Leonce and Lena,* on the other hand, does have a definite orientation: by analyzing this play in terms of the traditional elements of comedy and the comic, I attempt to defend the author's generic designation against the large number of critics who prefer to focus on the play's serious, even tragic, content and implications. Since the difference is largely one of attitude, the reader may reject my thesis and still find validity in my interpretation. It is possible to laugh and cry at the same thing, even, as the theater of the absurd has taught us, at the same time.

In *Lenz* Büchner depicts with extraordinary empathy and accuracy the psychic breakdown of the Storm and Stress dramatist J. M. R. Lenz. In this work Büchner's scientific attitude and medical interest in the nervous system, the brain, and the psyche, which are apparent in all of his works, combine with and entirely complement his poetic sensibilities in the creation of what has come to be recognized as a classic study of schizophrenia, a psychic disorder not yet isolated or named in Büchner's own time. My study follows Lenz's development and focuses on the medical accuracy and the artistic skill with which Büchner captures and recreates the fluctuating psychic condition of his subject.

Woyzeck contains Büchner's final statement on the nature of man and his role as a social animal. Before one can analyze and interpret this unfinished work, however, one must first come to terms with the problems involved in constructing a valid text. Readers may be surprised to discover that the text I propose deviates significantly from the text or texts with which they are familiar, since previous editors and translators have incorporated varying amounts of unauthorized material in their constructions, either by adding whole scenes from earlier manuscripts or by fleshing out or otherwise altering completed scenes. Through careful analysis of the extant manuscripts and the application of sound principles of editing I will delimit the narrow range of valid constructions and propose what I consider to be the best solution. Readers wishing to skip over this technical argumentation will find a complete text of my construction in the appendix. Also contained in the appendix is a brief survey of the reception of Büchner's works in the theater.

I am indebted to the Bouvier Verlag of Bonn, Germany, for permission to publish the chapter on *Woyzeck* in this English version. I wish to thank all those who have contributed, either directly or indirectly, to this study. I am especially grateful to Heinz Politzer, in whose seminar at Berkeley I first became interested in Büchner; to my friend and colleague Peter Heller for continued encouragement and valuable criticism; and to my wife Annegret for her patient support, for the many hours she has spent transforming barely legible manuscripts into clear typescript, and for preparing the index.

I. GEORG BÜCHNER, 1813-1837

Family Background

Büchner's father was pleased by his son's decision to study medicine as he, his father, and his father's father had done, but he was angered, embarrassed and disappointed by the younger Büchner's revolutionary political activities. Ernst Büchner had proudly served as a doctor in Napoleon's army; his ability and patriotism earned him the prestigious position of chief medical councilor in Darmstadt, the capital of Hesse. As a monarchist and prospering high civil servant, he had no reason to hope for a change in the existing political situation.

Büchner's loving, sensitive mother came from an old, upper middle class family of civil servants. Whereas her husband admired Napoleon—as the man who destroyed the French Revoluton—and things French, she sympathized with the national struggle for liberation; and whereas he was a positivist and atheist, she was deeply Christian, undogmatic and quietly secure in her faith. It was she who stimulated the imagination of their children and taught them to love nature and poetry. From her lips the young Büchner heard the fairy tales and folk songs he never ceased to love, and through her he was first introduced to the poetry of Schiller, Theodor Körner, and Friedrich von Matthisson and to the prose of Jean Paul.

At least two of Büchner's four siblings were better known than he throughout most of the nineteenth century: Ludwig was the author of *Force and Matter*, a popular and influential book on philosophical materialism; Luise was one of the most successful women writers of the time and an early champion of the feminist movement. Another brother, Wilhelm, a pharmacist and chemist, perfected a recently discovered method for producing artificial ultramarine and became wealthy as the owner of a dye factory. As deputy to the Hessian Diet and the Imperial Parliament, he also published political writings. After taking part in the revolution of 1848, Alexander became a respected professor of literature at a French university. Despite similar interests and outstanding contributions in pursuits related to those of their older brother, none of Büchner's siblings had any inkling of his true accomplishments, and all were embarassed by his political radicalism.

School in Darmstadt

While Büchner's interest was primarily in the natural sciences, the *Gymnasium* he had to attend in Darmstadt was more oriented to humanistic studies. Marginal comments in his school notebooks reveal that he was often bored by the uselessness and lifelessness of his studies. He enjoyed reading great works of literature, especially Shakespeare, but preferred doing so with his friends in an outdoor setting. Before *Danton's Death* he had never tried his hand at creative writing except to produce a few occasional poems in the manner of Matthisson. Unlike the poetry, his school essays reveal considerable independence of thought and the workings of a clear, logical, and bold mind. Comparison of the youthful idealism they disclose with later expressions of disillusionment will help to explain the crisis which accompanied the destruction of his boyhood beliefs and ideals.

In each of his three major essays Büchner deals with suicide, which he considered an affirmation of the existence of free will. By taking his own life or by freely sacrificing his life in a noble cause, a man can assert his freedom of will and his power of self-determination. Schiller's influence is clearly visible in Büchner's idealistic passion for freedom and in the language he uses to describe it: "It is grand and sublime to see man in his struggle with nature, as he forcefully opposes the fury of the unleashed elements and, trusting in the force of his spirit, subjects the raw forces of nature to his will. But it is even more sublime to see man fighting with his fate, when he dares to intervene in the course of world history, when he commits his highest and his all to the accomplishments of his goal (II.25).[1]

Whether he succeeds or fails, the heroic quality of the effort itself ensures his immortality. Especially praiseworthy are those men who have given their lives in the heroic fight for freedom. Büchner singles out Cato as a man whose "great soul was completely filled by the boundless feeling for fatherland and freedom which inspired his life," and who preferred death to life as a slave under the tyrannical rule of Julius Caesar. Cato could have withstood the fall of his country, had he been able to find "asylum for the other goddess of his life, for freedom." But when the "sacredness of the laws was violated and the altar of freedom destroyed," Cato was the only person in the world to take his own life in order not to live in bondage as a slave among slaves. "The Roman knew only *one* freedom: the law he submits to from *free* choice as being *necessary*; Caesar had destroyed this freedom; Cato was a slave if he yielded to the law of arbitrariness. *And if Rome was not worthy of freedom, freedom itself was worth living and dying for*" (II.29). In the hope of securing freedom of belief for future generations of their countrymen, the legendary Pforzheim soldiers, 400 in number, willingly sacrificed themselves in battle against the invading French troops during the Thirty Years' War: "thus, they did not even die for their own faith, not for themselves, but they bled for posterity. This is the most sublime thought for which one can sacrifice oneself, this is death for redemption of the world [*Welt-Erlöser-Tod*]" (II.13-14). Both Cato and the Pforzheim soldiers exercised their free will in performing acts of world-historical significance. Cato's suicide served as an indictment against tyranny, as an example to his fellow citizens, and as a logical conclusion of a life dedicated to the pursuit of freedom. The heroic self-sacrifice of the Pforzheim soldiers supposedly furthered the cause of freedom in Europe in much the same way as did the French Revolution.

Related to the problem of suicide is Büchner's attitude toward Christianity and the Christian dogma. In the essay on Cato he avoids a direct confrontation with Christianity by simply pointing out the untenability of judging the deeds of a Roman from a Christian perspective. A person must be judged from the standpoint of his time, his beliefs, and his character. As a Roman and a Stoic, Cato's action was completely justifiable and admirably heroic. In an earlier essay Büchner discusses suicide in more detail and states his attitude toward

Christianity more explicitly than in the essay on Cato, which
was written for public delivery as a valedictory address. In
opposition to the Christian view of the earth as a testing ground
and life as a means to some other end, he believes "that life is
its own end, for *development* is the goal of life; *life itself* is
development; therefore life is its *own goal*" (II.21).

If the purpose or end of life is considered to be life itself, the
only valid argument that can be made against suicide is the fact
that it contravenes nature and our purpose "by destroying
prematurely the *form* of life which is compatible with our
purpose and which nature has given us." There are circumstances, however, in which such an act is warranted. If a man's
condition becomes unbearable, it is in his nature to attempt to
change it and make it more tolerable, even when the result of
such a change is uncertain. Thus, if life itself becomes in-
tolerable, one might wish to escape it and risk the uncertainty
that gave Hamlet pause. The only criterion for judging someone who takes his own life is a subjective one, according to
Büchner, and any religious dogma which does not accept this
criterion is false, at least in this one regard, since "our religion
cannot forbid us from recognizing and respecting any *truth*,
magnanimity, *goodness*, and *beauty* besides itself, and it can
never permit us to disapprove of an action *recognized as moral*
because it is not in accord with one of its teachings. What is
moral must remain *moral* from *every* standpoint and according
to *every* doctrine" (II.20). Büchner carefully points out that he
is not condemning Christianity itself, but those who misinterpret it; and he argues rather sophistically that since Christianity is founded upon the principle of morality, it could not
condemn a moral act such as Cato's suicide. Besides defending
suicide for moral and patriotic reasons, Büchner also agrees
with Goethe's Werther in not considering the self-inflicted
death of someone suffering from physical or mental illness
to be suicide at all. Such a person has simply succumbed to
his illness (II.22).

Through the exercise of their free will, some men are able
to rise above the "disgraceful egoism" and animalism of the
masses of people and perform courageous deeds of world-historical importance:

I only need direct my attention to the fight which shook the
world just a few years ago, which furthered in one mighty

leap the development of mankind by more than a century, which revenged in a bloody but just war of extermination the atrocities that infamous despots had perpetrated on suffering humanity for centuries, which illuminated with its sunny rays of freedom the fog which hung heavily over the peoples of Europe and showed them that Providence had not destined them for the games of arbitrary despots. I mean the French fight for freedom. (II.8)

While the Germans seem to be sleeping at the moment, the young schoolboy can claim with pride that his people fought the noblest fight, the fight for freedom of belief:

The Greeks fought their heroic fight against the collected force of Asia, the Romans triumphed over the ruins of Carthage, the French gained Europe's political freedom, but the Germans fought the most glorious fight: they fought for freedom of belief; they fought for the light of enlightenment; they fought for man's highest and holiest possession. This fight was the first act of the great battle that mankind is fighting against its oppressors, just as the French Revolution was the second. As soon as thought was no longer bound in chains, mankind recognized its rights and its worth. All the improvements we now enjoy are the results of the Reformation, without which the world would have taken on a completely different appearance, without which eternal darkness would rule where the light of the Enlightenment now shines, and without which the human race that now raises itself to ever freer, ever more sublime thoughts would, like the animals, be deprived of its human dignity. (II.9)

Büchner is painfully aware that the time is not yet right for his countrymen to add a third act to the historical drama representing man's progress toward freedom and reason. He can only hope that they will at least regain a sense of national pride and not throw away the freedom won for them by their ancestors:

Oh, you Germans! In your provinces the most beautiful and glorious deed took place, a deed that ennobles the entire nation, a deed whose fruits you still enjoy; and you have forgotten the heroes who accomplished it, who dedicated themselves to death for you. You gape at things foreign in cold admiration, whereas you could suck glowing enthusiasm

for everything noble from the breast of your country. . . .
You no longer have to fight against external forces; your
freedom is secure against all challenges. . . . But still you
are not free, Germany. Your spirit lies in chains; you are
losing your nationality: In the same way you are now a slave
of things foreign, you soon will be a slave of foreigners.
(II.14-15)

The pessimism, cynicism, and despair later expressed in *Danton's Death* and the other poetic works is a pole apart from the
schoolboy's affirmation of free will, heroism, and such historical events as the French Revolution. Such a radical change
obviously presupposes a disillusionment of critical intensity.

Werner R. Lehmann has demonstrated that Büchner's concept of historical progress and his belief that the Reformation
led inevitably to the French Revolution was taken from Fichte's
Addresses to the German Nation (1807-1808).[2] Despite the fact
that the *Addresses* had been forbidden since 1824 by Metter-
nich's censorship, Büchner boldly incorporated passages from
them in his own essay, which was probably written shortly
before the revolution of 1830. Büchner's emphasis on life as its
own reason for being and its own end also agrees with Fichte's
philosophy. While it is interesting from the standpoint of intellectual history to locate this source of some of Büchner's
material and to note that his practice of freely borrowing from
others does not originate with the poetic works, it is also important to realize that he only borrows another person's voice
when it corresponds with and supports his own. Büchner's
reaction to the destruction of the beliefs and ideals expressed
in these essays clearly indicates how fundamental they were
to him.

Büchner was described by his school friends as being a
"quiet, thorough, somewhat reserved observer," who was slow
and carefully selective in choosing friends, but warm, even
enthusiastic, with those who shared his interest in what he
considered true or authentic life, his love of nature, and his
desire to keep abreast of current political and cultural developments. His friends recognized him as the "most outstanding,
independent, and energetic" member of their group. He went

"quickly and directly to the heart of what he recognized to be the essence and core of things . . . in all things his principle was freedom." He and his friend Minnigerode, who later became involved with him in the attempt to revolutionize the Hessian peasants, always greeted each other in their later school years with the words: *"Bon jour, citoyen."* Büchner was "entirely independent in thought and action through his striving for substantiality and truth." He was completely unimpressed by inconsequential appearances or by external authority, and he rejected dogmatism in every form, whether in society, philosophy, or art. "He deeply despised those who deceive themselves and others with trivial platitudes instead of seeking to gain truth for themselves and to impart it to others."[3] He was boldly skeptical toward religion, but tolerant of the ideas and beliefs of others. His taste for literature reflected his love for truth and authenticity. Among his favorites were Shakespeare, Homer, Goethe, all folk literature, Aeschylus, and Sophocles, followed by Jean Paul and the major Romantics. He admired Schiller, but objected to the artificiality of his rhetorical language. His favorite work of German literature was Goethe's *Faust* (B.556). One of the friends with whom Büchner read literature and discussed philosophy was convinced that his "unforgettable boyhood friend and *commilito in literis* was born to be a philosopher rather than a poet" (B.554).

Strasbourg

There was never any doubt in Büchner's mind but that he would become a physician like his father and grandfather. In the fall of 1831 he began his medical studies at the University of Strasbourg. His mother had relatives there who could look out for and keep an eye on him, and his father, a Francophile, was eager to have his son become acquainted with French life, culture, and politics, little realizing how much things had changed since he had served in Napoleon's army.

Strasbourg was a gathering place for both German and French revolutionaries. Its intellectual life and literature were predominantly German, but politically it was a part of France. Its citizens had taken part in the Revolution and had gained political rights and a degree of individual freedom unknown by their German neighbors, who were still oppressed by serfdom and at the mercy of the aristocracy. Whereas the political opposition in Germany had always suffered from the political indifference of the people and from its inability to convert ideas and ideologies into deeds, the people of France took an active interest in politics and had recently learned how to turn theory into practice. Büchner soon became an eager and receptive student. Only a few months after his arrival in Strasbourg he joined a group of students in breaking through a line of armed guards in order to celebrate Ramorino, one of the generals who had led the abortive uprising of the Poles in their fight for freedom:

> We gathered in the Academy. As we wanted to proceed through the gate, the officer, who had received orders from the government not to let us pass with the [black] flag, drew up an armed guard to prevent us. But we broke through with force and took our stand, three or four hundred strong, on the Rhine bridge. The National Guard joined us. Finally Ramorino appeared, accompanied by a host of cavalry. A student gives a speech to which he replies, and so does a National Guardsman. The National Guard surrounds the coach and pulls it. With our flag we take the head of the procession, which is preceded by a large chorus. Thus we march into the city, accompanied by a huge mass of people singing the Marseillaise and the Carmagnole. Everywhere the cry is heard: *vive la liberté! vive Ramorino! à bas les ministres! à bas le juste milieu!* (II.413: after 4 December 1831)

Büchner's letter to his parents may have been written the day of the demonstration and clearly betrays, notably in the shift from the imperfect to the present tense as he relives the event, the excitement he still feels and his enthusiastic commitment to the cause of freedom. Then, fearing how this news will be received at home, he belatedly tries to make the whole thing out to have been a playful prank, a "comedy." In a subsequent letter he freely admits that he would take up a rifle if the Russian oppressors of the Poles should cross the Oder river. Referring to the Russian Czar and his allies the Monarchs of Prussia and Austria, Büchner writes: "God may be merciful to the most illustrious and annointed jackasses [*den allerdurchlauchtigsten und gesalbten Schafsköpfen*]. Hopefully, they will no longer find mercy on earth" (II.414: December 1831).

When a group of about fifty naive and poorly organized conspirators attempted in April 1833 to stage a putsch in Frankfort, Büchner's fearful parents inquired of their son, whose political tendencies were now quite clear to them, whether or not he had been involved. Büchner immediately answered that he had not taken part in what had occurred and that he would not take part in what might still occur, not because he condemned such action, nor because he was afraid, but only because he believed that the time for revolution had not yet come, and because he did not "share the delusions of those who saw in the Germans a people ready to fight for its rights. This crazy opinion led to the events in Frankfort, and the error was very costly." Still, the use of force is justified, he maintained, for it is only through force that the people can wrest their human rights from the ruling oppressors: "If anything can help now, it is *force*. We know what we can expect from our sovereigns. Everything they have granted was wrested from them by necessity. . . . Are we not in an eternal state of force?" What follows this statement anticipates the message and tone of *The Hessian Courier* and sounds the chord of cynical pessimism later developed in *Danton's Death:*

> Because we are born and raised in prison, we no longer notice that we are stuck in a hole, with chained hands and feet and with gags in our mouths. What do you call the *lawful state [gesetzlichen Zustand]*? *A law* that makes the great masses of citizens into toiling cattle, in order to satisfy the unnatural cravings of an insignificant and spoiled minority? And this law, supported by a brutal military force and the foolish cunning of its agents, this law is an *eternal, brutal force* which violates justice and sound reason, and I will fight against it with *word* and *deed* wherever I can. (II.416: 5 April 1833)

Büchner recognized that revolutions are not brought about by the agitations of idealists and intellectuals, but by the angry uprisings of the masses: "I will always act according to my principles, though *recently* I have learned that only the urgent need of the great masses can bring about changes, that all activity and shouting of the *individual* is idle foolishness. They write, but no one reads them; they shout, but no one hears them; they act, but no one helps them" (II.418: June 1833).

Giessen

According to the laws of Büchner's native Hesse, he could not study more than two years on foreign soil. Consequently he had to leave Strasbourg and continue his studies at the Hessian State University in Giessen. Shortly before his departure, he assured his worried parents that he did not intend to get involved in the local "backwoods politics and childish revolutionary pranks" (II.418: June 1833).

Büchner returned reluctantly and sorrowfully to a land in which all opposition to the existing political system, whether in word or deed, was forbidden and in which social injustice and the brutal oppression and exploitation of the poor prevailed. He hated also to take leave of the outstanding young men, mostly students of medicine and theology, who had become his friends, and of his fiancée Minna (Wilhelmine) Jaegle, daughter of the prominent pastor in whose house he had resided.

Büchner describes his emotional and physical response to the unwelcome change in a letter to his friend August Stöber: "I often feel a true homesickness for your mountains. Everything here is so narrow and small. Nature and people, the most petty surroundings which do not interest me even for a moment. At the end of October I went from here [he is writing from Darmstadt] to Giessen. I spent five weeks there, half in muck and half in bed. I had an attack of brain fever; the illness was suppressed while just beginning, but I was still forced to return to Darmstadt in order to recover there completely" (II.421: 9 December 1833).

The poet is distinguished from other men, according to Goethe's Tasso, by his ability to express or explain his suffering. Büchner's example supports this statement, for it was his inner need to express and give form to his pain and anguish that awakened the poet in him. The letter to Stöber contains a hint of things to come: "Since the Wednesday evening five weeks ago when I last stuck my hands out of the carriage door to grasp yours, it seems to me as if they were broken off, and I think we squeeze each other's hands all the more firmly, the less frequently we extend them to each other" (II.421). The striking image Büchner uses here to express his inner state anticipates the fully developed poetic description contained in a letter to Minna written about three months later, parts of which appear still later in several of the poetic works:

The first bright moment in a week. Unending headache and fever. In the night scarcely a few hours of inadequate rest. I don't get to bed before 2 o'clock, and then repeated abrupt awakenings from sleep and a sea of thoughts in which my senses fail me. My silence tortures you as it does me, but I had no control over myself. Dear, dear soul, do you forgive me? I just came in from outside. A single, reverberating tone from the throats of a thousand larks sounds through the brooding summer air; heavy clouds wander above the earth; the deep roaring of the wind sounds like their melodic steps. The spring air has freed me from my catalepsy [*Starrkrampf*]. I was afraid of myself. The feeling of being dead has always hung over me. Everyone looked at me from death-masks, eyes glazed, cheeks like wax. And when the whole machinery then began to grind: the joints jerked, the voice creaked, and I heard the eternal organ-song warbling and saw the barrels and pins in the organ revolving and jumping—I cursed the concert, the instrument, the melody and—oh, we poor screaming musicians. The groaning on our racks: does it only exist in order to force its way through the rifts in the clouds and resound further and further until it dies like a melodious breath in heavenly ears? Could we be the sacrifice in the glowing stomach of Perilaos's steer[4] whose dying screams sound like the delightful cries of the God-steer consuming itself in the flames? I do not blaspheme. But the people blaspheme. And yet I am punished; I am afraid of my voice and—of my mirror. I could have sat for Callot-Hoffmann, couldn't I, my love? For modeling I could have received money to travel. I sense that I am beginning to become interesting. (II.424: 10 March 1834)

As if embarrassed by his poetic effusions, Büchner explains that he cannot work and that he has been overcome by a dull brooding in which he scarcely has a clear thought. "Everything is consumed within me. If only I had an outlet for what is inside me. But I have no cry for the pain, no shout for the joy, no harmony for the happiness. This silence is my damnation" (II.425). He attempts in this letter to gain clarity, to come to terms with his thoughts and feeling, and to relieve internal tensions and pressures by expressing, in the literal sense of forcing out, what was pent up inside him. It was written more for his own benefit than to communicate with Minna: "I have told you a thousand times already: don't read my letters—cold, sluggish words! If I could only pour a full tone over you; but in this way I drag you into my confused labyrinth. You sit now in your dark room alone with your tears; soon I will join you" (II.425).

It is not primarily the suffering and discomfort of illness, but, as the following letter makes clear, the absence of feeling and emotion about which Büchner complains:

> I curse my health. I was burning; the fever covered me with kisses and embraced me like the arms of my beloved. Darkness hovered over me. My heart swelled in boundless longing. Stars penetrated through the darkness and hands and lips bent down. And now? And otherwise? I do not even have the pleasure of pain and longing. Since I crossed the Rhine bridge, it is as if I were dead inside. Not a single feeling arises in me. I'm an automaton: my soul has been taken. (II.426: after 10 March 1834)

In *Lenz*, Büchner describes a similar state of inner numbness and deathlike rigidity as being symptomatic of the complete breakdown of the psyche.

Even allowing for some poetic exaggeration in Büchner's description of his condition, it is doubtful whether a disagreeable change in environment and the misery of illness could account for such an extreme state, and in fact, Büchner's letters reveal the occurrence of a much deeper and far more disturbing crisis, one involving the loss of his most cherished ideals and beliefs. Just before complaining to Minna about his inner numbness, he writes:

> I studied the history of the Revolution. I felt annihilated by the dreadful fatalism of history. I find in human nature a terrible uniformity, in human relations an inevitable force given to all [collectively] and to none [individually]. The individual is only foam on the wave; greatness is simply chance; the rule of genius is a puppet play, a ridiculous struggle against a pitiless law: to recognize it is the ultimate; to control it is impossible. It no longer occurs to me to bow to the parade horses and loafers of history. I accustomed myself to the sight of blood. But I am not the blade of a guillotine. *Must*

is one of the damning words with which man is baptized. The saying: offences must come, but woe to that man by whom the offence comes—is gruesome. What is it in us that lies, murders, steals? I don't want to pursue the thought. If only I could lay this cold and martyred heart on your breast! (II.425-426)[5]

After previously having celebrated heroism as the highest expression of man's freedom, he now discovers that man is no more than a puppet or an automaton whose actions are determined by forces he does not and cannot control. Without free will there can be no heroic deeds, nor any meaningful action whatsoever. Man can neither determine his own development nor willfully alter the course of history. Nor can he affect changes in the social or political structure of society. No longer can the likes of Cato, the Pforzheim soldiers, or the French revolutionaries inspire Büchner with their "sublime," selflessly heroic deeds.

Büchner's disillusioning discovery did not prevent him, however, from taking a leading role in an abortive attempt to overthrow the government. Motivated by the disgust engendered in him by renewed contact with the restrictions and injustices of the police state and by the sympathy he felt for the people who barely existed on a subhuman level while their productive labor enabled others to live in luxury, Büchner felt compelled to take up the cause of the masses of people who were too submissive and ignorant to help themselves.[6] "The political situation could drive me mad," he wrote to August Stöber. "The poor people tow the cart upon which the aristocrats and liberals play their fools' comedy. I pray every evening to rope and the street lamps" (II.422: 9 December 1833).

Büchner stood almost alone among the German revolutionaries of the time in his views on the goals and process of revolution. Whereas the liberals and the politically oriented students' associations *(Burschenschaften)* wanted to reestablish a unified German Empire under the strong leadership of an Emperor whose office would be hereditary, Büchner wanted to do away with the ruling class and establish a democratic, republican system of government that would recognize the equality of all men and eliminate the social injustice and material want which results from the exploitation of the poor by the rich and powerful. Such a revolution could only be accomplished, Büchner believed, by the people who stood to benefit most from it: the peasants and craftsmen. He considered the tactics advocated and occasionally even practiced by the student groups to be naive and ineffective. He must have had them in mind when he referred to the "revolutionary pranks" of Giessen's "backwood politics." He disagreed also with the bourgeois revolutionaries, whose main interest in overthrowing the government was to gain more power and wealth for themselves. Nor could he sympathize with the "revolution from above" as represented by the German intellectuals such as Heinrich Heine, Ludwig Börne, and the Young Germans. The intellectuals wanted above all to be free of censorship and to acquire freedom of speech and press; they believed that once the masses were sufficiently informed, freedom and equality would automatically follow.

Büchner criticizes this approach in a letter to Karl Gutzkow, one of the group's major representatives:

Incidentally, to be honest, you and your friends do not appear to me to have taken the smartest course. For the *educated* class to reform society by means of *ideas*? Impossible! Our time is entirely *material*. If you had proceeded more directly in a political fashion, you soon would have reached a point where the reform would have stopped on its own. You will never overcome the rift between the educated and the uneducated.

I have become convinced that the educated and wealthy minority, despite the many concessions it wants from the ruling power, will never give up its advantageous relationship to the masses. And the masses themselves? For them there are only two levers, material misery and *religious fanaticism*. Any party that knows how to use these levers will win. Our age needs iron and bread—and then a *cross* or something of that sort. I believe that one must proceed in social matters from an absolute principle of *justice,* that one must look for the formation of a new spiritual life in the *people* and let the effete modern society go to the devil. To what purpose should such a thing run around between heaven and earth? Its whole life consists only of attempts to drive away its terrible boredom. It may die out; that is the only novelty it can still experience. (II.455)

And again:

> The whole revolution has already split into Liberals and
> Absolutists and has to be swallowed by the uneducated and
> poor class. The relationship between poor and rich is the
> only revolutionary element in the world. Only hunger can
> become the goddess of freedom and only a Moses who would
> send the seven plagues of Egypt upon us could become a
> Messiah. Fatten the peasants, and the revolution gets apo-
> plexy. A *chicken* in the pot of every peasant causes the Gallic
> *rooster* to die. (II.441)

Büchner's ideas on the goals and tactics of revolution were
influenced by his study of the French revolutions and his direct
association with revolutionaries and revolutionary organiza-
tions in Strasbourg. Following the pattern of the most radical of
the French secret societies, the *Société des Droits de l'Homme,*
some of whose meetings he had no doubt attended in Strasbourg, Büchner founded in Giessen and later in Darmstadt two
sections of the *Gesellschaft der Menschenrechte* (Society for
Human Rights). Unlike the elitist, liberal student fraternities,
Büchner's society was constituted democratically of common
people and craftsmen as well as intellectuals and students. To
achieve its aim, which was nothing less than the revolutionary
overthrow of the government and the establishment of a democratic republic, members were trained in the use of weapons
and in the preparation and distribution of propaganda.

By the time the society was founded in March 1834, Büchner
had already made contact with Friedrich Ludwig Weidig, a
pastor and schoolmaster, who was also an experienced revolutionary and active propagandist. Büchner could not agree with
Weidig's desire to establish a unified German Empire with a
more or less democratic constitution, but he did agree with him
in recognizing that the revolution could not succeed without
the active support of the masses. The first step to success, then,
was to reach, win over, and arouse the people through the
extensive use of propaganda. To that end Weidig welcomed the
support of Büchner's keen analytical mind and powerful gift
of persuasion, and Büchner was glad to find an experienced
collaborator who had access to a printing press. The fruit of
this collaboration was what Viëtor calls "the most caustic and
brilliant of all the political pamphlets from the period of German reactionism."[7]

The Hessian Courier

Büchner wrote *The Hessian Courier* in the early spring of 1834. When Weidig read it, he was impressed by the lucidity and persuasiveness of Büchner's arguments, but shocked by their radicalism. He would not consent to have the pamphlet printed until Büchner agreed, however reluctantly, to let him revise it. Weidig had learned that the politically naive peasants were more likely to accept political arguments if they were supported by Biblical quotations and placed in a Christian context, since this was a language and a frame of reference they could understand and to which they could relate. Although these revisions weakened and distorted some of his arguments, Büchner could see their merit and was willing to accept them. But when Weidig also toned down the pamphlet's socialist tendency, he objected bitterly.

Büchner was the first of the German revolutionaries to consider the state to be the instrument of feudal class-rule, to interpret the existent situation from an economic and social standpoint, and to give his propaganda a social-revolutionary orientation.[8] He denounces and reviles the kind of state government which imposes heavy and unjust taxes on the peasants, sanctions the exploitation of their labor, and makes it possible for a small group of aristocrats and powerful representatives of the bourgeoisie to profit from their productivity. Not just the aristocrats, but the rich in general are identified by Büchner as the true enemy of the poor. But since Weidig did not want to offend and antagonize the wealthy bourgeois liberals on whose support he counted, he substituted the designation "the aristocrats" wherever Büchner had written "the rich." Besides interpolating some of his own ideas about constitutions and the rights of the people, Weidig also added a preface and reworked the conclusion. Büchner was so angered by these changes and additions that he no longer wanted to recognize the pamphlet as his own. He claimed that Weidig had deleted precisely those parts of the argument which he considered most important and which justified all the rest of it.[9] But Büchner finally accepted these changes, too, in order to get his pamphlet printed.

A major source of information about the origin and purpose of *The Hessian Courier* is the court record of the hearings of August Becker, a close friend of Büchner's and a member of the Giessen section of the Society for Human Rights.[10] At a time when his testimony could no longer harm those involved, he cooperated as the principal witness in the investigation of Weidig's revolutionary activities and provided the court with the requested information. When asked to discuss the purpose and the thesis of the *Courier*, Becker claimed that he could remember Büchner's words well enough to let the author speak for himself. Büchner argued, according to Becker, that all attempts to change the political system in Germany would continue to fail until the revolutionaries could muster more than the usual handful of undisciplined liberals to throw against the armies commanded by the various German governments. The only way to win the support of the politically indifferent peasants, according to Büchner, was through their purses. Material want is the first prerequisite of revolution.

In *The Hessian Courier*, Büchner uses richly metaphorical, strikingly graphical, predominantly rhetorical language to depict the contrast between the comfortable, extravagant life of the rich and the miserable, subhuman life of the peasants:

> The life of the aristocrats is a long Sunday: they live in beautiful houses; they wear elegant clothes; they have plump faces and speak a language of their own. The people, however, lie in front of them like manure in the fields. The peasant walks behind the plow, but the aristocrat walks behind him and the plow and drives him along with the oxen. The aristocrat takes the grain and leaves him the stubble. The life of the peasant is a long workday: strangers devour his field before his eyes; his body is a callus; his sweat is the salt on the aristocrats' table. (II.34, 36)

By using statistics obtained from Weidig, Büchner shows how the taxes of the poor are used to pay the bills of the rich. The poor also provide the rich with their servants, their prostitutes and—what terrible irony—with the very soldiers the rich use to protect themselves against and to suppress the poor:

> For those 900,000 gulden [for the military] your sons must swear allegiance to the tyrants and stand guard at their palaces. With their drums they drown out your sighs; with their clubs they crush your skulls whenever you dare to think that you are free men. They are the lawful murderers who

protect the lawful robbers. Think of Södel! [A peasant rebellion of 1830 which was crushed by the military.] Your
brothers and children murdered their own brothers and
fathers. (II.40)

He urges the people to discover for themselves how their
money is being used:

Go to Darmstadt and see how your masters enjoy themselves at
your expense. Then tell your starving wives and children that
their bread has stuck wonderfully onto strange stomachs.
Tell them of the beautiful clothes that are dyed in their sweat
and of the delicate ribbons cut from the calluses of their
hands. Tell them about the stately houses that are built from
the bones of the people. Then crawl into your smoky huts
and bend over your stony fields so that one day your children
can go there too—when a hereditary prince and a hereditary
princess want to find a means of creating another hereditary
prince—look through the open glass doors at the tablecloth
from which your masters eat, and smell the lamps which
provide light from the fat of the peasants. You endure all that
because the scoundrels tell you: "This government is from
God." This government is not from God, but from the father
of lies. (II.44, 46)

The state, he argues, consists of all its inhabitants, and the
laws of the state should exist for the protection and benefit of
everyone. Where the facts do not agree with the ideal, something should be done about it.

Büchner then directs the readers' attention to a land in
which something was done about it. The French decided that
the King is a man like all other men. Through his office he is
the first servant of the State. As such, he is responsible to the
people and can be replaced if he does not fulfill his duties
properly. The French also proclaimed that rights, privileges, or
titles cannot be inherited or purchased, and that government
should be democratic. The will of the majority should be represented by laws, and these laws should be uniformly enforced
by elected representatives. The French people got rid of their
King when he did not keep his promise to uphold the constitution. Frightened sovereigns of other European countries inter-
vened on behalf of the French King, but were defeated by the

people. After having resisted the force of kings, however, the French people succumbed to the promise of glory: by putting Napoleon on the throne, they sold out their own freedom. Napoleon's defeat led to the reinstatement of a hereditary monarchy, and in 1830 revolution broke out again. To pacify their rebelling subjects and avoid revolution in their own countries, many sovereigns promised their subjects constitutions. Unfortunately, the people trusted them and were betrayed by sham documents. Büchner hoped through his pamphlet to arouse the people from the apathy and false complacency which hypocritic promises and meaningless constitutions had engendered in them. "You are nothing; you have nothing!" he tells them. "You are without rights. You must give what your insatiable oppressors demand and bear the burden they impose on you."[11]

Anyone caught reading or even in possession of such a pamphlet could be tried for high treason, and some were. As Carl Vogt, a fellow student of Büchner's, relates in his memoirs, it made no difference how one came into possession of such material or whether or not guilt was proven:

> I knew people who were driven from their homes, torn away from thriving businesses and forced to earn their bread with great effort in a foreign country, simply because a spy had found a package of the odious journal under their gate, where it had been placed by some unknown person. I knew others who were held for years in the most miserable solitary confinement, where every activity, even of a manual nature, was denied them with refined cruelty, and who were then acquitted and dismissed as broken men from imprisonment and from an investigation which had yielded nothing. One of my cousins, Gladbach, spent, if I am not mistaken, fully eight years in this way.[12]

Little wonder, then, that most of the cowed and frightened peasants dutifully turned in their unread copies to the police. Germany obviously was not yet ready for revolutionary change. In the words of Becker:

> With the political pamphlet he wrote, Büchner wanted first of all simply to discover the mood of the people and the Ger-

man revolutionaries. When he later heard that the peasants had delivered most of the pamphlets they had found to the police, and when he learned that even the patriots had spoken out against it, he gave up all his political hopes for change. He did not believe that the *constitutional* opposition would be able to bring about a truly free condition in Germany. If these people should succeed, he said, in overthrowing the German governments and in introducing a general monarchy or even a republic, then we will get a monied aristocracy here as in France: it would be better if things remain as they are.[13]

But even without the timidity of the peasants and the opposition of the patriots, this bold adventure was doomed from the start by betrayal from within. Distribution of the *Courier* was undertaken by members of Büchner's Society for Human Rights as well as by some of Weidig's friends and collaborators. Among the latter was a Judas, who had been selling his knowledge to the state for some time. In the night of 30 July Karl Minnigerode, Jakob Schütz, and Karl Zeuner went to Offenbach, where the pamphlet had been secretly printed. The following day Zeuner returned to Weidig's house with an unknown number of copies for distribution under Weidig's direction. Returning with his copies to Giessen, Büchner's friend Minnigerode ran into the arms of the waiting police. As soon as Büchner heard about Minnigerode's arrest, he went to Butzbach to warn Weidig and Zeuner and then by night to Offenbach to warn Schütz, who left the next day for France.

When Büchner returned to Giessen, he found that his room had been searched and his letters and papers confiscated. Although he could have no idea how much was known about his participation in the conspiracy and his authorship of the treasonous pamphlet, he immediately called on the judge to express his indignation and lodge a formal complaint. The judge, Konrad Georgi, held a warrant for Büchner's arrest, but he was so confused and overwhelmed by Büchner's bold display of righteous indignation that he released him with his apologies. The search of Büchner's room had failed to uncover any incriminating evidence, and Georgi probably did not know why the arrest had been ordered. Büchner's voluntary appearance and indignant protestations convinced him that he would need more information before proceeding in the matter.

After warning Schütz in Offenbach, Büchner had proceeded to Frankfort, where he visited his friend from Strasbourg, Eugen Boeckel. Probably reckoning with the possibility of his arrest, Büchner had written his parents from Frankfort and informed them that he was traveling without a pass. This was a relatively minor infraction that could serve to explain his arrest, should it occur, without troubling his parents too much and without raising their suspicion. He also offered ingenious and harmless explanations for the highly suspect fact that he travelled at night and via Offenbach. Nevertheless, when Büchner's parents learned that Minnigerode had been arrested coming from Offenbach only shortly before Büchner's departure for the same city, they suspected a connection between the activities of their son and those of his good friend, and immediately sent off an anxious letter of inquiry. In his reply, Büchner feigns innocence and expresses indignation:

> I think I told you that *Minnigerode* was arrested half an hour before my departure. . . . I can't understand why he was arrested. Our brilliant judge got the idea, it appears, of making a connection between my trip and Minnigerode's arrest. When I returned here, I found my chest *sealed*, and I was told that my papers had been looked through. Upon my request, the seal was immediately removed. My papers (nothing but letters from you and my friends) were also returned to me. Only some of the French letters . . . were retained, probably because they had to send for a language teacher to read them. I am disgusted at such behavior. It makes me sick to think that my most sacred secrets are in the hands of these dirty people. And all of that—do you know why? Because I left on the same day Minnigerode was arrested. Based on a vague suspicion, my most sacred rights were violated and nothing more was required than that I should explain my trip!!! Of course I could do so without any difficulty. . . . I am free and it is impossible that a reason for arresting me will be found. But I am most deeply disgusted at the courts for breaking into my most sacred family secrets on suspicion of a possible suspicion. At the university court I was *only asked* where I had been during the three days. And to get information about that, they break open my desk on the second day of my absence and seize my papers! I will speak with some

lawyers to see if the laws afford satisfaction for such injury!
(II.430-431: 5 August 1834)

In his next two letters Büchner continues to express resent-
ment at the violation of his "most sacred rights" and family
secrets. In an even more confident and self-assured tone and
with obvious pleasure he reports how he "nearly killed" the
judge with his polite irony and scorn by asking him in the
presence of others the reason for the kind visit he paid him
during his absence. Since the search was conducted illegally
and, as he insists, with no good reason, Büchner feels it is his
duty to complain bitterly to the authorities. To do otherwise
would be an insult to the government and to justice.

Darmstadt: **Danton's Death**

Despite Büchner's assurances, his father thought it best that
he remain in Darmstadt during the winter semester and continue his studies under his supervision. But neither the unhappy
events of the summer nor the close surveillance of his father
intimidated Büchner enough to make him give up further political activity. Encouraged by the success of his bluff and confident that Minnigerode would not talk,[14] he reactivated the
Darmstadt section of the Society for Human Rights, recruited
new members, and slipped out two or three nights a week to
hold secret meetings.

At about the time Büchner may have been conceiving the
plan for his political pamphlet, he wrote his fiancée that he
could promise her love and loyalty, but could not yet say when
he would be able to provide for her: "Student for another two
years; the certain prospect of a stormy life, perhaps soon on
foreign soil!" (II.427: March 1834). This cryptic prophecy,
which must have disturbed and puzzled Minna, who probably
knew nothing of his political activities, reveals that Büchner
was well aware of the danger he was exposing himself to, and
that he saw exile as a very real possibility, if not likely consequence of his treasonous pursuits. While studying under his
father's tutelage in Darmstadt, investigations conducted by
Georgi and others were, in fact, steadily tightening the noose.
In the winter of 1834-1835 three members of the Darmstadt
section of the Society for Human Rights were arrested, and the
organization discontinued its meetings. In the second week of

January, Büchner received a summons to appear before the
court in Offenbach as a witness in the investigation of Jacob
Schütz, who had fled the country after Büchner's warning. Two
weeks later he was summoned to Friedberg to testify in the
investigation of Minnigerode.

At about this same time, in the early part of January, the
twenty-one year-old student also began to write his first play.
One must wonder if ever a literary work was written under
more unfavorable conditions. The author's house was being
watched by the police, and he by his father. Since he worked on
the play when he was supposed to be studying anatomy, he had
to be constantly on the alert for his father and ready to cover
his manuscript with anatomical charts. It was clear to him by
now that his arrest was imminent, and he hoped that his play
would provide him with the means for his escape into exile. He
also wrote to relieve that inner pressure he described in an
earlier letter. Some of the problems and decisions he faced
were similar to Danton's: should he leave his friends behind
and try to save himself? Was there any hope of success for
revolutionary activity at that time? Must he consider himself
responsible and guilty for the consequences of his political
actions? Or is the answer to these questions not contained in his
discovery of fatalism and the existence in man of an unknown
force that manipulates him like a puppet?

On 21 February Büchner sent the manuscript of *Danton's
Death* to the publisher Sauerländer. He was astute in request-
ing that it be forwarded for evaluation to Karl Gutzkow, who
edited the literary section of Sauerländer's periodical the *Phoe-
nix*. Since Gutzkow was a major spokesman for the Young
Germany movement, Büchner had reason to assume that he
would receive his play favorably and recommend it to the publisher. His desperate appeal to Gutzkow reveals his inner state
at this critical moment in his life:

> Perhaps observation or perhaps, less fortunately, your own
> experience has already taught you that there is a degree of
> misery which causes one to forget all considerations and
> deadens all feeling. Of course there are people who claim
> that it would be better in such an event to starve oneself out
> of the world, but I could seize on the refutation provided by a
> recently blinded Captain from the alley who explains that he

would shoot himself, if he were not forced to preserve his pay for his family by remaining alive. That is terrible. You will no doubt realize that there can be similar situations which prevent one from making one's life into a sheet anchor, in order to throw it into the water from the wreck of this world. And therefore you will not be surprised when I throw open your door, enter your room, place a manuscript on your chest, and demand alms from you. For I beseech you to read the manuscript as quickly as possible and, if your *conscience as a critic should allow it,* to recommend it to Sauerländer and to answer immediately. About the work itself I can say no more than that unfortunate circumstances forced me to write it in 5 weeks at most. I say this to influence your judgment about the author, not about the work itself. I do not know myself what I should make of it. I only know that I have every reason to blush vis-à-vis history. But I comfort myself with the thought that, with the exception of Shakespeare, all writers stand before history and nature like school boys.

I repeat my request for a prompt answer. In the case of a favorable outcome, a few lines from your hand, if they reach here before next Wednesday, can save an unfortunate person from a very sad situation. If the tone of this letter astonishes you, then consider that it is easier for me to beg in rags than to supplicate in evening dress, and almost easier to say with a pistol in my hand *"la bourse ou la vie!"* than to whisper with quivering lips "God bless you!" (II.434-435: 21 February 1835)

The desperate tone of this appeal accomplished its purpose: Gutzkow immediately began to read in the play and decided that very evening to recommend its publication.[15] He promptly sent Büchner an initial note of encouragement, which was soon followed by Sauerländer's offer of ten Friedrichsdor and a statement of terms, including the right to bowdlerize. But Büchner had not been able to wait.

Shortly after he had sent off the manuscript, Büchner received another summons, this time from the local court in Darmstadt. In order to gain some time, he sent his younger brother Wilhelm, who looked very much like him. The judge apparently knew the family, however, and was not fooled. He demanded that the right Büchner appear, but, probably in deference to the father's reputation as a respected physician, he gave him two days' time. It was more than enough, for Büchner had planned his escape well in advance.

Strasbourg: **Leonce and Lena** *and* **Lenz**

Büchner left Darmstadt on the morning of 1 March. Nine days later he entered France at Wissembourg, about sixty miles north of Strasbourg. In a letter written that same day he notified his family of his safe arrival in France and expressed the conviction that he would be able to return home in two or three years. He continued to feign innocence, stating that he was not afraid of the result of an investigation but only of the investigation itself: he would have had to stay in prison until it was completed and would have been physically broken and mentally deranged by the time of his release—a prediction entirely borne out by the tragic fate of his less fortunate fellow conspirators. During his stay in Strasbourg, Büchner was kept well informed about the situation at home: he knew who was arrested, how the prisoners were treated, and who had fled. The more he learned about the abuse, ill-treatment, even torture being suffered by his weakened, but heroically unyielding friend Minnigerode, the more grateful and justified he felt at having left when he did. Having escaped the constant fear of arrest, having emancipated himself from his domineering father, and finding himself once again in the freer air of France, Büchner was exultant with renewed courage and self-confidence:

> Now I have my hands and head free. . . . Everything now lies in my own hands. I will carry on my study of the medical-philosophical disciplines with the greatest diligence, and in *that* field there is still enough room to accomplish something significant. And our time is especially made for recognizing such accomplishments. Ever since I crossed the border, I have fresh energy. I now stand completely alone, but precisely that enhances my strength. To be rid of the constant, secret fear of arrest and other persecutions, which constantly tormented me in Darmstadt, is a great relief. (II.436: 9 March 1835)

But with freedom came the responsibility of having to support himself while trying to complete his studies. In expressing relief at having escaped arrest and optimism about the prospects for his future success, Büchner was more concerned with the effect his letter would have on his worried parents than with telling the whole truth. In a letter to Gutzkow he reveals, albeit in a playful tone and with some exaggeration, the new worries and uncertainties that now oppressed him:

> My future is so problematic that it even begins to interest me, which is saying a lot. I cannot easily opt for the subtle form of suicide through *work*. I hope to be able to keep my idleness alive for at least three months and will then take a handsel either from the Jesuits for service to Mary or from the St. Simonists for the femme libre, or I'll die with my sweetheart. We will see. Perhaps I'll be there when the minister once again puts on a Jacobin cap. What do you say to that? I'm only joking. But you shall still see what a German is capable of, when he is hungry. I wish the whole nation would fare the way I do. If there should once be a bad year in which only the hemp succeeds. That would be amusing. Then we would plait a boa constrictor. For the time being my Danton is a silk thread and my muse a disguised Samson. (II. 436-437: March 1835)

It is impossible to determine how accurate these letters are as an indication of Büchner's true feelings, since both were written with a definite purpose in mind: the one to reassure and comfort his parents, the other to induce Gutzkow to continue his efforts in his behalf, either by trying to get more money from the publisher for *Danton* or by helping him in other ways to earn money with his pen. We cannot judge the success of the letter home, but the one to Gutzkow brought a prompt and encouraging reply. Gutzkow praised Büchner for his play and assured him that the best way of earning money is by writing:

> You are still oppressed by want. I hope you now have what you earned ten times over [the payment for *Danton*]. The best means of existence remains writing, i.e., not the kind that is proscribed [*geächtet*], but the kind that is still somewhat respected [*geachtet*], or at least honored by the philistines, who have the money. Speculate with ideas, poetry, whatever your genius brings you. I'll be the canal or dealer who answers you with cash. (II.477)

Somewhat later Gutzkow wrote: "Tell me what you want to write. I'll find a place for everything" (II.478). Such encouragement from one of Germany's leading and most influential literary figures did a great deal to bolster Büchner's confidence, and it gave him something definite with which to reassure his parents: "I look to my future with confidence. In any event I could live from my writing. . . . I have been asked to send critiques of newly appearing French works to the literary journal. They are well paid" (II.437: 20 April 1835). It is ironic that the author of one of the most remarkable first plays ever written feels the need to defend his work from the anticipated rejection of his uncomprehending family and to assure them that his literary undertakings will not interfere with his studies:

> He [Gutzkow] seems to think highly of me. I am glad of that; his literary journal is well respected. . . . I learned from him that parts of my play have appeared in the *Phoenix*. He also assures me that it did his journal credit. The whole play is due to appear soon. In case you see it, I ask you to consider in your evaluation that I had to remain true to history and represent the men of the Revolution as they were: bloody, dissolute, energetic, and cynical. I see my play as a historical painting that must resemble the original. . . . Gutzkow asked me to write reviews [for his journal] as if requesting a special favor. I couldn't refuse. I spend my free time reading, and if I then occasionally take up my pen and write something about what I have read, it is no very great effort and does not take much time. (II.438-439: 5 May 1835)

Despite his declaration to the contrary, Büchner found idleness even more unbearable than that "subtle form of suicide through work," and he lost no time in responding to Gutzkow's encouragement to write. In a letter dated 12 May, Gutzkow refers to Büchner's intention of writing a novella about Lenz. The same letter also reveals that Büchner had already sent Gutzkow some comments on contemporary literature, and that he had been invited to contribute to Gutzkow's edition of Victor Hugo's plays (II.479). In the early summer of 1835 he translated *Lucretia Borgia* and *Maria Tudor* for that edition. In September he wrote his family that he had been invited to contribute regularly to a new periodical, the *German Review*

[*Die deutsche Revue*], which was to be edited by Gutzkow and Ludolf Wienbarg. To make regular contributions would interfere with his studies, he felt, but he did agree to contribute occasionally, including something at the end of that year (II.448). His subsequent letter, from October 1835, identifies the planned piece as an essay on Lenz. The same letter also contains a reassuring comment on the progress of his studies: "Now a period of constant study and the path is cleared. There are people here who foresee a brilliant future for me. I have no objection" (II.448: October 1835).

In a letter dated 2 November he informs his family that the *German Review* had been attacked and banned even before it had begun. While Büchner was undoubtedly quite pleased and flattered to have been named along with Heine, Börne, and other champions of freedom and justice as a potential contributor, his parents were angered and, especially after learning of Gutzkow's arrest, disturbed by their son's association with the prohibited journal. Either in response to their worried inquiry or in anticipation of it, Büchner assures them that he could not be harmed by the suppression of the *Review*. He also ridicules and denounces the moral and religious hypocrisy of those responsible for the ban and the ignorance of those who applaud it:

> I must laugh at how pious and moral our governments suddenly have become. The King of Bavaria has immoral books banned! He cannot have his biography published then, for it would be the dirtiest book ever written. The Grand Duke of Baden, first knight of the double order of blockheads, appoints himself knight of the holy spirit and has *Gutzkow* arrested; and the dear, plain and honest German, believing that it has all been done for religious and Christian reasons, claps his hands. (II.451)

After defending Gutzkow's character and denying that he has any knowledge of the books being attacked as "immoral," he disclaims association with the Young Germany movement:

> *For myself*, incidentally, I do not at all belong to the so-called *Young Germany*, the literary party of Gutzkow and Heine. Only a complete misunderstanding of our social conditions could make people believe it possible to bring about a complete transformation of our religious and social ideas through

popular literature [*Tagesliteratur*]. Furthermore, I *do not at all share their opinion about marriage and Christianity*. But it does irritate me when people who have sinned a thousand times more in practice than they have in *theory* make moral faces and throw stones at a youthful, competent talent. I go my own way and stick with the drama, which has nothing to do with all these controversial questions. I draw my characters in accordance with my understanding of nature and history and laugh at the people who want to make me responsible for their morality or immorality. I have my own ideas about that. (II.451-452: 1 January 1836)

Büchner did not agree with the utopian idealism of the Young Germans. He thought it naive to hope that educated, liberal writers communicating their ideas to a small number of educated, liberal readers could bring about political and social reform. As we have seen, he believed that only the suffering masses could bring about the revolutionary political and social change he considered desirable.

Having discovered that the time for revolution in Germany had not yet come, Büchner could now say and mean that he would not take an active part in political activity. During the fall and winter he dedicated himself entirely to the study of anatomy and philosophy. In the spring of 1836, just thirteen months after his arrival in Strasbourg and two years to the month after he predicted he would complete his studies in two years and probably on foreign soil, Büchner was invited to read his completed dissertation on the nervous system of the barbel fish in a series of meetings of the *Société d'Histoire Naturelle*, following which he was accepted as a member of that scholarly organization. Lorenz Oken, one of Germany's leading natural scientists and philosophers, was sufficiently impressed by Büchner's dissertation to recommend him for a doctorate at the University of Zurich and to invite him to join the faculty as a lecturer.

Following the completion of his dissertation, Büchner had more time to write. He was especially attracted by the prize money being offered by the Cotta publishing firm for the best German comedy. Büchner is reported to have said that he wanted fame from his writing, not "bread,"[16] but because of his financial situation the need for bread did, in fact, provide the more immediate and pressing motivation and impetus for all his creative writing. "When I have paid for my Doctor," he informed his friend Eugen Boeckel, "I will be broke, and I have not been able to do any writing for some time. I will have to live from credit for a while, and in the next 6-8 weeks I must see how I can cut myself coat and pants from the large white sheets of paper I must fill with my scribbling" (II.457: 1 June 1836).

The correspondence in tone and spirit as well as in specific detail between this letter and *Leonce and Lena* strongly suggests that Büchner was working on his comedy at this time. While Büchner hopes to convert empty paper into coat and pants, for example, his comic figure Valerio would like to dress his inner self by converting coat and pants into wine (I.120). With the peculiar mixture of playfulness and melancholy characteristic of his comedy, Büchner states on the one hand: "my frivolity, which basically is the most unlimited trust in God, has . . . again been greatly increased," while claiming on the other that he seriously contemplated shooting himself rather than have a tooth pulled. The ambivalence of his mood is reflected in the playfully serious sentence: "Life is generally something very beautiful, and in any event it is not as boring as if it were twice as boring" (II.457-458).

With scarcely a lag in the exhaustive pace to which he was by then accustomed, Büchner completed his comedy in a matter of weeks. The manuscript reached Cotta two days after the 1 July deadline, however, and was returned unopened. Not that it mattered, for it is most unlikely that the contest judges would have recognized the play's merits, just as they failed a generation earlier to award a prize to its predecessor and model, Brentano's *Ponce de Leon*.

Except for some worries about whether or not he, as a political exile, would be allowed to take up residence in Switzerland, Büchner's remaining summer months were relatively free of external pressure and threat. The preparation of his lectures for the fall notwithstanding, he had more time for writing than ever before. He may have worked on *Lenz* or the lost play about Pietro Aretino. He surely began or resumed work on *Woyzeck*. Early in September he wrote his brother:

I have now settled down completely to the study of the natural sciences and philosophy and will soon go to *Zurich* in order to lecture in my capacity as a superfluous member of society to my fellow men on something which is also extremely superfluous, namely, the philosophical systems of the Germans since Cartesius and Spinoza.—Meanwhile I am in the process of having some people killed or married on paper, and I ask the dear Lord for a gullible publisher and a large public with as little taste as possible. One needs courage for so many things under the sun, even to become a lecturer of philosophy. (II.460: 2 September 1836)

Another letter written in September indicates that two plays besides *Danton* were near completion: "I have not yet parted from my two plays. I am still dissatisfied and don't want to experience what I did the first time. These are works with which one cannot be finished at a definite time like the tailor with his garment" (II.460). One of these plays was *Leonce and Lena;* the other may have been "Pietro Aretino," but, as the letter to his brother suggests, was probably *Woyzeck*: the one play ends in marriage, the other in murder.

Zurich: Woyzeck

The day after celebrating his twenty-third birthday with his fiancée (17 October), Büchner left for Zurich. From all indications, the success that had been prophesied for him was assured. His academic career began auspiciously with the well received presentation on 5 November of his trial lecture on cranial nerves. Jean Strohl, a prominent zoologist, describes the trial lecture as a "distillate of the most subtle essences" of the dissertation. Büchner presented his findings with greater liveliness in his native language, and the meaning of the work emerged "in decidedly warmer tones and with deeper, more penetrating force."[17]

Büchner was undecided until almost the last minute whether he would teach science or philosophy. Considering his materialistic, empirical bent and his distrust of and antipathy toward idealism and abstract speculation, it is a surprising hesitation. Of course science was not yet as completely separated from philosophy as it is now, and those engaged in scientific research also endeavored to consider the broader implications and consequences of their findings, to relate their knowledge and theories to man and his place in the world. Büchner prefaced his lecture, for example, with a brief discussion of the philosophical context of his work. He rejects the teleological method of scientific investigation, which endeavors to explain the organs of an organism in terms of the purpose for which they are intended, in favor of what he calls the "philosophical" method. Reflecting his earlier argument against the Christian concept of this world as a testing ground, he maintains that the meaning and purpose of each expression of nature is to be found in itself, rather than in some external purpose it is meant to serve or in some goal toward which it strives. The task of the philosophical method of scientific investigation, in Büchner's view, is to search for the "law of existence," a law which explains the immediate function of the parts in their relationship to each other, to the whole organism, and to all of nature.

Büchner defines the fundamental law of nature in aesthetic terms:

> This question [of the philosophical school] . . . can only find its answer in a fundamental law for the entire organization. For the philosophical method, then, the whole physical existence of an individual is not produced for its own preservation, but is the manifestation of a primal and fundamental law [*Urgesetz*], a law of beauty, which produces the highest and purest forms according to the simplest plans and designs. For it [the philosophical method], everything, form and material, is dependent upon this law. All functions are effects of it; they are not determined by any external purposes, and their so-called purposeful actions upon and with each other are nothing more than the necessary harmony in the expressions of one and the same law, whose effects naturally do not destroy each other. (II.292)

Like Goethe, the Early Romantics, and Kleist, Büchner has a syncretic view of the world, according to which science, philosophy, and art do not represent isolated disciplines or "cultures," to speak with C. P. Snow, but different perspectives from which to view the same subject and somewhat different languages with which to describe it.[18]

When Büchner's mother and sister visited him in Strasbourg, they found him nervous and exhausted from the excessive demands he made on himself, and they heard him predict that he would not live long. He did not let up the pace in Zurich. His many interests, his superabundance of intellectual and creative energy, his ambition, and perhaps also his fear of emptiness did not permit him even to slow down, let alone to rest. His course of lectures on the comparative anatomy of fish and amphibians was especially demanding, since he had to prepare his own specimens for the demonstrations which were an important and memorable part of the course:[19] "I sit by day with my scalpel and spend the night with my books" (II.463).

Büchner enjoyed the new "surroundings, people, circumstances, and activities," but once the novelty had worn off and a routine very similar to the one he had just left was established, he became depressed and melancholy and yearned for reunion with his fiancée. Only through his active imagination was he able to forget himself and the monotony of his tiring work:

> The best thing is that my imagination is active, and the mechanical occupation of making preparations leaves it free. I always see you shimmering through between fish tails, frog's toes etc. Is that not more moving than the story of Abélard, as Héloise always intervened between his lips and his prayers? Oh, every day I become more poetic; all my thoughts swim in alcohol. Thank God I dream a lot again at night; my sleep is no longer so heavy. (II.463: 13 January 1837)

He longed for rest,[20] but allowed himself little, even when ill:

> I caught a cold and went to bed. But now it is better. When one is slightly sick, one has such a strong desire for idleness; but the mill wheel turns on and on without rest. . . . Today and yesterday, however, I allow myself a little rest and do not read; tomorrow it's back into the old routine: you can't believe how regularly and orderly. I'm almost as reliable as a cuckoo clock. (II.463: 20 January 1837)

In addition to thoughts and visions of his fiancée, a major source of pleasure and escape from routine was his writing:

> But still it's good: following all the excited, intellectual life —peace and with it the joy of creating my poetic products. Poor Shakespeare was a scribe by day and had to write at

night, and I, who am not worthy of untying his shoes, have it much better. (II.463)

Shortly before the first symptoms of a major illness became manifest, Büchner comforted his worried fiancée: "My dear child. You are full of affectionate concern and will get sick from worry; I even believe you are dying—but *I* have no desire to die and am as healthy as ever. I think fear of the care here has made me well; in Strasbourg it would have been very pleasant" (II.464: 27 January 1837). This letter, Büchner's last, ends in a rather different tone, however, as he expresses an inner need for her cheering and stabilizing influence: "You're coming soon? My youthful courage is gone; otherwise I'll get gray hair. I must soon strengthen myself again through your inner happiness and your divine ingenuousness and your charming frivolity and all your bad characteristics, bad girl. Adio piccola mia!—" (II.464).

On 2 February, less than a week after writing these lines, Büchner began to feel feverish. Although typhoid fever was prevalent in Zurich at the time, some days elapsed before his illness was so diagnosed. His last days were well documented by Karoline Schulz who, along with her husband and other friends of Büchner's, stayed with him and took care of him until the end. In his feverish delirium he was tormented by recurring delusions of being extradited and fear of being imprisoned. On several occasions he tried to get away, either to escape arrest or to break out of prison.

When the doctors gave up hope, Karoline's "otherwise pious nature bitterly asked Providence: 'why?'" Her husband comforted her with what he claimed were Büchner's own words: "Our friend himself answers you," he said. "After a powerful storm of fantasies was past, he said with a calm, raised, solemn voice: 'We do not have too much pain; we have too little of it, for through pain we go to God!'—'We are death, dust, ash. How could we complain?'" (B.580).[21]

As soon as it had become apparent that Büchner would not recover, Minna was sent for. She arrived on 17 February and had the "painful pleasure" of being recognized by the patient, who by this time was continuously delirious. The day after her arrival, Büchner conversed with her, took nourishment from her hands, and appeared so much improved that his friends began to hope again. It was apparent by evening, however, that the improvement was temporary. As Karoline and Minna sat together the following day, they knew their friend was dying. "I remember few hours in my life as solemn as this one," wrote Karoline. "A sacred peace poured over us. We read some poems, we spoke of him, until Wilhelm entered to call Minna, in order that she could perform the final act of love for her beloved. She did it with controlled calm, but then her pain broke out audibly. I took her in my arms and cried with her" (B.581). Minna described her last days with Büchner in a letter to his friend Eugen Boeckel:

> It was said that my appearance could not harm the patient, for he would not recognize me anyway—but I could not be allowed to see his distorted countenance. You can imagine that as long as it was only done for my sake they could no longer prevent me from entering the sickroom. Dr. Zehnder led me in. In front of the door he said to me: compose yourself; he will not know you. No, he will know me, was my answer. And he did recognize me. He felt my nearness and I brought him peace. He died gently; I kissed his eyes closed Sunday, 19 Februry at 3:30. The distress of his parents is boundless. A black veil is thrown over the rest of my life. May heaven have mercy on me and let me live only as long as my old father. (B.588)

Since none of the family members was present when Büchner died, Minna took possession of his literary remains. Using clean copies she sent him, Gutzkow published in the *Telegraph für Deutschland* a cut version of *Leonce and Lena* (May 1838) and *Lenz* (January 1839). When Büchner's family refused to cooperate with Gutzkow's effort to edit and publish a complete edition, Minna turned to Büchner's friend Georg Zimmermann, but Büchner's family had other plans. Because of basic disagreements and the unwillingness of either side to cooperate with the other, it was 1850 before Büchner's brother Ludwig published an edition that omitted *Woyzeck*—which he found to be almost undecipherable and too fragmentary for publication—and included only selections from the letters.

By the time Karl Emil Franzos began to prepare the first complete edition of the works and documents, some of the original manuscripts had been accidentally destroyed in a fire in the Büchner home, and Minna, now a stubborn and narrow-minded old woman, refused to turn over some of the material in her possession. She was motivated in part by her enmity toward the surviving members of Büchner's family and in part by her desire to protect her fiancé's memory and reputation: she considered some of the writings too atheistic and others too unfinished and fragmentary to be made public. Before her death in 1880—she never married—she destroyed his journal, many of his letters, and perhaps, though not probably, a play about Pietro Aretino.

II. *DANTON'S DEATH*

To finance his flight into exile and to satisfy a deep and compelling urge to express and come to terms with the thoughts and experiences of the recent past, Büchner wrote his first play, his first literary work of any kind, in the remarkably short period of five weeks. It seems almost inevitable that the young revolutionary should have looked to the French Revolution for subject matter, but it is somewhat surprising and quite significant that he did not choose a great moment of revolutionary action and decision as his topic, but rather the last days in the life of a revolutionary hero who has been superseded and is being destroyed by the very changes he helped to create. After having advocated the founding of a Republic which would fulfill the needs and guarantee the rights of the individual, and after having been moved by compassion to call for mercy and an end to the bloodbath that terrorized the people of France, Büchner's Danton has become motivated by his disillusionment with the course of the Revolution and by his despairing insight into the nature of man and his role in history to drop out of the political arena altogether, thus becoming vulnerable to attack by the radical revolutionaries in whose hands the power now resides and whose actions will determine, for the moment at least, the further development of the Revolution. Büchner's play about the death of Danton is also about the death of the French Revolution[1] and the futility of revolution in general. Its primary concern is not with a particular historical event or moment, but with the condition of man, his role in society, and his attitude toward life and death.

It is apparent from the beginning that Danton is not playing
the role that made him famous and feared, and that something
has happened to destroy his will to act and his belief in the
goals for which he had been fighting. Without a strong, perhaps
fanatical belief in the efficacy and obtainability, if not inevitability of his goals, a decent and humane leader cannot risk
the lives of his followers or even sacrifice his enemies. And an
honest man must be convinced he is right, before he can rally
the people to his cause. When it was a matter of getting rid of
the King and the privileged class, Danton was in the first ranks.
Now that he wants to join with the people in reaping the
benefits of their efforts, the Revolution has fallen into the
hands of ideologists who are more interested in abstract ideals
and personal power than in the material want and suffering of
the people.

Danton has learned through his own role in the Revolution
and through the course of its development that he has not so
much determined events as he has been determined by them.
This knowledge paralyzes his will to act. It is highly significant
that Danton, when tormented by feelings of guilt and a sense of
his impotence, should express himself in words recalling Büchner's letter on fatalism, and that the knowledge which crushed
the inexperienced young student can give a painful kind of
comfort to the bloodied revolutionary, as it may also have to
Büchner, too, at the time the play was written. By writing
Danton, Büchner not only came to terms with the recent past
and with the problems facing him at the moment, but also
prepared himself for the immediate future: the decision Danton faces after learning that the Committee of Public Safety has
ordered his arrest is fundamentally the same as the one confronting Büchner at the time he was writing, namely, whether
or not to seek safety in flight. In deciding to remain, Danton
suffered consequences similar to those Büchner foresaw for
himself, should he be arrested (see II.435-437).

Guilt and Punishment

Danton does not heed his friends' advice to flee Paris until
after his arrest has been ordered by the Committee of Public
Safety. Before he has gone far, however, he stops to reconsider.
Presupposing a peculiar distinction between his memory and

his person, he reasons that if he saves his memory, it will kill him, whereas if his memory is killed, he will be saved. Insofar, then, as the place to which he is fleeing will be safe for his memory, it will not be safe for him, since he can only hope to find safety in forgetting. As long as he is not yet fully convinced, or refuses to admit to himself, that his enemies can and will destroy him, Danton enjoys flirting with death and can view it as a desirable alternative to the anguish caused by his memory and conscience.[2]

The scene following this peculiar argument reveals why Danton wants to lose his memory: his conscience is tormented by guilt because of his leading part in the bloody September massacre. In his earlier confrontation with Robespierre, Danton called conscience a "mirror before which a monkey torments itself" (I.vi). His Epicureanism and belief in determinism would indeed seem to preclude the existence of a conscience and feelings of guilt. But while consistency may be an attribute of the artificially one-sided figures or "marionettes" of the idealistic drama, in which the characters can be equated with a specific "feeling, maxim, or concept" (II.iii), and in which man is presented as the dramatist thinks he should be, rather than as he is, it is not often found in life. In the complex interplay of such non-congruent categories as thought, feeling, and belief, there is always potential for discord and inconsistency.

In his sleep, or the semiconscious state which follows interrupted sleep, the cry of a child in the night apparently sounds in Danton's guilt-ridden subconscious like the word which names his guilt: "September!" Upon awakening, he goes to the open window, which often serves in the episodic play as the point of contact between the inner world of the individual and the world outside him,[3] and hears the name of the sin he would die to be rid of being "screamed and wailed through the streets." He then asks himself: "Will it never end? Will the light never burn out and the sound never cease? Will it never become still and dark, so we no longer see and hear each other's foul sins?—September!—" (II.v). Without being aware of it, Danton openly confesses what he scarcely thought and what he meant to keep hidden:

Julie. You spoke of foul sins and then groaned: September!
Danton. Me? Me? No, I didn't speak. I scarcely thought it.

Those were only very still, secret thoughts.
Julie. You are trembling, Danton.
Danton. And shouldn't I tremble when the walls speak like that? When my body is so broken that my thoughts wander restlessly about and speak with the lips of stones. It's strange. (II.v)

The guilt represented by the word that "stretches its bloody hands toward him" is connected in his mind with the fear and anxiety expressed through the nightmare from which the incriminating cry awakened him.

To justify himself and ease his conscience, Danton reconstructs with Julie the events of that fateful September in 1792, when he was forced by the political situation and his position of power to condone the murder of approximately 1400 imprisoned suspects, Royalists and clergymen, in order to save the Republic. He cannot understand on a rational level why he should feel guilty for responding to the situation in the only way he could. What force is it, he wonders, that compels one to act? And who can curse someone for doing what he must?

It was self-defense; we had to. The man on the cross made it easy for himself; offenses must come, but woe to that man by whom offense comes.

Must come; that was this must. Who will curse the hand upon which the curse of the must has fallen. Who spoke the *must*? Who? What is it in us that whores, lies, steals, and murders?

We are puppets, manipulated on our strings by unknown forces. We ourselves are nothing! Nothing! The swords that spirits fight with. One just doesn't see the hands—like in a fairy tale. (II.v)

Though presented here as if it were a new discovery and a convenient rationalization, the same awareness was expressed previously by Danton's identification of man with a player (II.i); it is also the implicit cause of the disillusionment, cynicism, and despair which characterize his attitude and behavior from the beginning. Danton's refusal to act and his denial of the real motives for his earlier action, his debilitating boredom, the futile attempt to find peace and forgetting in sensual pleasure, his belief that man is a player or a puppet, his nihilism—it all stems from or is an expression of his discovery of the "fatalism of history," of the individual's inability to determine the direction of historical development: "We didn't make the Revolution, the Revolution made us" (II.i). While reason tells him that he is not guilty, his feelings tell him that he is and that he will be punished accordingly: "offenses must come, but woe to that man by whom offense comes!" To the extent that Danton's political moderation and call for mercy are products of his guilt, that guilt does indeed become the cause of his death. Moreover, he is sentenced by the very Revolutionary Tribunal he helped to establish—with the intention of preventing a repetition of the September murders.

Danton uses the words of Jesus to explain and justify his action, but the mechanism of transgression and punishment he describes, and the one realized in the play, owes more to ancient Greece than to the New Testament. While Jesus foresaw the commitment of offenses in general as an inevitable consequence of man's imperfect nature, he assumed that the particular individual has the freedom to refrain from committing such offenses if he so chooses.[4] Danton agrees with the Greeks in denying man this freedom. The individual must act as he does, and is punished nevertheless. Such punishment is not an earned consequence of wrongdoing, but a necessary means of restoring a disturbed equilibrium or order. Like Schiller, Büchner postulates the existence of some power or force —Schiller called it Nemesis—which strives to restore the disturbed order by punishing the offender.[5] Of course Büchner differs from Schiller in his understanding of that higher law and the forces it uses: whereas Schiller considers it to be a moral, ethical absolute, Büchner locates it in nature. Schiller is famous as the dramatist of freedom, but even his figures, once they make the decisions or perform the actions that disturb the moral order, lose their freedom and are subjected to the forces which destroy the cause of the disturbance and restore the natural order. Mercier presupposes the action of such forces when he tells Danton: "The blood of the twenty-two [Girondists executed with Danton's approval] is drowning you" (III.i). Because he assumes that offenses will be punished, Danton is able to anticipate his own fate and to predict with confidence the fall of Robespierre and his followers.

Suffering and the desire for peace

If there is any sin in Büchner's world, it is causing others to suffer. After attempting to prove through philosophical argumentation that there is no God, Büchner's Payne comes to the crux of the matter, which is the existence in life of imperfection and suffering: "One can deny evil, but not pain. Only reason can prove the existence of God; the emotions revolt against such an assumption. . . . Why do I suffer? That is the bedrock of atheism. The least twitch of pain, and should it be felt only in a single atom, makes a tear through creation from top to bottom" (III.i).[6] If pain is the only sin and suffering the only vice, as Laflotte claims (III.v), the creator of this world must be the *summum malum* rather than the *summum bonum.*

The highest good conceivable by those who must inhabit such a world is the absolute peace of nothingness.[7] Danton is too cynical to be able to conceive of any form of existence that would be essentially different or any better than the one on earth. When Philippeau attempts to comfort him with the hope of an afterlife, Danton rejects the "divine theory of class" with its promise of promotion from one level to another, from one "pile of manure" to the next. What he wants is peace, and peace is not to be found in God but in nothingness:

> **Philippeau.** What is it you want?
> **Danton.** Peace.
> **Philippeau.** It is with God.
> **Danton.** In nothingness. Immerse yourself in something more peaceful than nothingness. And if the highest peace is God, is not nothingness God? But I am an atheist. The accursed theorem: something cannot become nothing! And I am something! That's where the misery lies! (III. vii)

Since the void has been filled and destroyed by the expanding creation, even the comfort of being able to believe in nothingness is denied him. By giving birth to creation, the void killed itself; the creation is its wound and cause of death. "We are its drops of blood and the world is the grave in which it decays." Danton realizes that his account of the creation sounds mad, but he claims some truth for it.[8] By equating the earth with the legendary Wandering Jew who cannot die, Camille seconds his friend: "The world is the eternal Jew; nothingness is death, but it is impossible. Oh, not to be able to die, not to be able to die, as it says in the song" (III.vii).[9]

When Philippeau later presumes the existence of a divine plan and a divine Being in whose ears "the screams and cries that deafen us are a stream of harmonies" (IV.v), Danton, Camille, and Hérault again cite suffering as the emotionally irrefutable argument against the existence of a benevolent divinity. Danton begins the "choral monologue" by cynically pointing out that we are the poor musicians and our bodies the instruments that produce those "screams and cries." He asks rhetorically if we exist in order that the ugly tones forced out of our suffering bodies should delight some heavenly listener? A series of parallel questions provides variations on the theme:

> **Hérault.** Are we suckling pigs that are whipped to death for princely tables, so that their flesh becomes more savory?
> **Danton.** Are we children who are roasted in the glowing Moloch-arms of this world and tickled with light-rays so the gods enjoy their laughter?
> **Camille.** Is the ether with its golden eyes a bowl of golden carp which sits on the table of the blessèd gods, and the blessèd gods laugh eternally and the fish die eternally and the gods are eternally amused by the colorful play of their death-struggle?[10]

Philippeau's optimistic belief in divine order and meaning is completely overshadowed by the emotional force and rhetorical power of his friends' bitterly pessimistic counterstatements. They can find little comfort or hope in a Being who takes sadistic pleasure in the agony of their suffering and death. "The world is chaos," Danton concludes with epigrammatic terseness; the only deity that could offer any hope to man is the one that no longer exists and never can again: "Nothingness is the world-god which should be born" (IV.v).[11]

The dilemma of a revolutionary

If contributing to the suffering of another person is the greatest, perhaps the only sin, then helping to alleviate that suffering must be the greatest good. The goal of Danton's political program, as of Büchner's, was to make the lives of the masses of poor people somewhat better by recovering and withholding from those living in luxury and excess the wealth which the poor had created through their productive labor, but which had been taken from them through unjust taxes. The situation of the masses in *Danton* is similar to that of the Hessians as described by Büchner in *The Hessian Courier*, and the tone of the political pamphlet echoes in the protests of the citizens. Their response to Simon's drunken attempt to imitate the Roman Virginius, who stabbed his daughter to save her virtue, may be cited as an example:

> Yes, a knife, but not for the poor whore. What did she do? Nothing! Her hunger whores and begs. A knife for the people who buy the flesh of our wives and daughters! Woe to them who whore with the daughters of the people! You have rumbling in your empty bellies, and they have pressure in their full stomachs; you have holes in your jackets, and they have warm coats; you have calluses on your fists, and they have hands of velvet. Ergo you work and they do nothing; ergo you have earned it and they have stolen it; ergo, if you want to get back a few coins of your stolen property, you must whore and beg; ergo they are villains and must be killed. (I.ii)[12]

Büchner's revolutionary efforts failed because the physical suffering of the people had not yet become severe enough to prevail over their docility, apathy, and fear of authority. Danton's revolution failed for the opposite reason: in their indignation, anger, and revolutionary fervor, the people became a mindless, directionless mob, bent on destruction, thirsty for blood, and ready to follow blindly the leaders who best understood how to control them and who promised them what they wanted. "The people are a Minotaur that must have its corpses every week." "The matter is simple," Lacroix explains after the meeting at the Jacobin Club, "the atheists and ultrarevolutionaries have been sent to the scaffold, but the people are no better off. They still run barefoot in the streets and want to make shoes from aristocratic leather. The thermometer of the guillotine must not fall; a few more degrees and the Committee of Public Safety can look for its bed on the Place de la Revolution" (I.iv). To answer the peoples' cry for more blood and to save his own faction, Robespierre promises a weighty head. "The Hébertists are not yet dead," Lacroix tells Danton, "the people are in material misery. That is a terrible lever. The scale of blood cannot be allowed to rise if it is not to become a lantern for the Committee of Public Safety. It requires ballast; it needs a heavy head" (I.v). That head, of course, is Danton's.

The hope and guarded optimism that must have motivated Büchner in his revolutionary endeavors is completely missing in *Danton's Death*. That Danton's pessimism and despair are shared by the author is apparent from the representation of the people the revolution is intended to benefit and upon whom its success depends. In their unquenchable lust for blood and will-less capriciousness, they throw away a unique opportunity to create a democratic republic and to accomplish meaningful social reform. Like mindless animals they follow and obey those few men who are clever and ruthless enough to control them. And because they lack judgment and experience, they have no sense of the ends they are being made to serve. In their ignorance they equate moderation with weakness and prefer a continuation of the bloodbath to mercy and consolidation, which convinces Danton that they actually enjoy the excitement and spectacle of their own misfortune and the tragedy befalling their nation. What more can they want, he responds, when asked by Philippeau whether France is to remain in the hands of its executioners, "in order to be sentimental, noble, virtuous or witty or in order not to be bored." It is better to die a theatrical death to the appreciative applause of spectators, than to die of fever or old age. "It is quite nice and appropriate for us: we always stand on the stage, even if we are finally stabbed in earnest" (II.i). The spectacle of the theater or the circus can help the people forget for the moment the pain caused by lack of bread:

> **A Woman with Children.** Make way! Make way! The children are screaming; they are hungry. I must make them see, so they will be quiet. Make way! (IV.vii)

Unless he is blinded by fanaticism, a revolutionary may find it difficult to avoid becoming cynical toward the people he is attempting to liberate. An artist wishing to indict a particular political system and its accompanying social conditions confronts a related problem: he will probably want to demonstrate what a dehumanizing, brutalizing effect such a system has on the people, but people represented as being dehumanized and brutalized will give the impression that they are not worth saving. In *Danton's Death* and again in *Woyzeck* Büchner faced the same problem that was to become a major dilemma for the Naturalists.[13] Danton's attitude toward the people and the author's portrayal of them suggest that the revolutionary impulse may in fact be better sustained by hate and disgust for the men in power, as Danton admits it was for him (I.i), than by love and sympathy for the poor.

Danton's description of the people indicates as well as anything that his career as a revolutionary is no longer tenable. What is more, he has given up trying to better their lot and is devoting himself instead to the pursuit of his own pleasure. This not only separates him from them, but also places him in conflict with them, for in their inability to enjoy, they hate those who can:

> **Lacroix.** And besides, Danton, we are depraved, as Robespierre says, that is, we enjoy ourselves; and the people are virtuous, that is, they do not enjoy themselves, because work has dulled their senses. They don't get drunk, because they have no money. And they don't go to the brothel, because they stink of cheese and herring, and the girls are nauseated by that. (I.v)

Under Robespierre's influence, the people also identify those who enjoy the material pleasures of life with the revolution's primary enemy, the aristocrats. Since depravity is the "most subtle, dangerous, and abhorrent attack on freedom," it threatens the existence of the Republic and becomes a political crime as well as a moral transgression (I.iii).

Conflicting political programs

The clash between Danton and Robespierre is inevitable, since they represent diametrically opposed political programs. Danton has given up fighting for his and seems unwilling, as he demonstrates in the first scene, even to recognize it as his own, but the program described by his friends is indeed his. In keeping with the shift of emphasis from God to man, which was characteristic of the times, and with his own Epicureanism and nihilism, Danton's politics concentrate on the rights, privileges, and pleasures of the individual. The state should recognize that

individuals vary, and it should assure each person the possibility
of achieving the maximal degree of pleasure obtainable without
infringing on the equal rights of others: "Everyone must be able
to enjoy himself in his own way, as long as no one is allowed to
enjoy himself at someone else's expense or to disturb others in
their own peculiar pleasures" (I.i). It is not the business of the
state to define virtue and duty and to punish those who do not
comply with its definition, but rather to assure each person his
rights and to provide for his health and welfare: "Our principles
of state must place justice above duty, well-being above virtue,
and self-defense above punishment" (I.i). All men are fools and
no one has the right to impose his particular foolishness on
another.

Robespierre and Saint-Just disagree. They are ideologists,
demagogues, and fanatics who claim for themselves the right
to define virtue and to intimidate and force others through
terror and bloodshed to comply with their definition:

> The weapon of the Republic is terror, the strength of the
> Republic is virtue. Virtue, because without it terror is perni-
> cious; terror because without it virtue is impotent. Terror is
> an outgrowth of virtue; it is nothing other than swift, severe,
> and unbending justice. They say that terror is the weapon of
> a despotic government and that ours therefore resembles a
> despotism. Certainly! But in the same way the swords in the
> hands of freedom fighters resemble the sabers with which the
> guards of tyrants are armed. If the despot rules his animal-
> like subjects through terror, he is right as a despot. Crush the
> enemies of freedom through terror and you, as founders of
> the Republic, are no less right. The revolutionary govern-
> ment is the despotism of freedom against tyranny. (I.iii)

They no longer believe in God either, but rather than put
man in His place, they deify Reason and make morality into a
dogma. By this means they retain an Absolute according to
which man's actions can be measured and judged. To their
way of thinking, ideas and concepts have the infallibility and
inexorability of natural laws and processes. Saint-Just asks:

> Should moral nature be more considerate in its revolutions
> than physical nature is? Should an idea be any less able than
> a law of physics to destroy what opposes it? Should an event

that transforms the whole configuration of moral nature, that is, mankind, not be permitted to shed blood? The world spirit uses our arms in the spiritual sphere just as it uses volcanoes and floods in the physical sphere. What difference does it make if they die from the Revolution or from an epidemic. (II.vii)

Robespierre's own supporters realize that he wants to make a religion of politics and that his opposition to Danton is as much moral as it is political: "They'll make the guillotine into a cure for venereal disease. They are not fighting moderates; they're fighting vice. . . . Robespierre wants to make the Revolution into a lecture hall for morality in which the guillotine will serve as a pulpit" (III.vi). They go along for self-serving reasons and will turn against him when the time is right. Büchner reveals through them that Robespierre's plans for the Revolution are as futile and unrealizable as Danton's and that the Revolution will discard him as surely and in the same way it has Danton.

Robespierre is not only the dogma of the Revolution, as Danton says, he is also the Messiah of the new political religion. He is deeply offended by the comparison, which he reads in Camille's newspaper *Le vieux Cordelier:*

This bloody Messiah Robespierre on his hill of Calvary between the two thieves Couthon and Collot: he sacrifices there and is not sacrificed. The Praying Sisters of the Guillotine stand at his feet like Mary and the Magdalene. Saint-Just, like John, is near to his heart and acquaints the Convention with the apocalyptic revelations of the master. He carries his head like a monstrance. (I.vi)

Because he is thus betrayed by his erstwhile friend, Robespierre consents to have Camille executed with the others. When left alone, however, he not only accepts the comparison between himself and the Messiah, but actually believes that his task has been more difficult and painful and has involved greater self-denial than the one faced by his predecessor:

Yes indeed, the bloody Messiah who sacrifices and is not sacrificed.—He redeemed them with His blood, and I redeem them with their own. He made them sinful, and I take the sin on myself. He had the pleasure of pain, and I have the anguish of the executioner.

Who denied himself more, He or I? (I.vi)

At the same time, and under the influence of Danton's visit, Robespierre recognizes that all men suffer as Jesus did in the garden of Gethsemane and that no one is able to relieve the suffering of anyone else. Like Danton, he realizes that man is alone, and he suffers acutely from the awareness of his own isolation: "Truly, the Son of Man is crucified in all of us. We all struggle in the garden of Gethsemane bathed with bloody sweat, but no one saves the other with his wounds. My Camille! —they all forsake me—everything is desolate and empty—I am alone" (I.vi).

Danton and Robespierre

The only direct confrontation between Danton and Robespierre takes place near the end of the first act. What we actually witness is only the conclusion of an argument which began well before the opening of the scene, but our knowledge of their respective views enables us to pick up the thread without difficulty. In agreement now with the program defined by his friends, Danton has advocated mercy and demanded an end to the bloodbath. Robespierre informs Danton that anyone who opposes or hinders him is his enemy. "The social revolution is not yet finished," he insists. "Whoever leaves a revolution only half completed digs his own grave. The good society is not yet dead; the healthy strength of the people must replace this thoroughly degenerate class. Vice must be punished; virtue must rule through terror" (I.vi).

Robespierre uses words and concepts which have no meaning for Danton, since they have no place in his view of life. Danton does not understand the word "punishment," because he denies the existence of sin and guilt. Since he accepts no absolute system of moral values according to which human actions can be measured and judged, he also denies the existence of virtue and vice, the very foundation of Robespierre's Puritanical, Rousseauist ideology. Danton considers every person to be an Epicurean; everyone follows his own nature in doing what he enjoys: "All men are Epicureans, some crude and some refined. Christ was the most refined. That is the only difference that I can discern between men. Everyone acts according to his nature, that is, he does what he enjoys."

Whereas Robespierre condemns Danton's vice as the "aristocracy's mark of Cain," Danton recognizes that Robespierre's
supposed morality gives him the aristocratic pleasure of finding others inferior to himself: "I would be ashamed to run
around for thirty years between heaven and earth with the
same moral physiognomy, just so I could have the miserable
pleasure of finding others inferior to me."

It is one thing for Robespierre to delight in his own virtue,
it is another for him to want to impose his peculiar tastes and
standards on everyone else and to condemn and even put to
death those who fail to comply with them. Speaking from the
standpoint he refused earlier to recognize as his own, Danton
censures Robespierre for attempting to force his "peculiar foolishness" onto others, thereby denying them the right to enjoy
themselves in their own way:

> Everyone may defend himself when others try to spoil his fun.
> Do you have the right to make the guillotine into a washtub
> for the filthy linen of other people and to use their chopped-
> off heads as spot remover for their dirty clothes, because you
> always wear a well-brushed coat? Yes, you can resist when
> they spit on it or tear holes in it, but what does it concern
> you as long as they leave you in peace. If they are not
> embarrassed to go around like that, do you then have the
> right to bury them in their graves? (I.vi)

If he is offended by the way others live and cannot bear to
see what even God tolerates, then he should cover up his eyes
with a handkerchief rather than set himself up as the "police-
man of heaven."

Communication between men holding such divergent views
is not possible. When Danton recognizes to what extent Robespierre has been blinded by his fanaticism, he gives up and
leaves in disgust. But as Danton rightly assumes, his accusa-
tions have hit the mark. Left alone, Robespierre attempts to
convince himself of the political necessity of getting rid of Danton, but Danton's disquieting words repeatedly intrude into his
attempted self-justification and cause him to question his own
motives and arguments. He realizes, finally, that no amount
of rationalization can cover the wounds Danton has inflicted:
"Why can't I get rid of the thought? It always points with

its bloody finger there, right there! No matter how many rags I wrap around it, the blood always comes through" (I.vi). He tries to collect himself but must admit that he is confused and uncertain.

The unity of Robespierre's fanatically monolithic personality has been shattered by his confrontation with Danton, and a new or previously suppressed voice emerges to question his integrity and challenge his motives. It is a voice very much like Danton's, and for a moment it becomes predominant. As in Danton's later confrontation with otherwise suppressed fears and feelings of guilt, inner and outer reality interact through the symbolical open window, and Robespierre gains some clear insight into himself, his actions, and his relationship to the world. And like Danton, he also expresses awareness of his guilt and sin, for "sin is in our thoughts." In realizing that man is not master of his actions, but controlled, rather, by dark and unknown forces, he reaches a conclusion, or reveals a hitherto suppressed realization, similar to the one which paralyzed Danton's will to act:

And isn't our waking a brighter dream? Are we not sleep-walkers? Isn't our action like that in our dreams, only more distinct, definite, and complete? Who would blame us for that? In one hour our mind carries out more deeds of thought than the sluggish organism of our body can imitate in years. Sin is in our thoughts. Whether thoughts become deeds, whether the body carries them out—that is only chance. (I.vi)

Though he shares Danton's disillusioning insight, his response is and has been fundamentally different. Whereas Danton despairs and becomes thoroughly introspective, questioning the meaning of words and actions and life itself, Robespierre repudiates the self and concentrates his attention and energy in an idealistic attempt to change the world.[14] To replace a discarded belief in religious salvation, he substitutes a concept of political salvation—"He [the Messiah] redeemed them with his blood, and I redeem them with their own"—and attempts to create through political means a new religion and to cast himself in the role of the new Redeemer.[15]

Büchner has no sympathy for a political program which is more concerned with abstractions than with empirical reality

and which sacrifices humans to ideas, but he can sympathize
with the discontent which underlies such a program and with
the anguish and suffering of a man who is no less determined
than Danton in his effort to destroy an undesirable system and
replace it with something better. He can sympathize, too, with
the isolation of a man who, unlike Danton, is not surrounded by
true friends, but by callous and calculating opportunists, and
whose moments of anguish are not interrupted by a comforting
and tender Julie, but by a Saint-Just demanding more blood and
bringing the news that Camille, the one person he considered a
true friend, has also turned against him. Robespierre had evidently resisted the demands of his followers for the blood of the
Dantonists—his remarks at the Jacobin Club were meant only
to frighten them, he says—but now that Danton's accusing
words are threatening his inner peace, and now that he is
completely alone, he nervously consents: "Quickly then, tomorrow. No long death struggle! I have been sensitive for some
days now. Just do it quickly." Robespierre's example gives
further support to Danton's claim that isolation is an inherent
part of the human condition. We must pity a man who cries out
of his loneliness: "My Camille!—They all forsake me—everything is desolate and empty—I am alone." The tragic implications of this emotion-charged statement of isolation and loneliness make it highly effective as a curtain speech.

Death

No less important than the conflict between political programs, *Weltanschauungen,* and personalities is the confrontation of Danton and his associates with death. At a time
when Büchner was threatened by arrest and its possible consequences, he attempted through his art to come to grips with
death and dying. What is death, and what does it mean to die?
Can there be any meaning in death for those who no longer find
meaning in life? How does one react when one knows that one's
death or the death of a loved one is imminent? Büchner thus
presents and attempts to come to terms with various aspects of
one of man's most fundamental and universal concerns, the
terrible inevitability of death with all its consequences.

As long as Danton is not convinced that his enemies will dare
to destroy him, he carries on a playful "flirtation" with death.

He resembles Hamlet in his ambivalence: he would welcome death as an escape from the slings and arrows of outrageous fortune, but his uncertainty and fear of the unknown make him rather bear those ills he has than fly to others he knows not of. Of course Danton's situation is more dangerous than Hamlet's, since he does not control the blade with which he flirts. In facing the tragic dilemma of having to decide whether to flee his internal or external enemy, he rather light-heartedly decides to do what is easiest, namely, to remain passive and leave the next move to his opponents. (Despite Danton's passivity, there is dramatic tension in this situation, since the spectator is aware that Robespierre has already given the order to have Danton arrested and killed.)

In the first act the opposing political programs are defined and brought into direct confrontation; the act ends with Robespierre's decision to eliminate his enemies. The second act focuses on Danton's philosophy of life, his feelings of guilt, and his attitude toward the danger that confronts him. It ends with his arrest and denunciation by Robespierre, Saint-Just, and the Deputies of the National Convention. The third act alternates between the proceedings of the Revolutionary Tribunal—including the behind-the-scenes machinations of Danton's opponents—and the dialogues of the imprisoned friends, as they attempt in one way or another to come to terms with their fate. Having been aroused by the nearness of death and provoked by the falsehood of the calumniating charges against him and the injustice of a trial which denies him the right to call witnesses or question his accusers, Danton finally begins to fight for his life or, more accurately, since he knows that his trial is only *pro forma* and that the outcome has already been determined, for his reputation.

Büchner includes only a small part of Danton's trial in his play. The fact that he does not take full advantage of the inherently dramatic trial scenes as recorded in his sources indicates that he was less interested in dramatizing history than in presenting what he thinks might have, or could have, taken place behind the scenes. He shows how the outcome of the trial is predetermined by the careful selection of jurors; how the fanciful plans of the imprisoned Dillon—Barrère calls them "fairy tales"—reach Saint-Just and are used by him as a weapon against Danton and Camille: "But we will put them to sleep

with the fairy tale" (III.vi); and how a hastily contrived decree
from the Convention is used to prevent Danton from speaking
and to end the proceedings. Given the methods used by the
present leaders of the Revolution and the hypocrisy, brutality,
and opportunism of the men in whose hands the fate of the
country and its people now rests, Danton's pessimistic forebod-
ings for the future of the Revolution and the country appear
entirely justified.

The primary concern of the third act, then, is not so much
with the trial, as with the way Danton and his friends respond to
their new situation and with the effect that situation has on
their attitudes toward life and death. For his part, Danton
intends to accept death with resignation and courage—"I'm
being sent to the scaffold. All right then! I won't stumble"
(III.i)—but he no longer welcomes it. The flirtation has ended,
and Danton now tries to keep death at a distance and to
suppress his fear by minimizing through cynicism and wit the
significance of his terrible opponent: "one must go laughingly
to bed" (III.i). Only Camille is so crushed by the prospect of
death and separation from his beloved Lucile that he not only
cannot join his friends in their exchange of witticisms but
repeatedly attempts to confront them with the frightening reality of their situation: "Just don't trouble yourself. No matter
how far you may stick out your tongue, you still can't lick the
death-sweat from your brow" (III.i).

Though he talks about mounting the scaffold, Danton still
oscillates between the conviction that he is doomed and the
hope that his opponents will not dare to eliminate a revolutionary hero of his stature and potential usefulness. He talks and
behaves as he did at the beginning of the second act when he
attempted to justify his inaction by admitting that he was already a dead saint and a relic, only to end his defense of an
early death with the self-confident or self-deluding claim that
his opponents would not dare to kill him. Following his appearances before the Revolutionary Tribunal, however, Danton's attitude changes. Once he smells death's stinking breath,
he overcomes his lethargy and boredom, drops the various
defense mechanisms through which he had attempted to keep
death at a distance, and begins to fight in earnest. But as
Lacroix indicates, it is too late: "You shouted well, Danton. If
you had taken such trouble for your life somewhat earlier, it

would be different now. Isn't it so, when death comes so shamelessly close and stinks out of the throat like that and becomes
ever more obtrusive?" (III.vii).

Furthermore, it is no real fight. The worst part about death,
they discover—and upon this they are in agreement—is that its
mechanical nature precludes the possibility of a fair fight, and
that its slow, systematic manner of grinding the life out of them
is far less tolerable than if it would do its work quickly and
cleanly:

> **Danton.** If it were a fight in which arms and teeth seized each
> other! But it seems to me as if I had fallen into a mill and my
> limbs were slowly and systematically being twisted off by
> cold physical force. To be killed so mechanically!
> **Camille.** To lie there alone, cold, stiff in the damp fumes of
> decay. Perhaps so death can slowly torture the life out of our
> fibers, perhaps with the consciousness that we are rotting
> away. (III.vii)

Whereas Danton had hoped to find the peace of nothingness in death, he now agrees with Camille that it will only bring
a continuation of the suffering they know from life. Since the
creation destroyed the void, and since life itself is only a form
of death—"We are all buried alive and entombed like kings in
triple or quadruple coffins: under heaven, in our houses, in our
coats and shirts" (III.vii)—there can be no hope of finding
peace and an end of suffering in death: "There is no hope in
death. It is only a more simple and life a more complex, more
highly organized form of decay. That is the whole difference!"
(III.vii).

Entirely inconsistent with his rational assumptions about
death and what follows it are the hope that Julie will not let him
go alone and the essentially religious feeling that it could make
a difference for him if she would join him. "Oh, Julie! If I
should go *alone*! If she left me in solitude! Even if I completely
disintegrated, completely decomposed—I would be a handful
of tormented dust; each of my atoms could find peace only
with her" (III.vii).

Each success by Danton's opponents allows death to loom
ever larger and more threatening until it completely dominates
the final act. The various countenances it shows there are
determined by the different perspectives of the people who

face it. For Julie death is beautiful and desirable, because it will enable her to follow and remain with Danton. No theological or philosophical speculations can cause her to question the truth of her feelings. She welcomes without hesitation the death-containing vial as the priest whose blessing will permit her to enter her lover's bed. Though Danton is dissatisfied with the chaotic state of the world and tormented in life by suffering and despair, he fears and hates death. Julie, on the other hand, loves life and considers the earth to be beautiful and desirable, yet she leaves it willingly and gladly. Her lyrical description of the earth's appearance at sunset, as the light gradually grows dimmer and dimmer, reflects the gradual dimming or fading of her life. She goes into death as serenely as the earth slides into darkness at night:

> The sun has set. The earth's features were so sharp in its light, but now its face is as still and solemn as the face of someone dying. How beautifully the evening light plays on its brow and cheeks.

> It steadily grows paler and paler; it drifts down like a corpse in the flow of the ether. Will no arm grasp it by the golden locks and pull it out of the stream and bury it?

> I go quietly. I won't kiss it, so no breath, no sigh will wake it from its slumber.

> Sleep, sleep. (*She dies.*)[16] (IV.vi)

In stark contrast to Julie's beautiful death is the example of the callous man who willingly, perhaps eagerly, sacrifices his wife to the Revolution. Dumas compares himself to the Roman Consul Brutus, who killed his sons for plotting against the Republic. An incredulous Citizen claims he admires the legendary Brutus with all his soul, but he rejects nevertheless as monstrous and dreadful the deed of his would-be imitator.[17] One must have looked at the list of players to realize the full significance of the statement "The Revolutionary Tribunal will proclaim our divorce; the guillotine will separate us from table and bed" (IV.ii), for Dumas is himself one of the Presidents of the Revolutionary Tribunal.

As they await execution, Danton and his friends, each in his own way, must prepare to die. Lacroix and Hérault try through their witticisms to minimize the importance of death and to keep it at a distance. Camille is especially tormented by concern for Lucile and the possible consequences of her having been denounced during the trial for supposedly attempting to free him. He cannot bear to think that she might be harmed, and he does not want to believe that beauty such as hers can be destroyed (IV.iii).

While his friends sleep, Danton's mind wanders, as in modern stream-of-consciousness writing, along an associational path from one thought to another. As the clock ticks off the passing time he feels the walls closing in on him "until they are as narrow as a coffin." This simile reminds him of a frightening story he read as a child. "As a child," he repeats, and adds cynically: "A lot of good it did to fatten myself and keep myself warm. Just more work for the gravedigger!" "Gravedigger" suggests corpse, and Danton has the sensation of already being a stinking corpse, but, in order not to offend the body with which he has spent so much time, he will hold his nose and imagine the smell is something else. Still addressing his body, he states through a series of analogies that it will soon be a lifeless, useless, worn-out thing:

> Tomorrow you'll be a broken fiddle: its melody has been played out. Tomorrow you'll be an empty bottle: the wine has been drunk, but I'm not intoxicated and go to bed sober. They are lucky people who can still get drunk. Tomorrow you'll be a worn-out pair of pants: you'll be thrown in the closet and the moths will eat you, no matter how much you stink. (IV.iii)

But Danton can no longer find comfort in the playful manipulation of language and ideas. Finally he must agree with Camille: "Yes, having to die is miserable." He especially objects to the manner of his death, its ugliness and untimeliness. Consistent with his Epicureanism, he would have preferred an easy and beautiful end: "But I would like to have died differently, completely without effort, as a star falls, as a tone fades away, kissing itself to death with its own lips, as a ray of light is buried in clear streams." The discrepancy between things as they are and things as they should be seems to him to be the cause of such great suffering that it must be felt throughout the universe: "The stars are sprinkled through the night like sparkling tears. There must be great sorrow in the eye from which they have flowed" (IV.iii).

Lucile

Julie and Lucile have very minor roles in the first three acts, but they add an entirely new dimension to the play in the final act, Julie through her desire to follow Danton into death and through the lyrical beauty of her dying, and Lucile through the effect Camille's imminent death has on her psyche and through her pathetic, half-mad attempt to understand the meaning of death and dying.

When Lucile hears that Danton's arrest has been ordered, she fears for Camille and urges him to talk to Robespierre. The premonition that she will not see him again first gains expression through the folk song she sings almost unconsciously:

> Oh parting, oh parting, oh parting,
> Who ever conceived of such pain?

"How did that, of all things, come into my mind?" she asks herself. "It is not good that it found the way by itself." But now that it has, she admits having felt as Camille left "that he couldn't return and that he would have to go further and further from me, further and further." The sequence ends with her prophetic or anticipatory sensation of being in a room recently occupied by a corpse: "How empty the room is. The windows are open as if a corpse had lain in it. I can't stand it up here" (II.iii).

Lucille asks Camille if she is mad for even thinking that his head might fall. When her premonition proves true and he is sentenced to death, she does in fact lose her sanity. Looking at the prison window behind which Camille is standing, she cannot distinguish between him and his surroundings (IV.iv). The walls of the prison appear to her like a "stone coat" Camille is wearing and the bars of the window like an iron mask. After singing one strophe of a folk song in which the setting for a nocturnal rendezvous between lovers is described, she pathetically imagines herself in the position of the waiting girl and invites her friend up to her room. But he cannot pass through the gate, dressed as he is in his "insufferable costume." Frightened by his silence and immobility, she tells him to end his bad joke.

The loss of her sanity protects Lucile from fully comprehending what she could not bear. "Listen! The people say you must die, and they make such solemn faces." She cannot understand how a simple word like "die" can be taken so seriously: "Die! I must laugh at the faces. To die! What kind of word is that? Tell me, Camille. 'Die!' I will think about it." She attempts to grasp the word's meaning by repeating it again and again. When that fails, her mind transforms the abstraction into a concrete entity which can more easily be pursued: "There, there it is. I will chase it. Come, sweet friend, help me catch it. Come! Come!" (IV.iv).

Because of his preoccupation with Lucile and her madness, Camille is unwilling to discuss with his friends the political consequences of their impending execution. He had been unable to arouse Danton from his political indifference while it still mattered and is unwilling now to engage in useless *ex post facto* speculation and analysis. He is the only member of the group who is unselfishly in love, and he wants to be left alone to think about Lucile and her condition. He apparently feels the need to convince himself that he is not responsible for her madness: "Madness sat behind her eyes. Lots of people have gone mad. That's how it goes. What can we do about it? We wash our hands. And it is better that way" (IV.v). Anticipating Valerio from *Leonce and Lena*, he concludes that madness is a more comfortable *idée fixe* or delusion than the one generally called reason, because it can offer escape from the suffering and anxieties of an absurd life: "May heaven help her to a comfortable fixed idea. The common fixed ideas, which are called healthy reason, are intolerably boring. The happiest person was the one who could imagine that he was God the Father, the Son, and the Holy Ghost." His only regret is that he cannot remain to enjoy her madness with her: "What a charming child is the madness she has born. Why must I leave now? We could have laughed together with it, could have rocked and kissed it" (IV.v).

Through the contrast created by interposing Julie's private and beautiful suicidal death between the final scene at the Conciergerie and the ugly spectacle of the public execution to which Danton and his friends are submitted, Büchner greatly enhances the effectiveness of those scenes. Especially the jar-

ring transition from Julie's quiet death to the raucous singing
and dancing of the celebrating public and the singing of the
"Marseillaise" by the Dantonists creates a startling and powerful dramatic effect. Also theatrical is the execution itself, as
one after the other the condemned men mount the guillotine
they helped to erect.

The play does not end with this dramatic execution, however, but with Lucile's continuing attempt to find some meaning for what has taken place. She enters the scene as she
previously left it, still in pursuit of the significance of "dying."
She is beginning to understand it, she says, but she cannot
comprehend how someone as important as her Camille could
be affected by it, while the insignificant fly and the bird live on.
Camille said of Lucile that the earth would not dare to ex-
tinguish her beauty (IV.iii). She now echoes this sentiment with
respect to him: "The stream of life would have to stop if only
one drop of his blood were spilled. The earth would have to be
wounded by the blow" (IV.iii). These words are a poetic re-
statement of Payne's emotional argument: "The least twitch of
pain . . . makes a tear through creation from top to bottom"
(III.i). Camille's life is of such absolute importance for Lucile
that she thinks all life should cease if his does. But that is not
the case. Everything continues as before, as if his life and death
had meant nothing: "Everything is in motion, clocks run, bells
ring, people walk, water flows, and so, so everything goes
on. . . ." Unable to bear this situation, she decides to sit down
and scream so loud that everything will stop from fright: she
will force acknowledgement of Camille's death. When nothing
happens, she must finally admit to herself that his life is indeed
insignificant and that she can change nothing. She comes in her
own way to the insight she now shares with Danton, Saint-Just,
and Payne: "We must suffer it" (IV.viii).

In a historical moment dominated, as Büchner wrote in his
letter, by coarse and vulgar men (II.443-444), the important
women of the play appear only infrequently. They seem too
tender and delicate to be drawn into the intrigues and brutal-
ities of politics and government. Since they constitute one of
the few positive and beautiful aspects of an otherwise ugly and
meaningless reality, they are able to provide a last hope and
refuge for their disillusioned men. They are totally committed
to the men they love, or, in the case of Marion, to love itself. In

her four brief appearances Julie speaks only to Danton, twice directly and once through a messenger. Her last speech is a monologue. Lucile also appears four times, if we count the last two scenes separately. Except for two brief exchanges with Camille in one scene, all her speeches are monologues. The importance of these two women in the play, however, is far greater than the number of their speeches would indicate, partly because they, especially Lucile, frequently influence and occupy the thoughts of their husbands, and partly because they reveal through their voluntary deaths that man is free to make at least this one important decision.

Danton and his friends must die because Danton was either too indifferent or too consumed by despair to save himself and them. Julie, on the other hand, freely decides to take her life in order to be united with Danton in death. Lucile's similar decision provides the play with a moving conclusion. While sitting on the steps of the guillotine, she is approached by a patrol and asked to identify herself. She thinks for a moment and then makes her suicidal decision. "Long live the King!" she cries and is arrested "In the name of the Republic." Her decision and action do not reverse the deterministic implications of the rest of the play, as has been claimed, but emphasize rather the arbitrariness and absurdity of historical events and demonstrate the lie of Robespierre's pious assumption that the Revolution has claimed no innocent victims. Nothing could be more brutal, meaningless, and unjust than the arrest of this politically naive woman, who lives only to love her husband, and who makes what must be the only political declaration of her life in order that she can be rocked to sleep in the same "dear cradle" and sung to death by the same "sweet tongue" that took away her Camille.

(1) Language: lack of communication

The reader or spectator need not be familiar with the historical facts nor aware, even, of the play's title to realize from the beginning that Danton is doomed. When his cynical and morbid conversation with Julie is interrupted in the first scene by his friends, who bring news of the execution of Hébert and his followers, express outrage over the most recent developments of the Revolution, and describe with persuasive enthusiasm and rhetoric their own political intentions, Danton remains completely silent. He does not speak until after Camille urges, or commands, him to act: "Danton, you will attack at the Convention" (I.i). The nature and tone of his reply contrast sharply with his friends' aroused concern and eagerness to act, thus indicating the distance that separates him from them: "I will, you will, he will. If we live that long, say the old women. At the end of one hour, sixty minutes will have passed. Isn't it so, my lad?" Rather than attempt to explain to them why he is unwilling to act as they demand, he shows through the absurdity and inappropriateness of his answer that he considers their words and demands to be equally inappropriate and without meaning.

When pushed for an explanation, Danton asks a most surprising question for one whose oratory had once so effectively roused the masses to revolutionary action: "Who is to accomplish all those nice things?" And when Philippeau suggests that they will be joined in their efforts by the honest people— "We and the honest people"—Danton expresses doubt in the possibility that such a coalition could be formed or that it could serve a useful purpose even if it were: "The *and* in there is a long word. It holds us rather far apart. The stretch is long; honesty loses its breath before we come together. And even if we did!—One can lend money to the honest people and act as their godfather and marry one's daughters to them, but that is all." Danton's cynical answer contains none of the republican, humanistic sentiment just expressed by his friends. His lack of regard for the very people the Revolution was meant to benefit, and without whose support it cannot succeed, causes Camille to wonder why Danton began the fight in the first place. Conspicuously missing from Danton's reply is any reference to altruistic, idealistic, or socialistic goals: "Those people disgusted me. I never could look at such would-be Catos without giving them a kick. That's just my nature."

Whatever Danton's original motivation for taking up the revolutionary struggle may have been—his responses cannot always be taken at face value—it is clear by the end of this scene that he no longer shares the revolutionary fervor and program of his friends and that his experience of the Revolution has left him disillusioned, cynical, and largely indifferent to its future course. Bored and irritated by his friends' political discussion, Danton leaves. On his way out he prophesies that before the "statue of freedom" mentioned by Camille is cast, they can all burn their fingers. Notwithstanding his protestations, Danton's friends know that he will be with them when it comes to action, if "only for amusement, the way one plays chess" (I.i).

Having become alienated from his friends and politics, Danton seems to find diversion and enjoyment in the arms of women. Yet the play opens with his witty attack on the deceitful women playing cards with Hérault and the implication that all women, including Julie, at whose feet he is sitting, are liars. "See how cleverly the pretty lady turns the cards! She certainly knows how. It is said that she always presents the *coeur* to her husband and the *carreau* to the others. You women could make a man fall in love with a lie." As a masked expression of repressed aggression, wit generally intends to injure. A cynic may use this form of aggression in a particularly callous manner in order to defend himself against depression.[18] Danton's opening remark may well express in this disguised manner an unconscious and irrational disappointment at the failure of women, including his wife, to give his life meaning and to help him escape boredom.

But beyond that, like his impatience with his friends, his disregard for the "honest people," and his disgust with the political opposition, Danton's playfully serious statement about women expresses his dissatisfaction and disillusionment with the nature and condition of man in general. The real object of his anger and aggression is not specific individuals or groups, but the world as a whole and the forces which made it and make it as it is. "A mistake was made at our creation," he says later: "we lack something. I have no name for it. We won't tear it out of each other's guts, so why should we break open our bodies? Go on, we are miserable alchemists." Or, in the echoing words of Camille:

How long shall mankind devour its own limbs in eternal hunger? Or, how long shall we float on this shipwreck and suck the blood from each other's veins in unquenchable thirst? Or, how long shall we algebraists of the flesh continue to write our calculations with mutilated limbs in our search for the unknown, eternally withheld X" (II.i).

Danton might be able to come to terms with the hopelessness of bringing about the desired political and social changes and improvement if he could at least find meaning and a degree of fulfillment on the personal level, but in that regard, too, he has become disillusioned and skeptical. When Julie tells him that he knows her, he continues in the same brutally frank and serious manner to question the relevance and validity of a kind of knowledge which cannot penetrate beneath the physical appearance of a person to the thoughts and feelings that are hidden in the brain cells:

> You have dark eyes and wavy hair and a fine complexion and always say to me: dear George. But *(he points to her forehead and eyes)* there, there—what lies behind that. Go on, we have crude senses. Know each other? We would have to break open our skulls and tear the thoughts from each other's brain cells. (I.i)

Danton attributes man's isolation at least in part to the fact that the subjective and unsharable nature of his thoughts and feelings precludes meaningful communication. Julie's inability to understand even the immediate meaning of his words, let alone their deeper significance as expressions of his inner condition, tends to substantiate his assertion. If she did understand him, she would not misinterpret and be hurt by his remark: "No, Julie, I love you like the grave."

Whereas Julie assumes that Danton must know her, since otherwise he could not love her, his answer indicates that he does not love her because he knows her, but because he finds in her the peace he wants and needs, the peace he hopes and expects to find in the grave: "No, listen! They say there is peace in the grave and peace and grave are one. If that is so, I already lie under the earth in your lap. You sweet grave, your lips are death-bells, your voice is their knell. Your breast my burial mound, and your heart my coffin." While the Lady's cry of "Lost!" which follows this statement refers directly to the card game, it serves also as an ironic comment on Danton's condition and as a foreshadowing of his fate.

Communication between individuals is limited by the lack of a common and therefore sharable fund of knowledge, thoughts, and experiences and by the unreliability of sensual perception. It is also restricted by the ambiguity of language. By disregarding the conventions upon which verbal communication depends and by using words, concepts, and images in an idiosyncratic and arbitrary manner, Danton severely aggravates the very condition about which he complains. His absurd and confusing response to Camille's call-to-action is a case in point.

(2) Language: wit

In the puns and witticisms which abound in the "conversations" of Danton and some of his friends, language is not used for communication, but as an end in itself. In the context of wit, words and concepts take on an independent existence. They can be played, or played with, like the cards which provide a frame of reference for some of the puns and witticisms of the first scene. Because of its agonistic nature, the exchange of witticisms between two or more speakers may be compared to a game or contest: each participant attempts to outdo and triumph over the opponent or opponents. This is true of the erotically oriented punning which accompanies the card game between Hérault and the Lady as well as of the verbal contests engaged in by Danton and his friends. The following exchange between Lacroix and Hérault, who must spend their last night in prison sharing a bed, illustrates both the agonistic use of wit and its use as a defense against death:

> **Lacroix.** One's hair and nails grow so much—one must really be ashamed.
> **Hérault.** Be a little careful. You are sneezing my whole face full of sand.
> **Lacroix.** And don't you step like that on my feet, my good man, I have corns.
> **Hérault.** You still suffer from vermin.
> **Lacroix.** Oh, if only I could once get rid of the worms.
> **Hérault.** Sleep well, now. We have to see how we will get along together. We don't have much room. Don't scratch me with your nails when I'm asleep. So! Don't pull on the shroud. It's cold down there. (IV.iii)

The aggressive tendency of wit makes it a fine weapon for attacking, overcoming, and even destroying—through ridicule —one's opponent.[19] Of course the use of wit as a weapon has its limitations. To reduce through ridicule such humorless, brutal, and powerful opponents as Robespierre and Saint-Just can prove fatal. Robespierre's decision to eliminate Camille, for example, is provoked, as we have seen, by the witty attack Camille published in his paper.[20]

In their death-oriented witticisms the condemned men attempt to render the butt or object of the wit ridiculous and risible and therefore less threatening and painful. In addition to the exchange between Hérault and Lacroix cited above, Hérault's joking commentary at the execution itself is illustrative:

> **Lacroix.** The tyrants will break their necks over our graves.
> **Hérault** *(to Danton)*. He considers his corpse to be a hotbed of freedom.
> **Philippeau** *(on the scaffold)*. I forgive you. I hope your hour of death will not be bitterer than mine.
> **Hérault.** I thought so. He must expose his bosom again and show the people down there that he has clean linen.
> **Fabre.** Farewell, Danton. I am dying twice.
> **Danton.** Adieu, my friend. The guillotine is the best doctor.
> **Hérault** *(wants to embrace Danton)*. Oh, Danton, I can't even make another joke. Now it's time. (IV.vii)

Hérault does not want to outlive his ability to joke and to laugh at life.

Because of its aggressive, agonistic quality, wit is inherently dramatic. The wit is a performer who requires an audience, someone to appreciate the skill of his performance and to laugh with him at the victim of his verbal assaults. The prominence in this play of witticisms, jokes, and puns supports Danton's claim that all men are players (II.i). The player is more concerned with displaying himself and his talents than with the give and take of authentic conversation. He is alone and lonely. Behind the comic mask of the wit is a suffering, hostile, despairing individual.[21] It is appropriate that Camille, the opponent of idealism in art, should encourage his friends to remove their masks and face the ugly truth of reality:

> We should once remove the masks; we would then see as in a room filled with mirrors just the one primeval, numberless, indestructible jackass [*Schafskopf*], nothing more, nothing less. The differences are not so great. We are all scoundrels and angels, fools and geniuses; in fact we are all those things together. . . . Sleeping, digesting, making children—all do

that. The other things are only variations in different keys on the same theme . . . so scream and whine when you feel like it.

Just don't make such virtuous and such witty and such heroic and such sagacious faces. We know each other after all. Save the effort.

Hérault agrees:

Yes, Camille, let's sit with each other and scream. Nothing is more foolish than to press our lips together when something hurts us.

The Greeks and the gods screamed, the Romans and the Stoics made heroic grimaces.

But in this, too, Danton differs from his friends. He believes that the Greeks and gods enjoyed their screaming as much as the Romans and Stoics did their heroic posturing; each acted out the role which pleased him best. Consistent with his view of men as actors, Danton thinks it natural that they should be concerned with how they play and how their performances are received: "The ones were Epicureans just as much as the others. . . . It's not so bad to drape yourself in a toga and to look around to see if you are casting a long shadow" (IV.v).

(3) Rhetorical language

As a successful political leader and orator, Danton knows well how language is and must be used to manipulate people and to hide and distort the truth. While it is primarily Robespierre and Saint-Just who hold the public stage in the period covered by the play, Danton is once again cast in the role of public performer by the necessity of defending himself before the Revolutionary Tribunal and by his desire to "cast a long shadow." In his self-defense, as in the previously discussed witty exchanges and heroic posturing, Danton does not use language to express his inner thoughts and feelings, but to convince those listening of his importance for the Revolution and to persuade them that he should be freed and that his accusers pose a far greater threat to the Revolution than he does. Rhetorical speeches, like theatrical performances, cannot be judged by the degree of truth they contain, but by their ability to move and persuade. Danton has become disillusioned with this type of performance precisely because it has no regard for the truth, because it precludes the possibility of authentic interpersonal communication, and, what is more, because it reduces human beings to the level of things. In its ability to manipulate and destroy men, language can be a powerful weapon in the service of those who wield it, but like the Revolution itself, it can escape the control of those who create it and destroy it too.[22]

Danton's unwillingness to continue wielding the rhetorical sword makes him vulnerable to the attack of those who do not share his compunctions. (Thus, in this regard, too, his conscience is responsible for his death.) When Robespierre first appears, it is to take control of an angry mob and to use its energy and momentum to serve his purpose. At first the discontented citizens refuse to listen to him: they want blood, not words. But once a fanatical woman persuades them to listen to "the Messiah, who is sent to choose and to judge," he easily convinces them that in order to prevent their enemies, i.e., the Dantonists, from turning their own force against themselves, they need the leadership which he and his party can offer. "Your lawmakers are watching; they will guide your hands. Their eyes are undeceivable, your hands are inescapable. Come with me to the Jacobins. Your brothers will open their arms to you. We will sit in judgment of our enemies" (I.ii).

Through his clever use of language and imagery, Robespierre demonstrates to the people that their interests coincide with those of the Jacobins and that they and the Jacobins belong together like separate organs of a single organism. In his historical speech at the Jacobin Club, Robespierre referred to his own actions in the first person singular and addressed his listeners in the second person plural. More skilled in the use of rhetoric, Büchner's Robespierre uses the first person plural to emphasize his unity with the group he is addressing. For example, what appears in Büchner's source as "*Vous* n'avez donc rien fait s'il *vous* reste une faction à détruire,"[23] becomes in the play: "We have done nothing, if we still have another faction to destroy."

Robespierre's public speeches here and throughout reveal the mentality and method of the political demagogue.[24] He is completely uninhibited in his public statements by Danton's sense of the complexity and ambiguity of life and language. He employs simple syllogistic logic, albeit with false premises and vague, unfounded generalities, to prove his points. The passion of his rhetoric, the persuasive quality of his imagery, and the rhythm of his language sweep his listeners along with him, without giving their benumbed and uninstructed intellects the chance to question the soundness of what he says. In this way he can persuade them to accept the self-contradictory designation of the Revolutionary Government as the "despotism of freedom against tyranny;" he can make the humane plea for mercy seem like a crime against the Revolution: "It [Danton's faction] drives us to weakness; its battle cry is: 'Mercy!' It wants to tear from the people the weapons and the strength that wields those weapons in order to deliver them up, naked and enervated, to the kings;" and he can convince people that terror and virtue are inseparable attributes of an attitude or quality more desirable than mercy: "The weapon of the Republic is terror, the strength of the Republic is virtue. Virtue, because without it terror is pernicious; terror, because without it virtue is impotent. Terror is an outgrowth of virtue; it is nothing other than swift, severe, and unbending justice." Where virtue is the strength of the Republic, vice must be not only morally but also politically condemnable: "This is the subtlest, most dangerous and abominable attack on freedom. Vice is the aristocracy's mark of Cain. In a Republic it is not only a moral but also a political crime. A depraved man is a political enemy of freedom. The greater the services which he has apparently rendered to it, the more dangerous he is" (I.iii). By not mentioning names while painting his portrait of the one remaining enemy of the Republic, Robespierre avoids a direct personal attack and seems to leave it to those listening to draw their own conclusions from his remarks—the conclusions his skillful use of rhetorical language has carefully and unequivocally led them to.

(4) Lyrical language

At the opposite extreme from the coldly logical, goal-oriented, rhetorical language of Robespierre and Saint-Just is the simple, spontaneous, lyrical language of Marion and the monologues of Julie and Lucile. The differences in language cor-

respond to the basic differences in the nature and interests of
Büchner's male and female figures as suggested above. The
women lead intensely personal lives and have no need or desire
to persuade and convince others. Emotions and feelings are
more important for them than ideas, political programs, and
power. Especially Marion represents in a pure form what Danton defines as Epicureanism. She is completely at one with
herself and acts entirely in accordance with her nature: "I
know nothing of breaks and changes. I am always the same. An
uninterrupted longing and grasping, a burning, a stream" (I.v).
Unlike most people, who work six days a week and pray only
on Sunday, she prays every day, as it were, because she lives for
pleasure, and "whoever enjoys the most, prays the most." The
days are all alike to her and so are the men: "For me there was
only one contrast; all men melted into one body." Consonant
with her refusal or inability to establish logical or chronological
interrelationships between individual moments, persons, or
events, her language is almost free of subordination and the
establishment of interrelationships: each statement has about
the same importance as every other statement. Thus her inner
being is appropriately expressed through the simple, spontaneous flow of her language: "But I became like a sea that
swallowed everything and dug in deeper and deeper;" "I sank
into the waves of twilight;" "I am . . . a stream."

Danton would like to be a part of that stream, to be more like
Marion, but his experience and intellectual sophistication have
destroyed his innocence and the unity of his being. However,
through the inspiration of Marion's uninhibited vitality and the
harmony of her being, he can momentarily free himself from
the cynicism and pessimism which are products of his disillusionment and inner discord. In such moments he also overcomes his distrust of language and expresses himself lyrically:
"Why can't I take your beauty entirely into myself and completely enclose it? . . . I would like to be a part of the ether, in
order to bathe you in my flood and to break on every undula-
tion of your beautiful body" (I.v).

To the extent that it does not demand or expect an answer,
rhetorical language is fundamentally monologic. In *Danton*
such language is the idiom for public speeches, the formulation
of political programs, and the polemical statement by the cit-

izens of their political and social demands. In general, however, the language in the play tends toward the lyrical. Lyrical language is also monologic. In a world where there is no real communication and where the individual is essentially alone and isolated, language tends to be rhetorical in public and lyrical in private moments. A speaker either attempts to convince and persuade his listeners through logic and pathos or to express lyrically his thoughts and feelings. Because it is the essence of the lyrical idiom to express directly and spontaneously the feelings of the moment, it is the ideal mode for realizing Büchner's intention of creating characters rather than characteristics, of capturing the contradictions, paradoxes, and inconsistencies that distinguish human beings from the mechanical and lifeless marionettes of idealistic art. Because of its focus on the moment, the lyrical idiom and mood are especially compatible with the Epicurean outlook on life and the episodic, or paratactic, structure. It also provides the means for creating the atmosphere which is so important in Büchner's plays.

The lyrical idiom also constitutes a high style by means of which elevated moments of intense feeling are set off from the realistically presented background. Julie's death-monologue, Lucile's expressions of foreboding and madness, Danton's account of his tormenting dream, and his expression of the desire to die a beautiful death may be cited as examples. Even Robespierre's language becomes lyrical when suppressed suspicions and fears emerge from the lower depths of his mind to question his motives and challenge his rigid and lifeless ideology. Lyrical moments sometimes culminate a longer monologue or monologic dialogue. Where the realistic style reaches its uppermost level of intensity, the change to the lyrical mode provides a qualitative leap into a higher plane, into the realm of dreams, magic, and ecstasy, a realm in which the normal exigencies of time, space, and logic no longer apply.[25] The short exchange that follows and contrasts with Marion's story of her life, the climax of Robespierre's monologue (I.vi), and the words and gestures of the Dantonists following the climax of their common expression of nihilism and protest (IV.v) may serve as illustrations.

(5) Colloquial language

At the other extreme is the coarse and vulgar language of the common people. The discrepancy between the two levels is effectively revealed through Simon's attempt to speak in the elevated style and with the pathos of the plays familiar to him in his occupation as theater-prompter. He first appears like a figure of low comedy, beating and cursing his wife: "You procuress, you mercuric pill, you worm-eaten apple of sin!" (I.ii). Having attracted a crowd, he begins to reach for a higher level by assuming the role of a Roman republican—"No, leave me be, Romans. I want to smash these bones! You vestal virgin"—and by attempting to imitate the style of the classical drama:

> Thus I tear the dress from your shoulders,
> Then hurl naked your carcass into the sun.

The comic incongruity between language and speaker and between the form and content of language is clearly demonstrated by Simon's inability to find an appropriate designation for his daughter: "Where is the maid? Speak! No, I cannot say that. The girl! No, not that either. The lady, the woman! Not that, not that either! Only one name remains! Oh it chokes me! I have no breath for it." Instead of arousing pity, Simon's affected pathos exposes him to ridicule; taking his metaphor literally, the Citizen replies: "That's good, for otherwise the name would smell of booze." Simon's wife finally explains in the coarse idiom of the people what Simon could not express with his inflated language and imagery. She praises her daughter for becoming a prostitute and providing for her parents. In her eyes Simon is not comparable with Virginius, who killed his daughter to save her virtue, but with Judas:.

> You Judas. Would you have a pair of pants to pull up, if the young gentlemen didn't let their pants down with her? You barrel of brandy. Do you want to die of thirst when the fountain stops running? Eh? We work with all our parts, so why not with that one too? Her mother worked with it when she came into the world, and it hurt. Can't she also work with it for her mother? Eh? Even if it does hurt her in the process. Eh? You blockhead. (I.ii)

The scene ends with a capricious reversal similar to the one later demonstrated by the people's fickle change from support to condemnation of Danton (III.x): Simon invites his virtuous wife" to go with him to the daughter he has wronged.

The people's coarse and vulgar jesting, an incongruous and parodistic attempt to imitate the high style of classical drama, polemical speeches meant to inflame the people and whet their appetite for blood, a revolutionary song, the witty remark that saves a young aristocrat's life, argument between the people and Robespierre and the latter's rhetorically skillful manipulation of the people—such is the variety of a single scene. It is characteristic of this type of play that each scene strives, through its diversity and range, to convey the impression of life, to suggest life's fullness and complexity. As a self-contained unit, each part is a miniature or reduced reflection of the whole. At the same time, each part reaches beyond its borders to imply what preceded and to suggest what will follow.

Dramatic unity

Unity of impression, the only unity that matters in the drama, is achieved when all the constituent parts are subordinated to a central spirit or idea. The well-known classical, or classicistic, unities of time, place, and action may provide useful means for achieving this end, but there are others as well. One of these, the use of recurring motifs, will be discussed in some detail in the chapter on *Woyzeck*. Especially important in *Danton* is the associative or contrasting interconnection of individual parts: a particular thought or occurrence may be followed by a contrasting one, which often provides ironic comment, or by a similar and thus reenforcing one. By shifting perspective the author can present different points of view on a particular matter, and he can provide comment on the characters of the play, showing them from various aspects and in various situations, as they see themselves and as they are seen by others.

Büchner uses contrast for variety, emphasis, and as a means of controlling the spectators' responses. Contrasts occur between scenes, parts of scenes, speeches, and individual sentences. High rhetoric contrasts with vulgar slang, personal action contrasts with public, comic scenes with serious ones.[26]

Seemingly unrelated elements are combined in metaphors and images to produce striking and surprising effects, as in the identification of Julie with a grave or Robespierre with the Messiah.

The respective reactions of Lucile, the spectators, and the executioners to the death of the Dantonists effectively illustrate the juxtaposition of contrasting episodes. In her attempt to understand death, Lucile learns how absurd the world is and how meaningless the life of an individual. It is a crushing insight that destroys her will to live. The women spectators, on the other hand, take sadistic pleasure in death as a public spectacle:

> **First Woman.** A handsome man, that Hérault.
> **Second Woman.** As he was standing by the Arch of Triumph on Constitution Day, I thought to myself: he would certainly look good on the guillotine. That was a kind of a premonition.
> **Third Woman.** Yes, you have to see the people in all situations. It's very good that dying is becoming so public. (IV.viii)

And it is all in a day's work for the executioners, one of whom nonchalantly sings a folk song while cleaning off the instruments of his profession. The magnitude of Lucile's suffering and the deeply human and loving nature of her response to the same instrument and to the day's events are emphasized by the contrast with the callous indifference of the executioners and the perverse delight of the women; but at the same time, the fact that her reaction is seen as only one of a number of possibilities relativizes it and prevents it from having a sentimental effect.

Almost any sequence of episodes contains similar contrasts. Marion is contrasted with Adelaide and Rosalie, for example, when the latter arrive with Lacroix and disturb her and Danton. The fact that she does not take part in their vulgar conversation and exchange of witty obscenities reveals that she is different from them. A change in tenor from the erotic to the political follows, as Paris arrives with news of the meeting of the Jacobins. Actually, the two seemingly unrelated spheres of activity are intimately connected, since Danton's enjoyment of life has become a political issue. The meeting with Marion makes it possible for the spectator to judge the validity of Robespierre's claim that Danton's so-called vice is counterrevolutionary. In fact, only Danton's friends could consider it so: since Danton's interest in women is an escape from the political arena, it weakens their position and makes them vulnerable. When Marion finally speaks again and tells Danton: "Your lips have become cold; your words have suffocated your kisses," he regrets the time he has wasted with political concerns and dismisses his friends with the promise that he will go to Robespierre, albeit not until tomorrow. Lacroix's parting remark explicitly connects the political and erotic spheres in another striking metaphor: "Good night, Danton," he says, "the thighs of the women are guillotining you, the mons veneris is becoming your Tarpeian Rock" (I.v).

Analysis of the first scene reveals a similar alternation between contrasting moments. It begins with a clear division into two separate groups, one composed of Danton sitting at Julie's feet and the other of Hérault playing cards with some women. Danton's opening remark refers to the card game, but leads immediately into matters of a very serious and personal nature, namely man's inability to know the true thoughts and feelings of others. His exchange with Julie is interrupted and ironically commented upon by the playful conversation of the card players, through which the suggestion is made that life, especally in its erotic aspect, is a game. Parallel to the scene with Marion, the entrance of Camille and Philippeau causes a shift from private and personal to public and political matters. Hérault's playful tone carries over into the beginning speech of the new episode, but his humor now contains more bitter and aggressive undertones. He exposes the serious business of the Revolution to scorn and laughter by making it appear ridiculous and petty. Camille continues in the same vein when he contemptuously contrasts the present "guillotine Romanticism" with the classical Republicanism of the likes of Alcibiades and Socrates. It is a comparison that is made or implied again and again during the play, always to the detriment of the modern republicans, who attempt to imitate but actually parody their classical counterparts. As the scene with Marion begins and ends in the erotic sphere, so this one begins and ends with references to games, and again the apparently distinct spheres are implicitly and explicitly connected through juxtaposition, analogy, and metaphor. In both cases the scene concludes with a metaphoric association of the basic themes, politics and sex in the one, politics and game-playing in the other.

Episodic or paratactic structure

As if anticipating the public's lack of understanding for the kind of play he was writing, Büchner includes in *Danton,* as he later does in *Lenz,* a brief statement of his aesthetic position.[27] At the time Büchner was writing, the stage was dominated by classicistic, idealistic plays and sentimental melodramas performed in a declamatory, hence stilted and artificial style. It is these types of plays and this style of acting that Camille attacks:

> I tell you, if they don't get everything in wooden copies, scattered about in theaters, concerts, and art exhibits, they have neither eyes nor ears for it. If someone carves a marionette, whose controlling strings one sees and whose joints creak in blank verse at every step — what character, what consistency! If someone takes a little feeling, a maxim, a concept and dresses it in a coat and pants, makes hands and feet for it, colors its face, and lets the thing agonize around for three acts until it finally either marries or kills itself — an ideal! If someone fiddles an opera that reproduces the soaring and sinking of the human emotions as a clay pipe with water does the nightingale — oh, the artistry! (II.iii)

In place of a non-existent, idealized world peopled by artificial and lifeless figures, the artist should attempt to capture in his art the "glowing, roaring, shining creation that . . . renews itself every moment." "In my opinion the dramatist is nothing but a historian," Büchner wrote to his family in defense of his play:

> He stands *above* the latter, however, through the fact that he creates history a second time, and instead of giving us a dry narration, he transposes us directly into the life of a time, giving us characters rather than characteristics, figures rather than description. His highest task is to come as close as possible to history as it really occurred. . . . The poet does not teach morality. He discovers and creates figures, he makes the past live again, and the people may then learn from it as well as from the study of history and from the observation of what takes place around them in life. (II.443-444: 28 July 1835)

In terms similar to Camille's, Büchner criticizes the idealist writers for creating "nothing but marionettes with sky-blue noses and affected pathos" rather than people of flesh and blood, "whose suffering and joy cause me to empathize and whose actions inspire me with loathing or admiration" (II.444). He admires Shakespeare and the early Goethe and follows their example in using the episodic form of drama to place his hero in the broad context of his time. With the figure of Danton as the integrating point, the diverse elements of the broadly drawn scene and the multiplicity of figures form a large-scale montage, a cross-section of an important moment in history.

The "Promenade" scene, which immediately precedes Camille's statement on aesthetics, illustrates on a small scale how this technique works. This scene contains fourteen different speaking roles and includes representatives from all social levels. It touches upon matters of such basic human interest as love, sex, pregnancy, birth, death, patriotism, work, leisure, material possessions, technical progress, the theater, fear, desire, optimism, and pessimism. Its seven different episodes fill only three pages. While each episode is complete in itself, its meaning and dramatic effect are also influenced by its relationship to the others. Episodes often begin *in medias res,* as when Danton enters with Camille and exclaims: "Just don't expect anything serious from me." When walking by a moment before, he took obvious pleasure in the sensuality surrounding him and felt inclined to participate. Now he cannot understand why the people do not stop on the streets and laugh in each others' faces.[28] The abrupt change and nihilistic reply are the only indications of what preceded, but Danton's short answer to Camille and the extremity of his disgusted response are enough to suggest that Camille has again importuned Danton to act.

The individual parts or units of the episodic drama are arranged, like the episodes of the "Promenade" scene, in a predominantly paratactic relationship. The structural difference between the episodic or open and the classicistic or closed form of drama can be roughly defined as the difference between parataxis and hypotaxis.[29] As opposed to the hypotactic structure, in which the complex logical and hierarchical interrelationship of parts is clearly established through the use of complex structures, the simple, serial arrangement of parts is ideally suited to the presentation of a fragmented world, a world in which clearly defined relationships are lacking, and in which the individual stands alone. It is also compatible with the spontaneous, natural, and simple form of expression and the orientation toward the moment which is characteristic of the Epicurean attitude toward life as defined by Danton. *Danton's Death* is predominantly paratactic on the higher structural levels, i.e., in the arrangement of scenes and episodes within scenes, but not on the lower. The "Promenade" scene, in which there are no subordinating conjunctions, is one of only a few passages that anticipate the fully developed and consistent use of the form as it later occurs in *Woyzeck*.

The growing appreciation of Büchner's dramatic achievement has depended upon the increase in importance of this type of drama. Since it demands more from the reader or spectator, who must make connections, supply missing but implied information, and draw his own conclusions, the public had to be prepared for it. The use of a similar form in the early cinema and the expressionistic drama, which was strongly influenced by Büchner, helped to prepare for the reception of Büchner's works when they finally reached the stage.[30]

III. *LEONCE AND LENA*

Though it is without doubt Büchner's weakest play, *Leonce and Lena* definitely is not the embarassingly simple and derivative piece of hack work some have considered it, and it has probably been Büchner's most successful play as far as frequency of performance and favorable public reception is concerned.[1] If each of the many generic designations assigned to it by critics actually represents a valid and justifiable possibility, the play must be far more complex than has generally been assumed. In that case each narrow and restrictive label will prove to be the product of reductionistic interpretation which tends to obscure the true essence of the play by focusing on one or the other of its constituent parts. A brief survey of such designations reveals a bewildering range of possibilities.

Genre

Writing at the time of a neo-romantic reaction against Naturalism, one of the earliest editors and analysts of Büchner's works noted the similarities between *Leonce and Lena* and the Romantic comedies of Musset, Brentano, and Tieck. He considered Büchner's play to be the "Ideal of a Romantic comedy" and the realization of what the Romantic poets themselves had failed to achieve.[2] A recent essay agrees with this interpretation and adds that the "fulfillment" of the form made its further use untenable.[3] Another critic demonstrates that *Leonce and Lena* is not a Romantic comedy at all, but a comedy of the Romantic, a realistic *"selbst-reductio ad absurdum"* of Romanticism and Idealism.[4] While it has been hailed as the most enchanting[5] and

most successful[6] German comedy, it has also been dismissed as
an unoriginal and unimportant "reversion to the simple literary
comedy of Romanticism based on Shakespeare's pattern."[7] One
critic considers it to be realistic like Büchner's other works,[8]
whereas another believes that it completely lacks the social
realism of Büchner's other works and stands apart from them in
its presentation of an unreal, fairy tale world.[9] Or realism and
fairy tale may be combined to yield *"Märchenrealismus."*[10]
Emphasis on the non-realistic nature of the play is reflected
in such designations as "Utopian fairy tale" *(Schlaraffenmär-
chen),*[11] "sad fairy-tale-comedy,"[12] and "dream play."[13] In addition to some of the terms already cited, the comic nature of the
play has been emphasized by such a wide diversity of designations as "ironic comedy,"[14] "satirical comedy,"[15] "inverted comedy,"[16] "comedy of mood,"[17] and "parody of comedy."[18] Some
critics have chosen to give greater emphasis to the serious and
even tragic aspects of the comedy by calling it a "tragicomedy,"[19] "a melancholy masterpiece, a tragicomedy of idleness and frustration,"[20] a "pantragic comedy"[21] and a "nihilistic
drama."[22] This seemingly endless list can be extended to include such fanciful suggestions as a "Mozartian pastorale,"[23] a
"festival play,"[24] and "a kind of fate play."[25] When confronted
with such an array of designations, we face the same problem
King Peter does in attempting to identify Valerio under all his
masks. The conclusion is similar in both cases: no single mask
or designation represents or names the total phenomenon.

Determination of the type or intrinsic genre of a work of art
is both a prerequisite and a goal of interpretation: operating
within the hermeneutic circle, the interpreter's notion of the
type of work he is dealing with influences his interpretation of
details, just as his interpretation of details influences his notion
of the type of genre of the work. E. D. Hirsch defines "intrinsic genre" as "that sense of the whole by means of which an
interpreter can correctly understand any part in its deter-
minacy."[26] When a critic assigns a particular label to a work of
art, he indicates, whether consciously or not, the generic concept which determines his interpretation. Such a label is an
integral part of the interpretation and should be questioned and
analyzed as such.

When an artist moves into new territory, he and his interpreters may be hard-pressed to discover a generic label that

adequately describes the new phenomenon. Since new types are created either by extending or recombining old ones, the critic may feel that he can name the new thing by identifying its constituent parts; but this is as futile as attempting to identify a metaphor with its component parts instead of with the new meaning that results from the combination of those parts. The critics who fail to recognize the originality of Büchner's comedy and who attempt to identify it with one or another of the sources from which the author borrowed ideas, motifs, and even direct quotations are guilty of doing just that: while identifying the component parts of Büchner's dramatic metaphor, they fail to recognize that an altogether new meaning is created by the new and unique combination of its parts.

To be as specific as possible without excluding any of its attributes and without unduly focusing attention on any particular facet of the whole, we can probably do no better than settle for the broad generic designation chosen by the author himself. In doing so, we also accept his right to suggest the point of view from which we should approach his work. Büchner wrote the play to compete for a prize being offered for the best German comedy *(Lustspiel)*, and that is what he called it.

Büchner's sense of the comic

A principal cause for misinterpretations of this comedy has been the failure to recognize that gravity or levity do not reside in the characters and events themselves, but in the manner in which they are represented and viewed. From the fact that Leonce is similar in many respects to Lenz and Danton and to a number of tragic or serious figures of world literature, it does not necessarily follow that Leonce must be taken seriously as an almost tragic figure.[27] In their eagerness to penetrate through the supposedly superficial and inconsequential veneer of comic appearance in order to get at the play's real, i.e., serious, content and meaning, most writers have failed to notice Büchner's sense of humor and his ability to perceive comic elements in the most serious situations. No matter how often he was threatened by his emotional involvement in futile political activity and by his disturbing insights into the nature of man, history, and life, he was able to preserve or regain some degree of the intellectual detachment and emotional balance which is

characteristic of the comic attitude. It is obvious from Büchner's letters and from his use of witticisms and puns in *Danton's
Death*[28] that he was quite aware of the distancing function of
humor, wit, and the comic attitude.

Büchner frequently uses comic devices in his letters to express detachment from external events and to alienate his own
thoughts and experiences. In some instances he reveals his
ability to see himself and others from a comic perspective; in
others he wants to give the impression that he is detached,
when in fact he is quite involved; and in still others he seems to
be making a desparate attempt to save himself from extreme
melancholy and despair. After having described the enthusiastic reception accorded the Polish freedom fighters by the students of Strasbourg, for example, Büchner apparently felt that
he had revealed too much of himself to his parents, whereupon
he attempted to estrange himself from the affair by dismissing it
as comedy: "Then Ramorino appears on the balcony and expresses thanks. The crowd shouts 'Vivat!'—and the comedy is
finished" (II.413: December 1831).[29] A description of the serious political situation in Strasbourg written a year later ends
similarly: "I do not have enough time for a political essay, and
it would not be worth the effort anyway. The whole thing is
really only a comedy" (II.415: December 1832). He reveals the
same ambivalence in his attitude toward people. While he was
deeply moved and troubled by the problems and suffering of
others, he could also laugh with critical detachment at man's
inherent and inescapable foolishness:

> I am accused of *mockery*. It is true; I often laugh. But I do
> not laugh at *how* someone is a man, but at the fact *that* he is a
> man, about which he can't do anything anyway, and at the
> same time I laugh at myself, for I share his fate. People call
> that mockery. They cannot bear it, that someone plays the
> role of a fool and becomes familiar with them. They are
> contemptuous, scornful, and arrogant because they look for
> foolishness only *outside themselves*. (II.423)

Büchner's more candid letters to his fiancée and friends also
contain numerous examples of his ability to shift from a committed attitude of emotional involvement to a self-alienated,
comic attitude of intellectual detachment. He concludes the
darkest, most disturbed letter he ever wrote by calling it a

"*Charivari,*" i.e., a mock serenade (II.426: after 10 March 1834). Another time he wrote: "If I want to do something serious, I appear to myself like Larifari in the comedy: if he wants to draw his sword, it's a hare's tail" (II.427: March 1834).

Leonce and Danton

One critic writes that "comedy at its most penetrating derives from what we normally regard as tragic."[30] *Leonce and Lena* provides convincing support for this statement. Leonce derives not only from figures such as Brentano's Ponce de Leon and Musset's Fantasio, but also from the likes of Werther, Hamlet, and especially Danton. The serious implications of his character and condition with their inherent proximity to and potential for tragedy are necessary prerequisites for comedy, which depends for its effect on the "minimization of the claim of some particular thing to be taken seriously, either by reducing that claim to absurdity, or by reducing it merely to the negligible in such a way as to produce pleasure by that minimization."[31] We do not take Leonce or his situation seriously, because the fairy tale improbability of events, the absence of any real pain or threat, and the apparent non-involvement of good or evil forces prevent us from identifying with him emotionally.[32] We view him with the intellectual detachment and the light-hearted, playful attitude characteristic of the comic perspective.

The importance of perspective and manner of presentation can be demonstrated by contrasting Leonce and Danton. In *Leonce and Lena* Büchner parodies the attitudes and ideas of the hero of his serious play: Leonce is a Danton-like figure transposed from the grim reality of the French Revolution to a comedic world of fantasy and illusion in the Kingdom of Popo. If the world is a stage and life but a play, as Danton maintains, then *Leonce and Lena* presents the illusion of an illusion. With a fine sense of romantic irony, Büchner engages in what Friedrich Schlegel called "transcendental buffoonery."[33]

Like Danton, and like Lenz after his breakdown, Leonce is a reflective man whose will to act is paralyzed by the realization that all men, whether heroes, geniuses, fools, saints, or sinners, are fundamentally alike: all are nothing but "cunning idlers" whose various activities are motivated by the desire to fill the emptiness of their lives and to escape boredom. Unlike Danton and Lenz, however, Leonce has not gained his insights and knowledge from fighting a losing and disillusioning battle with reality and historical forces. For Danton and Lenz, idleness and boredom are the void that remains after they lose the beliefs and ideals that once gave their actions purpose and meaning: Danton no longer believes in freedom of action or the possibility of controlling political revolution, and Lenz loses his faith in God.[34] Unlike Danton and Lenz, Leonce has no prehistory. (He is the only one of Büchner's "heroes" who is not based on a historical figure.) His dramatic life beings, as it were, near the point where theirs end. He represents the continuation and attempted reversal of their situations: he would like to find some ideal that could fill his empty life and give meaning to his senseless actions. But from the standpoint of the real, historical world of Danton and Lenz, Leonce's idealistic longing is ridiculous self-delusion and romantic escapism. Büchner's satire of idealism and parody of the idealistic drama demonstrates that if the idealistic alternative can exist at all, it is only in the unreal, fairy tale world of the comedy. And even there it is ridiculous.

Leonce as a comic figure

It is apparent from the moment the play opens that Leonce is not to be taken seriously. Incongruity is a major source of the comic,[35] and the play begins with a striking example of an incongruous situation: while half-reclining on a bench, Leonce tells his Tutor that he is too busy to prepare for his profession: "I've got my hands full; I have so much work, I don't know where to begin" (I.i).[36] His words are contradicted by his posture as well as by the ridiculous activities he considers to be "work": spitting on a stone 365 times in succession; throwing sand in the air, catching it on the back of his hand, and betting on whether he has an odd or even number; and thinking about what he would have to do to see the top of his head. Leonce ends the description of his work by asking: "Am I an idler? Do I have no occupation?" Assuming that the description of his various activities should have made it unmistakably clear what the answer to his rhetorical question must be, he pauses briefly, sighs perhaps, and changes the subject: "Yes, it's sad. . . ." But before he can complete the sentence, the Tutor finally manages to get in a word of agreement. Like all the other courtiers in the play, the Tutor is either unable or afraid to express a thought or opinion of his own. He refrains from attempting to answer Leonce's questions, because he is afraid he might say the wrong thing. When it appears that Leonce is answering them himself, however, it seems safe for him to concur: "Very sad, Your Highness." His ironically ill-timed reply effects a reversal of Leonce's intended meaning; it bisects Leonce's sentence and causes the independent clause, "Yes, it's sad," to refer syntactically to what preceded rather than to what follows, thus causing Leonce's words to be understood as the affirmative answer to his question rather than the beginning of a new statement.

This deceptively simple device reinforces the spectator's initial impression. Leonce's posture and his description of the activities that occupy him indicate that he is indeed an idler. The comic incongruity between his words and actions causes the spectator to view him with skepticism and detachment and to realize that he cannot be taken seriously. When Leonce completes his Hamletian statement of melancholy: "[Yes, it's sad] That for three weeks the clouds have been moving from west to east. It makes me awfully melancholy,"[37] the syco-phantic Tutor agrees that it is a "very well-founded melan-choly," but the spectator is not convinced.[38] And Leonce's own response reveals that his statement was meant to provoke disagreement, or, failing this, to expose the Tutor as an inade-quate partner for dialogue.[39] Taking part in verbal battle can provide another means for killing time, as Leonce's repartee with Valerio demonstrates. When the Tutor fails to take the challenge, Leonce dismisses him with scorn: "Man, why don't you contradict me? You're in a hurry, aren't you? I'm sorry I held you up so long."

The comic attitude continues to prevail in the following monologue. When Leonce describes bees, the very emblem of diligence and industry, as sitting indolently by flowers, and the sun's rays, the source of light, heat, and life, as lying lazily on the ground, the potentially serious implications of his statement are undermined by the incongruity between the meaning con-ventionally ascribed to these symbols and the meaning Leonce gives them. In fact, Leonce himself views life from a comic perspective. Since he recognizes that boredom is the source of all activity, he must laugh at the people who perform their absurd activities in all seriousness: "What people don't do out of boredom? They study out of boredom, they pray out of boredom, they fall in love, marry, and procreate out of boredom, and finally they die out of boredom and—and that's the humor of it—all with the most solemn faces, without realizing why and thinking God knows what in the process."

It may be possible to draw serious consequences from Leonce's situation and disposition, but readers who are responsive to the author's use of comic devices will recognize and laugh at the ridiculous nature of Leonce's desires and ambitions, the comic inconsistency between his various statements, the incongruity between the form and the content of his language, and the playful tone of the scene as a whole. Directors can greatly enhance the comic effect on the stage through the use of appropriate gesture, tone of voice, manner of speaking, and the kind of mimic action that will provide ironic comment upon the words spoken.

Marionettes

With its romantic plot, idealized characters, and fairy tale setting, *Leonce and Lena* scarcely complies with Büchner's demand that art contain "life and the possibility of existence" (I.86-87). By presenting the very type of lifeless puppets he so strongly rejects, Büchner's comedy seems to go against the most fundamental tenets of his own aesthetics as expressed by Camille in *Danton* (II.iii), by Büchner in defense of his play (II.444), and again by Lenz: "They wanted idealistic figures, but all I saw of it was wooden puppets. This idealism is the most shameful contempt for human nature" (I.87). While rejecting the artificiality of the figures which people idealist art, Büchner also claims that man *is* merely a puppet. The explanation for this apparent contradiction lies in the fact that he uses the metaphor of the puppet in two different contexts and with two different meanings. The figures in idealist art give the impression that they actually are puppets, he maintains, because they speak an artificial, affectedly pathetic language, and because they lack flesh and blood. Take an abstracted emotion, maxim, or idea, dress it up like a man, and manipulate it through three acts, and you have the kind of lifeless puppet Camille and

Büchner object to. When Büchner or Danton call themselves puppets, however, they mean that their actions are determined by elements beyond their control, such as their own nature, their social condition, and the forces of history. This in no way detracts from the impression of life they convey.[40]

The figures in *Leonce and Lena* are satires of their idealist counterparts. The immediate model for *Leonce and Lena* is Romantic comedy, especially Brentano's *Ponce de Leon* and Musset's *Fantasio*. Büchner borrows a standard Romantic plot and configuration of characters; Romantic motifs, imagery, and language; and quotes and paraphrases from the works of several Romantic writers.[41] He also employs hyperbole in his language and imagery with the intention of "outdoing"[42] the Romantics in the use of one of their own favorite devices. By fully developing tendencies inherent in the form, he pushes Romantic art to such an extreme that it becomes a caricature and satire of itself.

Thus Büchner takes up a favorite Romantic form, the ironic, satiric literary comedy, and turns it against Romanticism and against itself. The form allowed him to indulge in the free play of his creative impulses and talents, for the very essence of comedy, especially romantic comedy, is the sovereign and playful manipulation of language, illusion, plot, the characters, and ideas. It was common in Romantic comedy for the author to break into the illusionary world of the play to reveal himself as its god-like creator. Büchner's use of Valerio as an "interior dramatist" serves a similar purpose, but more subtly and with greater dramatic skill.

Valerio as interior dramatist

Valerio is by no means the fool that some would make him out to be,[43] and he is much more than simply a coarse, materialistic antipode and foil to Leonce's refined idealism.[44] As is often the case in comedy, the servant behaves more intelligently and with greater emotional maturity than his master. Valerio's moderating influence and guidance prevent Leonce from losing himself in the bathos of his self-pity, and his clearheaded realism deters Leonce from ending his life in a senseless display of "Lieutenants' Romanticism." As interior dramatist, Valerio appears to be responsible for bringing Leonce and

Lena together, and their marriage takes place according to his plan.

Leonce derives as much pleasure from his boredom and melancholy as he does from being in love. (When Rosetta asks: "So you love me out of boredom?" he answers: "No, I'm bored because I love you. But I love my boredom as I love you" [I.iii].) He also enjoys posing as a suffering tragic figure and intoxicating himself with the rhetorical beauty of his soliloquies. The more serious Leonce tries to be in delivering his monologues, i.e., the more the actor playing Leonce affects seriousness, the greater will be their comic effect, since the formal texture of these speeches—the tone, imagery, and hyperbolically pathetic manner of delivery—is ironically incongruent with their content.

The incongruity is further emphasized in each case by the appearance of Valerio who gives the impression that he has been sent in from the wings to remind Leonce that he is playing comedy, not tragedy. If we assume that Valerio does indeed represent the author or author-director,[45] the meaning of the puzzling exchange that follows Leonce's first monologue becomes clear. Leonce breaks off his speech when he sees Valerio approaching on the run. By expressing the wish for something that could make him run like that, he suggests to the spectator that Valerio must have some reason for his haste, and when Valerio confronts him with a stare and a meaningful gesture, Leonce understands him:

> **Valerio** (positions himself right in front of the PRINCE, places his finger on his nose, and stares at him fixedly). Yes!
> **Leonce** (likewise). Right!
> **Valerio.** Did you understand me?
> **Leonce.** Perfectly.
> **Valerio.** All right, let's talk about something else then. (I.i)

This exchange may be interpreted as a meaningless bit of comic nonsense, or as an illustration of how well Leonce and Valerio understand each other. But it may also be seen as a clue to Valerio's function as an interior dramatist, who enters the play at this point in order to remind Leonce not to stray from his role. An audience familiar with the Romantic comedy and its peculiar form of irony might be prepared in this way to expect a fanciful *jeu d'esprit* involving the amalgamation of reality and illusion, or various levels of illusion. A more explicit example of this type of irony is found at the play's conclusion, when Leonce sends the minor figures home and instructs them not to forget their roles, "for tomorrow we will begin the joke [*Spass*] again from the beginning in leisure and comfort" (III.iii).

A related form of ironic double-perspective is contained in the monologue which follows Leonce's meeting with Rosetta. Leonce comments on the peculiar transitoriness of love and wonders how many women one would need in order to experience love's full range of possibilities. Like an operatic aria, his monologue transcends its dramatic function to become an independent show-piece. Because his speech is so skillfully artistic in its formulation, so rhetorically brilliant in its accumulation and variation of similies and metaphors on the theme of his empty and monotonous life, and because it is so beautifully presented, it demands, and Leonce would like to have, an audience to admire and applaud it. In addressing himself to an imagined audience, he appears to break through the play's illusion and to speak directly to the real audience: "Gentlemen, gentlemen, do you know what Caligula and Nero were? I know." But this suggestion of romantic irony lasts only a moment. Returning to his proper sphere, though perhaps not entirely to the script, Leonce is willing to accept the normal dramatic conventions and to find his audience within the play, even though he must assume a double role to do so: "Come, Leonce, deliver a soliloquy. I'll listen to you" (I.iii).

In cheering and applauding his fine performance, his response to himself becomes so excessive that he seems to lose control. His narcissism threatens to degenerate into schizophrenia: "I enjoy it very much, when I call to myself like that. Hey, Leonce! Leonce!" Once again it becomes necessary for Valerio to bring Leonce to reason and prevent him from overplaying his role. This time he seems to be anticipating his duty and does not have far to go:

Valerio *(coming out from under a table)*. Your Highness really seems to me to have found the best way for becoming a genuine fool.
Leonce. Yes, when seen in the light, it actually appears that way to me too. (I.iii)

As in the first scene, an extended passage of comic dialogue follows, and again the scene ends with joyful optimism and enthusiasm—expressed this time in the decision to go south.

A variation of the cycle which leads from melancholy self-pity through comic repartee to enthusiasm is repeated just before Leonce meets Lena. Leonce not only continues to pity himself for not knowing how to fill his empty life, but is also oppressed and frightened by nature, which he describes in terms similar to those Büchner uses in his novella to indicate Lenz's disturbed mental state:

> What an eerie evening! Down here everything is still and up there the clouds change and pass by and the sunshine comes and goes again. Look, what peculiar figures chase each other there! Look at the long white shadows with the terribly skinny legs and bat's wings and everything so fast, so confused; and down here no leaf, no grass is stirring. The earth has curled up in fear like a child, and above its cradle the spirits stalk. (II.ii)

The severity of Leonce's melancholy state calls for a more extreme remedy than the usual repartee, and Valerio has it. After suggesting metaphorically that life is a game and should therefore not be taken too seriously, he deals out the cards, as it were, for a new hand. A "queen" is needed to complete the constellation, and one enters as if on cue:

> I don't know what you want. I'm feeling quite comfortable. The sun looks like the sign of an inn and the fiery clouds above it like the inscription: "The Golden Sun." The earth and the water down here are like a table upon which wine has been spilled, and we're lying on it like playing cards with which God and Satan are playing a hand out of boredom. You're the king and I'm the jack. Only the queen is missing, a lovely queen with a big gingerbread heart on her breast and a huge tulip in which her long nose sinks sentimentally, *(the GOVERNESS and the PRINCESS appear)* and, by God, there she is![46] (II.ii)

When Leonce overreacts to his brief meeting with Lena, Valerio once more calls him a fool and implies that his ecstatic romanticism is entirely incongruous with the situation.

As part of his scheme to help Leonce and Lena get married, Valerio introduces them at the court disguised as automatons. In the play's longest speech, a multilayered masterpiece of Pirandellian complexity, he attempts to describe and define the automatons and himself according to two or three different systems of reference or levels of reality. In answer to the King's question as to the identity of his masked visitors, Valerio removes one mask after the other and wonders himself which one he is or whether he is, in fact, any of them. Like every individual, Valerio has various roles or forms of appearance, which are represented here by his different masks. He fears that he may be like an onion, under whose layers there is no kernel; or he may be like the boxes placed one within the other: when the smallest one is reached, it is found to be empty.[47] When the King tells him he must be something, Valerio agrees to let his existence be defined by one particular mask, but only if all mirrors and shiny buttons are covered and all eyes averted. He does not want to see his reflected image, since it might confuse or frighten him.

Excursus: the mirror motif

The mirror recurs in Büchner's works as a symbol of man's disharmony with himself and the world.[48] This is a new meaning for a symbol which until the eighteenth century had been used, especially in mystical writing, to represent the still passivity of man's soul and its ability to absorb and reflect God's image in the *unio mystica*. In the eighteenth century the traditional meaning was extended to refer to the artist, who, as an "original genius," was seen to resemble God in his creative function. The moment of artistic conception was considered to be similar in essence to the mystical union with God: in both cases something divine enters the soul, which is a still, passive and reflective mirror of the world. At the same time the symbolical meaning of the mirror was being secularized and reinterpreted as a metaphor for the artist's soul, a major change in man's consciousness of himself and his relation to the world was causing it to undergo an even more decisive and essential transformation. Man's awakening self-consciousness made him increasingly aware of an inner discordance between the perceiving subject and the object perceived. Notwithstanding its painful implications, this knowledge of the disharmony and incongruity that exists between the individual and the world and even within the individual himself gave rise to a new sense of humor.[49] In this connection the mirror became a symbol of division rather than unity. A person who looks into the mirror sees his double staring back; he sees the suffering countenance of his own soul. This fills him with fear and causes him to avoid confrontation with his reflection.

The breaking of mirrors in a symbolical expression of the desire to destroy one's *Doppelgänger,* the sight of whom causes fear, disgust, or horror, became one of the most typical expressions of the new symbolism, and one which characterizes the spiritual condition of the new generation.[50] Fear of one's mirror image is a typical motif in German Romantic literature, especially in the works of E. T. A. Hoffman. A letter Brentano wrote, but never sent, to Hoffman indicates through direct application of the motif to his own life that its relevance was not just literary:

> What you have written has pleased me in many ways, but the fact that you did it has astonished me just as much. For just imagine: I would like to put out the lights in order not to see my shadow and cover the mirrors in order not to see my reflection [*Spiegelbild*]. And for that reason this shadow, this reflection of me in your book has often frightened me. Consequently, I cannot understand that you want to see and show your own in it. For some time now I have had a certain dread of all literature that reflects itself and not God.[51]

In one of his most personal letters (see above p. 11) Büchner, an admirer of Hoffmann's works, expresses a similar fear of his reflected image and of the sound of his own voice. The artistic quality of his expression and the reference to Hoffmann and Callot may indicate that he wrote with a high degree of aesthetic self-awareness, but the authenticity of the underlying experience and mental state can scarcely be doubted. After having become aware of the lifeless, mechanical appearance and behavior of the people who stared at him from behind masks of death, Büchner, who claims that the feeling of being dead has always hung over him, was afraid to look in the mirror and see his own death-mask staring back at him.

Man as a machine or a puppet

Like Brentano and Büchner, Valerio fears that seeing his reflection might increase his uncertainty about his identity or result in a terrifying discovery, and like Büchner, he too identifies himself with an automaton or an organ-like mechanism for producing speech:

> But actually I wanted to announce to this exalted and honored society that the two world-famous automatons have arrived here and that I am perhaps the third and most remarkable of the two—if I really knew myself who I am, about which you should not be astonished, by the way, since I myself know nothing about what I am saying; indeed, I don't even know that I don't know it; thus, it is most probable that I am simply being *made* to speak this way, and it is actually nothing but barrels and windbags that are saying all this. (III.iii)

When a man actually appears to resemble a machine or a thing, he loses his human dignity and becomes comic and risible.[52] That is the case here with Valerio, who is dehumanized by his masks and by his mechanical movements and speech.

Valerio assumes that he may be the "most remarkable" automaton, because his role as interior dramatist adds a dimension to his existence which the other figures lack: he represents the author in manipulating the others, and is at the same time manipulated by the author, who "makes him speak." Furthermore, as the dramatic representative of a real person, he is also controlled by the forces which control all men. It is no wonder that he is confused and uncertain about his identity.

The situation of Leonce and Lena in this scene is only slightly less complex and ironic. In the context of the play, they represent people imitating marionettes or automatons. In donning their masks, however, they are actually showing their true faces, since they are in fact puppets, both in the sense that they are manipulated by the author and by Valerio, and in the sense that all men are puppets. Although indistinguishable from "other people," they are indeed "nothing but artifice and machinery, nothing but cardboard and watch springs." Wind them up, and they run a full fifty years, the approximate lifespan of a man.[53] Once Valerio has identified the automatons with people in everything but construction, his comments about the behavior and qualities of the one may also be considered applicable to the other; thus human qualities are equated with superficial behavioral patterns; and morality, conscience, and love are defined in terms of reiterative behavioral mechanisms:

> They [Leonce and Lena] are very noble, for they speak High German. They're very moral, for they get up on the stroke of the clock, eat on the stroke of the clock, and go on the stroke of the clock to bed. They also have good digestion, which proves they have a clear conscience. They have a fine sense of decency, for the woman has no word for the concept of pants, and it is impossible for the gentleman to go up the stairs behind a woman or down the stairs in front of one. They are very educated, for the woman sings all the new operas and the man wears cuffs. Pay attention, ladies and gentlemen, they are now in an interesting stage: the mechanism of love is beginning to express itself. The gentleman has already carried the lady's shawl several times. The lady has already rolled her eyes and looked heavenward several times. Both have already whispered several times: faith, love, hope! Both already look to be in full agreement with each other. All that is missing is the tiny word: Amen. (III.iii)

The kingly puppet as puppetmaster

Man is determined by his nature and by the condition of the world in which he lives. He is also controlled and therefore determined by other men, especially those whose high political and social positions give them power over others. It is in terms of such power that Valerio describes the kingly prerogatives:

> Well, you're to become King. That's a lot of fun. You can drive for pleasure all day and cause the people to ruin their hats by doffing them so often. You can cut proper soldiers from proper people, so that everything becomes very natural. You can make black dresscoats and white ties into state officials. And when you die, all the shiny buttons will blush and the bell-ropes will break like thread from all the ringing. Isn't that entertaining? (I.iii)

And when Leonce does become King, he pictures his newly acquired powers in even more explicit terms:

Well, Lena, do you see now that our pockets are full, full of
puppets and toys? What shall we do with them? Shall we
make mustaches for them and hang sabers on them? Or shall
we dress them in frock coats and have them engage in
infusorial politics and diplomacy while we sit beside them
with microscopes? Or do you desire a barrel organ on which
milk-white, aesthetic shrews scamper about? Shall we build
a theater? (III.iii)

Kings and other rulers are puppetmasters, but they are also
puppets. Through King Peter, Büchner presents a caricature of
the "princely puppet" he described in *The Hessian Courier*
(II.42). King Peter has high regard for his ability to think and to
make and carry out decisions, but his empty words and actions
and his jerky, disjointed motions reveal that he, too, is a marionette or an automaton. His attempts to appear profound and
philosophical are ridiculous, because he does not understand
the philosophical terminology he uses, and because his borrowed words and phrases lose their meaning when taken in-
discriminately out of context. One is reminded of the Fool in
Woyzeck, who recites disconnected phrases from various fairy
tales; the words are there but not the meaning. More serious
and ominous than the disjunction between the words and their
meaning is the one between the speaker and his own voice:
"When I speak so loud, I don't know who it really is, me or
someone else. That frightens me" (I.ii). The integrity of the
King's personality appears to be threatened by a schizophrenic
dissociation. Following a long, tension-filled pause, he recovers
himself, however, and declares confidently: "I am I." This
Fichtean assertion of absolute ego restores the comic tone,
which is sustained to the end of the scene.

The autonomy of language

The figures in *Danton* often become instruments of their
language, but for the most part they appear to be more than the
language they speak; language alone is not enough to capture
the essence of a complex human being. In *Leonce and Lena,* on
the other hand, the figures are their language and no more. In a
reversal of the usual relationship, language appears to become
active and the speaker passive: instead of serving the speaker
as a means of communication, language seems to use the
speaker for its own ends.

An extreme example of this relationship is provided by the witty exchanges between the Prince and Valerio which fill a large part of the first act. For the most part, this dialogue adds little or nothing to the development of plot or character or to the thematic substance of the comedy. It exists for its own sake as an example of verbal *agon*, a form of play.[54] In dialogue of this type the speakers are secondary and interchangeable. They are automatons whose machinery is used for producing sounds, as Valerio says *"in a rattling tone of voice,"* but they do not control, not completely in any event, the sounds that will be produced, since their various responses are determined to a large extent by the inherent logic and structures of language itself.

In one of their verbal battles, Leonce defines Valerio in terms of language, equating him metaphorically with a play on words: "Man, you're nothing more than a bad pun. You have neither father nor mother, but were engendered by the five vowels" (I.iii). Leonce's description corresponds with Valerio's speculation that he is probably just a machine for producing speech: both metaphors refer ironically to the same *tertium comparationis*, namely, Valerio's fictional existence as a literary figure, as an instrument or puppet of the author. Valerio "outdoes" Leonce by describing him as "a book without letters, with nothing but dashes." According to Valerio's metaphor, Leonce is less than a machine for producing language and less than language itself: as a book, he is a lifeless container of language in its most lifeless form; and he is an empty container at that, since he contains only pauses. As absurdly hyperbolical as it may seem, Valerio's metaphor merely repeats what Leonce had previously stated in the form of a simile: "My life yawns at me like a large white sheet of paper that I must fill with writing, but I can't produce a single letter" (I.iii). Where existence is created by language, being equated with the absence of language must constitute the strongest possible negation of existence. Having thus vanquished his opponent, Valerio wins the contest.

Satire

Automatism, according to Bergson, is a primary source of laughter: "The comic is that side of a person which reveals his likeness to a thing, that aspect of human events which, through its peculiar inelasticity, conveys the impression of pure mechanism, of automatism, of movement without life."[55] As a source of the risible, automatism relies for its effect on the disparity between man's concept of himself as a dignified, exalted being and a mode of action incongruous with that concept. *"The attitudes, gestures and movements of the human body are laughable in exact proportion as that body reminds us of a mere machine,"*[56] that is, of something not compatible with our concept of what is human. When we are confronted by the incongruity of a being who can defy the gods and strive for the infinite, but who is bound to the finite through the demands and restrictions of physical necessity such as sex, eating, and elimination, tears of laughter and weeping mix in our response.

Satire, too, can be comic, since it also depends for its effect upon the awareness of incongruity. According to Schiller, for example, the object of satire is to present the contradiction between reality and the ideal. The latter, which for Schiller is the highest form of reality, need only be implied in the comparison. By portraying man at his most finite, that is, man as he is confined and restricted by material reality, the satirist presents reality as a "necessary object of distate."[57] By equating the "reality" of Schiller's definition with the object of satire, and by allowing for a less abstract and exalted definition of the "ideal," we can arrive at an acceptable definition. Satire casts derision and scorn upon persons or things which fall short of our concept of what they should be. It ridicules and renders risible ideas and behavior which are incongruous with commonly accepted ideals. Where pure comedy evokes laughter as an end in itself, satire uses laughter as a weapon with which to attack something outside the work, such as an individual, a class, a nation, or a form of government, in the hope of provoking correction and change. "We really do not laugh at the satirical as such; we laugh at the purely comic qualities with which it is accompanied or in which it is enclosed."[58] The division between comedy and satire is so slight that it may easily become lost behind the mask of laughter. Clear distinction between the forms is possible only at the extremes.

Büchner describes a satiric attitude when he notes in a letter the fact that he frequently laughs at man, not because of the *manner* in which he is a man, but because of the fact *that* he is a

man (II.422-423). This attitude is the result of his discovery that
man is determined, which caused him to experience personally
and profoundly the disparity between reality and the ideal.
But if man is ridiculous in his real limitations, when measured
against conventional ideals, he may be even more ridiculous,
and here Büchner reverses his great predecessor, in his attempts
to deny or transcend those limitations.

German Idealist philosophy, politics, and literature are
among the principal objects of Büchner's satire. The disparity
between the ideal and reality is especially pronounced in the
ridiculous figure of King Peter, who likes to think of himself as
a philosopher king, but who is really an empty-headed and
lifeless puppet. As with Leonce's opening monologues, the
incongruity between his words and the real situation immediately becomes evident. He must think for his subjects, he
says, since they cannot think for themselves. But his "thinking"
is no less absurd than Leonce's spitting on rocks or attempting
to see the top of his head. He begins by equating himself with
the *"Substanz,"* which is the same as the *"An-sich,"* namely, the
central part of the philosophical system whose terms he is
using, i.e., Kant's and Fichte's. The system is completed by the
addition of the "attributes, modifications, characteristics, and
accidences" along with "morality" and the "categories," all of
which he identifies with the articles of clothing he is donning.
When he finds that too many buttons are buttoned and that his
snuffbox is in the wrong pocket, he considers the whole system
to be ruined. Like the philosophy he parodies, the King attempts to introduce order into a chaotic reality, but the absurdity of his words and actions only subject that philosophy and
the concept of the enlightened, metaphysical monarch he supposedly represents to ridicule.[59]

As the absolute, feudal monarch in a land so small it can be
traversed in minutes, King Peter also serves as a vehicle for
satirizing political and social conditions similar to those Büchner exposed and attacked in *The Hessian Courier.* When
preparations are being made for the wedding in the last act of
Leonce and Lena, for example, the peasants are told that they
should appreciate being placed in such a way that for once in
their lives they will be able to smell a roast. This corresponds to
the passage in the *Courier* where Büchner tells the peasants to
go to Darmstadt and see how the aristocrats live in luxury from

the fruits of their, the peasants', productive labor (II.44,46). And like the petty princes described in the political pamphlet, King Peter also has a condescending, patronizing attitude toward his subjects. He must tie a knot in his handkerchief to remind him to remember his people; and even then he forgets what he was supposed to remember. German civil servants are satirized by the entourage of obsequious, sycophantic servants and councilors which surrounds the muddle-headed monarch, echoing and agreeing with his every remark. The King's satellites also serve as distorting mirrors for the King; their replies to his statements and questions reflect the confusion and absurdity of his words translated into the clumsy syntax of bureaucratic German.

Despite the striking similarities, however, the comedy differs considerably from the pamphlet, both in its intent and in the manner of presentation. The pamphlet presents the situation from the standpoint of the poor, who suffer needlessly because they are deprived of the products of their own labor. In keeping with its revolutionary intent, it stresses the urgency of changing the outrageously unjust and brutally inhumane conditions of their existence. The comedy reflects the author's critical detachment from the people who failed to respond to his efforts to help them. Büchner's cynical attitude toward the people is expressed in the docility and servility of the peasants, who allow themselves to be trained and manipulated like domestic animals or puppets, and in the remarks of those who do the manipulating: the School Master and the District President, King Peter and Leonce. Since they appear as caricatures in an anonymous group, the peasants scarcely possess the kind of presence and real humanity required to arouse the sympathy of the spectator.[60] They function as a source of laughter rather than as a vehicle of social criticism. Without the accusatory evidence which the example of a repressed and abused people could supply, the potential for criticism and censure inherent in the satire of the King is not realized.

Leonce and Rosetta

In contrast to King Peter, who is comical and ridiculous, but not callous and cruel, Leonce, especially as he appears in the first act, represents the kind of aristocratic arrogance and disdain that Büchner despised and subjected to the ridicule of satire (II.423). He knows what Caligula and Nero were (I.iii), because he has much in common with them. He shares their idleness and boredom and their propensity for entertaining themselves at the expense of their subjects. He indulges that inclination in his selfish and abusive conduct toward his Tutor, the King's councilors, and Rosetta.

Leonce is brutally insensitive to the anguish he causes Rosetta when he trifles with her emotions and casually announces the death of their love. To increase her suffering and his pleasure, he purposely makes the setting for their encounter as romantic as possible. With all the conventional requisites of seduction—soft lights, wine, roses, and background music—he sets out to destroy their love. He leaves it to her to begin a conversation, then mimics her. When he does speak, he insults and offends her by equating love with work and by identifying her as the source of his boredom.

Like Narcissus, Leonce loves only himself. He equates Rosetta with his emotional reaction to her, because what he really enjoys is the emotional state she helps produce in him: "*O dolce far niente*. I dream over your eyes as beside wonderfully mysterious, deep springs; the caress of your lips lulls me to sleep like the rushing of waves" (I.iii). His egocentricity is reflected in the monologic nature of the dialogue. When he does finally speak to Rosetta, he does not communicate with her. Instead of attempting to make himself clear, he entertains himself by playing with words and concepts and with her emotions. Even his description of his own emotional state is determined to a considerable extent by his desire to see how she will react. A detached sense of purely aesthetic pleasure pervades the entire scene. Although she is emotionally too involved to enjoy it the way Leonce does, Rosetta realizes what game is being played with language and joins in:

Leonce. . . . we can take time to love.
Rosetta. Or time can take love from us.
Leonce. Or love our time. Dance, Rosetta, dance, so that time will pass with the beat of your pretty feet.
Rosetta. My feet would rather pass out of time.

Leonce's talk about boredom lacks the seriousness of tone and the underlying sense of despair that would make it seem sincere and credible. He talks with Rosetta as he does with Valerio, using language as something to manipulate and play with. Or is it language that is using him? The more language frees itself from its pragmatic function of relating *res* and *verbum,* and the more it becomes capable of indulging in the free play of images, rhetorical figures, and meanings, the more it is able to realize its potential of creating its own reality. To the extent that language gains autonomy, the speaker loses his, in which case he is reduced more and more to the role of an instrument or "mechanism for producing sounds." A consequence of such a development is the dissociation of the speaker from his words, as is clearly the case when Leonce applauds his own speech, or when the King becomes frightened and confused by hearing his own voice. Because Leonce is alienated from his language, his speeches about boredom, love, and suffering fail to give the impression that he is expressing his innermost thoughts and feelings. He lacks the subjective involvement that would qualify him as an authentic example of the Romantic *Weltschmerzler* he resembles. He serves, rather, as a parody of such types and as a vehicle for satire.

Leonce's aesthetic enjoyment of suffering and death also satirizes a romantic attitude. While Rosetta expresses through song and dance her melancholy longing for death, Leonce daydreams about the beauty of his dying love:

> Oh, a dying love is more beautiful than a growing one. I am a Roman; at the lavish feast the golden fish play for dessert in their dying colors. How the glow dies from her cheeks! How quietly her eyes burn out! How lightly the waves of her limbs rise and fall. Adio, adio my love. I will love your corpse.

The role Leonce assumes for himself is similar to the one Camille attributes to the gods, who take pleasure in witnessing the colorful agony of the eternal battle with death. Leonce's statement is not of that order, however, and should not be interpreted as an expression of inherent sadism or necrophilia. The "dying love" he describes is not Rosetta, as some interpreters have assumed, but a personification of love itself. With the surrealistic vision of a dreamer—he speaks these words *"in a state of reverie"*—Leonce sees love as temporarily coincident with, but separable from Rosetta's person. While Rosetta dances, Leonce's love leaves her body, as it were. The "corpse" of his love is a memory that he will continue to love. He refuses to allow Rosetta to embrace him, because he does not want her to disturb the corpse of their love, i.e., the memory, that is buried in his head:

> Be careful! My head! I have buried our love in it. Look in the windows of my eyes. Do you see how beautifully dead the poor thing is? Do you see the two white roses on its cheeks and the two red ones on its breast? Don't jolt me, or one of its little arms might break off. That would be a pity. I must carry my head straight on my shoulders, as the pallbearer carries a child's coffin.

Despite the seriousness of what he is saying, Leonce's jocular manner and playfully original imagery makes Rosetta forget her tears. Imitating his tone, she calls him a "fool." The flirtatious and comprehending nature of her response threatens to reawaken the dead love. He therefore takes advantage of her grimace at him by thankfully closing his eyes and refusing to look at her again. As long as he retains this unflattering and aesthetically unappealing impression in his mind, it will be impossible for his dead love to reawaken.

Leonce as idealist

Leonce wants to be active, since inactivity is accompanied by melancholy and boredom and may end in madness or despair, but he recognizes that the only activities consistent with the absurdity or purposelessness of life, or his princely station, are absurd and purposeless activities. Just as Danton reveals the futility of Camille's call to action by the absurdity of his reply (I.i), Leonce reveals the absurdity of his life by the nature of his activities and proposed activities:

> Come on, Valerio, we must do something, do something. Let's occupy ourselves with deep thoughts. Let's investigate how it happens that a chair can stand on three legs but not on two, or that we clean our noses with the help of our hands and not with our feet like the flies. Come on, let's dissect ants and count the threads of cobwebs. I'll succeed yet in acquiring some sort of princely hobby. (II.ii)

He realizes that such pursuits fulfill the same function as play does for children. "I'll succeed yet in finding a rattle," he adds, "that will not fall out of my hand until I'm gathering wool and plucking at the blanket." He resembles a child also in the shortness of his attention span and in his inability to carry an activity through to its conclusion: "I still have a certain dose of enthusiasm to use up; but when I have thoroughly warmed everything up, I need infinite time to find a spoon with which to eat the dish, and by then it has gone stale."

In his discontent with the real possibilities and options open to him and in his desire to attain the impossible, Leonce resembles Faust[61] and other Romantic figures—resembles them, that is, as the distorted image of a fun-house mirror resembles the thing reflected. The serious and idealistic nature of Faustian striving and Romantic longing is parodied by the absurd and banal nature of Leonce's ideals and by the manner in which he states them. "Half of my life shall be a prayer, if only I'm granted a blade of straw which I can ride like a stately steed until I myself lie on the straw." He rejects the goals of his Romantic predecessors when he refuses to become a scholar, hero, genius, or useful member of society. Since he considers all activities to be of equal value, the ideal for him would be the kind of activity which yields a maximum of pleasure with a minimum of effort. And like Faust, he, too, has his Helen:

> But Valerio, ideals! I've got the ideal of a woman in me, and I must look for it. She is infinitely beautiful and infinitely simple-minded. The beauty in her is as helpless and touching as a newborn child. It is a delightful contrast. These sublimely stupid eyes, this divinely simple mouth, this sheep-nosed Greek profile, this mental death in this spiritual body. (II.i)

Leonce shares his Romantic predecessor's yearning to transcend the limitations of reality and to realize or reify the ideal. But the ridiculous nature of his ideals and the alienating contrast between his romanticism and Valerio's realism is comical and satirical.

Valerio as realist

One of Valerio's functions in the play is to provide ironic and satirical comment on Leonce. He accomplishes this directly in his role as interior dramatist and indirectly in his role as Leonce's foil. Like Leonce, who would like to be what he is not and to do what he cannot do, Valerio also has his "romantic" longing or "ideals": "Oh Sir, what a feeling I have for nature! The grass is so beautiful, that one would like to be an ox in order to eat it, and then a man again in order to eat the ox that has eaten such grass" (I.i).

Encouraged by Leonce's sympathetic understanding—"Unfortunate man, you also seem to be afflicted with ideals"—Valerio laments the sad state of the world in which such ideals cannot be realized: "It's a pity. One can't leap from a church tower without breaking one's neck. One can't eat four pounds of cherries, pits and all, without getting a stomach ache." Since he cannot do what he would like to, Valerio concludes that he might just as well sit in a corner singing unending repetitions of his nonsense verse: "Hey, there sits a fly on the wall, fly on the wall, fly on the wall!" Valerio's speech disturbs Leonce precisely because it is an extreme expression of his own idealistic longing and his attitude and reaction to the absurdity of life. Not wanting to face the logical consequence of his idealism, as formulated by Valerio, Leonce will hear no more: "Shut up with your song. It could drive a man mad."

Valerio only pretends to be an idealist. In fact, he is too much of a realist to be able to trade his reason for the self-deceptive escapism of such idealistic foolishness, though he would like to do so: "Who will trade me his madness [*Narrheit*] for my reason?" According to Valerio, a fool or madman is the purest kind of idealist. In his world of fantasy a madman can even realize Leonce's desire to be someone else, as Valerio demonstrates by pretending to be a madman imagining himself in another role. Ironically, he chooses a role similar to the one that Leonce will inherit when he becomes king. And since the unfettered imagination need settle for nothing second rate, Valerio chooses to be the greatest and most powerful ruler he can think of: Alexander the Great. The difference between the petty and the sublime is only one of degree: the *tertium comparationis* lies in the power each king has to give orders and to manipulate others:

Ha! I'm Alexander the Great! How the sun shines a golden crown into my hair! How my uniform sparkles. Generalissimo Grasshopper, assemble the troops! Minister of Finance Lord Spider, I need money! Dear Lady-in-waiting Dragonfly, how is my cherished wife, Queen Beanstalk? Oh, my most excellent Doctor Spanish-Fly, I am in need of a princely heir.

An especially appealing benefit of being mad—or a king—is the fact that all one's material needs are taken care of:

And with these delightful fantasies you get good soup, good meat, good bread, a good bed, and your hair cut for nothing—in the madhouse, that is—whereas I with my sound reason could at best hire myself out to a cherry tree for the promotion of its growth . . . .

Both the fool and the idealist want to be what they are not. Valerio would like to be free from material want, and he would like to imagine himself a great ruler. As Prince and heir to the throne, Leonce is already free of care and already has the power to give commands. Consequently he can entertain even "higher," that is, more foolish, ideals. The motto of the first act, words spoken by melancholy Jaques in Shakespeare's *As You Like It,* represents Leonce's desire just as much as it does Valerio's:

> O that I were a fool!
> I am ambitious for a motley coat.

Valerio also resembles Leonce in his disinclination to prepare for a profession. When Leonce asks: "But, most noble friend, your craft, your profession, your trade, your station, your art?" Valerio answers: "Sir, I have the great occupation of being idle. I have an uncommon skill in doing nothing. I possess extraordinary perseverance in being lazy. No calluses defile my hands. The earth has not yet drunk a drop from my brow. I am still a virgin as far as work is concerned." Leonce is so pleased by this reflection of his own attitude that he enthusiastically embraces him and welcomes him as "one of those godlike beings who wanders effortlessly and with a clean brow through the sweat and dust of life's highway and who enters Olympus like the blessed gods with gleaming feet and thriving bodies." By singing his nonsense verse, which calls to mind its original context and the meaning it received there, Valerio provides ironic comment on Leonce's response and reveals how dissimilar they actually are. Again like Danton's answer to Camille's call-to-action, Valerio's ditty suggests that Leonce's words are absurd nonsense. Throughout this scene Valerio plays with Leonce in order to unmask and expose him as the romantic idealist he is. This is another of his functions as interior dramatist.

A basic difference between Leonce and Valerio is revealed by their language. Valerio's idiom tends to be earthy and concrete; he even describes his "ideals" in terms which reflect his preoccupation with physical, material concerns, especially with eating and drinking. When he uses figurative language, it is generally more rational and rhetorical than Leonce's, and it either provides a means for showing off his wit or has satiric intent, as when he makes fun of romantics: "Meanwhile I will lie down in the grass and let my nose blossom out from between the blades and derive romantic sensations when the bees and butterflies sway to and fro on it as on a rose" (I.i).

Leonce's language reflects his higher social status[62] and is predominantly figurative. It resembles Valerio's in being generally self-conscious and rational, but differs from his in the abstract, poetic quality of its metaphors. At times, such as when he joins Valerio in the battle of wits, he succumbs to Valerio's influence and speaks on his level. On the rare occasions when he becomes enthusiastic, as when he speaks with Lena or when he conceives his plan to go south, his language is lyrical.

Lena

Lena's name stands with Leonce's in the play's title, but her role is very small compared to his. She is not introduced into the play until after Leonce has announced, in what is clearly a curtain speech, his intention of fleeing to Italy. As an appendage to the first act, this scene receives special emphasis; the importance of Lena's brief appearance is enhanced because she has the last word. Little time is required for her to reveal the profundity, authenticity, and substantiality of her personality and thus to establish herself as an adequate dramatic counterpart to Leonce. Her melancholy is more real and more deeply felt than his, and her close relationship with nature contrasts strikingly with his penchant for artificiality and with the idealist or utopian longing expressed in his desire to go south. Leonce and his position are relativized and ironically commented upon by such contrasts and by the fact that Lena is just as unwilling as he is to enter into a marriage of convenience with an unknown and unloved person.

Unlike Leonce, Lena lives in complete harmony with nature. She is like a flower: "You know I really should have been placed in a flower pot," she tells her Governess in a later scene. "Like flowers, I need dew and night air" (II.iii). After having existed like a flower in a world without conflict, the prospect of being forced into an unwanted marriage makes her melancholy. She does not want to be a "poor, helpless spring," which must passively reflect the image of every Narcissus who should happen to bend over it. She knows loneliness and wants to find a person to love, but she objects to marrying someone she does not love and thinks she should be allowed at least as much freedom as the flowers have: "The flowers open and close their cups at will to the morning sun and the evening breeze. Is the daughter of a King less than a flower?" (I.iv). She would rather be buried in nature than robbed of her "fragrance and radiance" by being sacrificed on the altar of marriage. Such a prospect is so painful to her that it threatens to destroy her faith in life and causes her to ask the despairing question: "My God, my God, is it true, then, that we must save ourselves with our pain? Is it true that the world is a crucified savior, the sun his crown of thorns, and the stars the nails and spears in his feet and loins?" (I.iv). Lena's Governess cannot bear to see her suffer and decides to help her escape. Her thorough knowledge of Romantic literature gives her the hope that they might meet a straying Prince on their journey.

Through the juxtaposition of their respective reactions to the natural surroundings, the fundamental contrast between Leonce and Lena continues to be stressed in the first part of the second act. When Lena escapes the threatening marriage, she leaves her melancholy mood and dark thoughts behind her. Unlike the Governess, who is exhausted from the seemingly unending journey and concerned about finding a place to spend the night, Lena thoroughly enjoys herself and has no concerns or worries whatsoever. She loves the natural world whose beauty and harmony she perceives and shares. For her the world is "beautiful and so vast, so endlessly vast!" (II.i). She would like to go on forever, day and night.

When Valerio, who is panting under the pack he is carrying, echoes the Governess's complaint about the vast expansiveness of the world, Leonce, too, disagrees, but for reasons entirely different from Lena's: "Not so! Not so! I scarcely dare stretch out my hands in this narrow hall of mirrors for fear of colliding everywhere, so that the lovely figures would lie in pieces on the floor and I would be standing in front of blank, bare walls" (II.i). As a Fichtean idealist and romantic subjectivist, Leonce creates his own world from within; he experiences his surroundings in terms of his sensations, impressions, ideas, and ideals.[63] He aptly describes the situation of the idealist when he compares the world to a hall of mirrors in which the observer perceives multiple images of himself. His uncertainty with regard to the substantiality and durability of his self is expressed in the fear that the reality he has created for and around himself may be extremely fragile. He completely lacks Lena's sense of kinship and harmony with nature. Rather than accept nature for what it is, he prefers either the futile search for a utopian natural setting that would correspond with his ideal and in which he would not experience fear and uncertainty, or the creation of artificial surroundings, as in the scene with Rosetta.

Leonce and Lena

As if in answer to Leonce's rhetorical appeal to God for something to fill his empty life, and as if to supply the missing card for the game being played in bored idleness by God and Satan, Lena enters the scene. For some unspecified reason, her initial melancholy has returned. She no longer wants to "go on forever, day and night." Now she asks the Governess: "My dear, is the way so long, then?" The tone and mood of her question strike a responsive chord in Leonce. Lost in reverie, he answers her in kind: "Oh, every way is long! The ticking of the deathwatch in our breast is slow, and every drop of blood measures its time, and our life is a creeping fever. For tired feet every way is too long" (II.ii). Lena understands him, too, as she listens *"anxiously reflecting."* Without quite realizing what is happening, she takes up his speech where he leaves off and continues it in the same vein: "And for tired eyes every light too bright and tired lips every breath too heavy . . . ."

Becoming fully conscious again of herself and the situation, she smiles and concludes her sentence with a touch of irony: ". . . and tired ears, every word too much."

Before Leonce and Lena are even aware of each other's physical presence, their voices blend and unite to form a single statement of melancholy. This harmony of voice and expression contrasts markedly with the discord that characterized Leonce's conversation with Rosetta. And whereas his meeting with Rosetta left him feeling melancholy and cold—"It's as if I were sitting under an air pump. The air is so sharp and thin that I'm freezing" (I.iii)—the short exchange with Lena has the opposite effect: "Thank God I'm beginning to be delivered of my melancholy. The air is no longer so light and cold; the sky sinks, warmly glowing, close around me, and heavy drops are falling" (II.ii).

The meeting between Leonce and Lena takes place more in the realm of language than in physical reality. Leonce is transposed into a dreamlike trance when he hears her melancholy question. She speaks his language and he understands her: "Oh, that voice: is the way so long, then? Many voices speak above the earth and we think they are talking of other things, but I understood it" (II.ii). The motto of this act, an inexact quotation from *"Die Blinde,"* a poem by the Romantic poet Adalbert von Chamisso, refers to this meeting and its consequences:

> Oh how a voice did ring
> Deep inside of me,
> Thereby extinguishing
> All my memory.

Leonce does seem to overcome and forget his past and to feel new life and hope awakening within him: "It [Lena's voice] rests on me like the spirit, as it hovered above the water before there was light. What a ferment deep inside me! What a becoming within me! How the voice flowed through space!—Is the way so long then?"

It is paradoxical that Leonce should be cured of his melancholy by hearing and understanding the melancholy question of a strange female voice. And Lena's question itself seems to be curiously at odds with her earlier statement: "I would like to go on like this forever, day and night." It is also at odds with the actual situation, since she asks it while standing in the garden of

the inn that is her day's destination. But scenes such as this and
the one later that night are governed by other laws and logic
than those of reason and causality. It is an ironic comment on
what occurs that such meetings do not and cannot take place in
reality, but rather in dreams, fairy tales, and the imagination.
The ideal medium for presenting such a world of unreality is
the comedy, since it "specializes in the improbable, the re-
versible, the redemption that comes from nowhere *(deus ex
machina)*."⁶⁴ Leonce's meeting with Lena is a midsummer
night's dream—from which Valerio awakens him.

Saddened by her meeting with a man whom she recognizes as
being "so old under his blond curls," and disturbed by the
"horrifying thought" that "there are people who are unhappy,
incurably so, simply because they *exist,*" Lena leaves the oppressive closeness of her quarters to go into the garden, where
she meets him again. Leonce's ecstatic reaction to the night
would seem to indicate that he has in fact been changed by
their first meeting. Nature no longer seems "eerie" to him, and
he can feel comfortable in a natural, outdoor setting. In contrast to his meeting with Rosetta, he no longer feels the need
to be surrounded by artificiality as a shield against the natural
world or to behave and speak in a playfully insincere manner as
a protective barrier against close human contact. His language
becomes correspondingly less rhetorical, witty, and intellectual
and more subjective and lyrical.

Lena, on the other hand, is now preoccupied with death
and her feelings of loneliness and melancholy. Her surrealistic
vision reveals that she experiences the surroundings from a
highly subjective perspective, or as if in a dream:

> The warbler has twittered in its dream. The night sleeps
> more deeply; its cheek grows paler and its breath stiller. The
> moon is like a sleeping child; its golden curls have fallen over
> its dear face.—Oh, its sleep is death. How the dead angel
> rests on its dark pillow, and the stars burn like candles
> around it. Poor child, will the black men soon be coming to
> fetch you? Where is your mother? Doesn't she want to kiss
> you once more? Oh, it's sad—dead and so alone. (II.iv)

When Leonce enters her reverie, identifies himself as a dream,
and asks her to let him be her "blissful dream," she answers:
"Death is the most blissful dream." In that case Leonce would

be the angel whose kiss will bring her the death she desires. After kissing her, he addresses her as a corpse: "Lovely corpse, you rest so beautifully upon the black pall of night that nature hates life and falls in love with death." Their voices blend as they weave the key words "death," "dream," and "blissful" into a gossamer expression of mutual understanding and harmony.

Leonce feels that his whole being has become concentrated in his meeting with Lena. Realizing that he can experience no greater joy, and knowing that his ecstasy cannot last, he decides to end his life while it is at its highest point, and while the earth seems meaningful and beautiful:

> Too much! Too much! My whole being is in that one moment. Now die. More is not possible. Creation is struggling out of chaos toward me, breathing freshly and radiant with beauty. The earth is a bowl of dark gold. How the light froths in it and flows over its rim, and the stars bubble brightly out of it in pearls. My lips suck on it: this one drop of bliss transforms me into a precious container. Away, sacred chalice!

But before he can act, it is already too late. Valerio destroys his mood and shatters his illusion with his sobering wordplay—the intellectual nature of his wit counteracts the emotionalism of Leonce's response—and with his exposure of Leonce's behavior as "Lieutenants' Romanticism." When forced to view his situation with objective detachment, Leonce admits that Valerio is right. He expresses regret at having been deprived of this most opportune chance for a beautiful suicide, but the tone of his language clearly reveals how complete the reversal in his attitude has been and how far from ecstasy he now is: "Man, you have deprived me of the most beautiful suicide. I'll never again find such an opportune moment for it, and the weather is so splendid. Now I'm already out of the mood." Romantic ecstasy and yearning for death give way to a more worldly and realistic wish: "May heaven grant me a very sound, heavy [*plumpen*] sleep."

Is Leonce cured?

This meeting of the lovers who are attempting to escape each other is the heart and climax of the play. According to the Romantic scheme upon which the plot is based, Leonce should be cured of his suffering and sorrow and should find happiness and meaning for his life through Lena. He should be able to start filling in those blank pages. And Lena should find the hand she has been groping for, the man she can love and share her life with. But such a fairy tale conclusion would seem peculiarly incongruous with the tendency of this comedy to ridicule and satirize Romantic literature and its conventions. And in fact, nothing in this, the most Romantic scene of the play, gives us any reason to expect such a happy resolution. On the contrary, the Romantic aspects of the scene are thoroughly alienated by Valerio's speeches.

Furthermore, Leonce's ecstatic reaction to his second meeting with Lena is absurdly out of proportion to, and thus incongruous with, the actual event. The comic nature of his response will be enhanced in performance, if this speech is delivered with exaggerated pathos, thus emphasizing its parodistic and satiric intent. The spectator must be able to agree with Valerio, when he refers to Leonce's behavior as "Lieutenants' Romanticism"; even Leonce accepts that judgment. Just as his kiss shattered Lena's romantic reverie, his own romantic ecstasy is interrupted and destroyed by Valerio's sobering influence. It was a whim and no more—"Now I'm already out of the mood." Once the transitory mood has past, Leonce quickly gains sufficient detachment to speak of it in a disparaging manner. The incongruity of extreme moods has a comic effect, as does the rapidity of the transition from "Away, sacred chalice!" to "May heaven grant me a very sound, heavy sleep."

Leonce is not cured or even significantly changed by his meeting with Lena. It is entirely unwarranted to assume on the basis of Leonce's whimsical and ambiguous statement to Valerio which opens the third act—"Do you know, Valerio, that even the least of men is so great that life is still much too short to be able to love him?"—that Leonce has undergone a major change or transformation. Leonce is still more concerned and involved with his emotions than with the objects that stimulate them. And while Lena understands and pities Leonce, nothing in the text indicates that she has found the man she can love.

While the conventions of the Romantic plot and the comedic form demand that Leonce and Lena get married, nothing guarantees or even suggests that marriage can or will cure Leonce of his boredom and melancholy. In Leonce's dying love for

Rosetta, his inability to sustain enthusiasm, and the short duration of the romantic ecstasy he feels immediately after his meetings with Lena, the author establishes a pattern which indicates to us that Leonce's love for Lena will soon cool down and that the bored apathy which is his normal state will be restored, thus completing one more cycle in an unending chain of cycles. Following his break with Rosetta, Leonce expressed doubt in the possibility of finding the fullness of love in any one woman; there is no reason to assume that this statement no longer applies: "My God, how many women does one need in order to sing up and down the scale of love? One woman scarcely fills out one note. Why is the haze above our earth a prism that breaks up the glowing white ray of love into a rainbow?" (I.iii).[65]

Rosetta represents only one note on the scale of love; it is enough to occupy Leonce for a while, but not enough to fill his life forever. "Love's a peculiar thing," he says. "You lie for a year, half asleep, half awake in bed, and on one beautiful morning you wake up, drink a glass of water, put on your clothes, pass your hand over your forehead, and recollect yourself—recollect yourself" (I.iii). Having awakened from his love affair with Rosetta, Leonce was ready for a new love: "In what bottle is the wine for today's drunkenness?" But he is not sure he can go through the whole process again. His boredom and melancholy are so severe, and his life so empty, that he no longer feels he can or will make an effort to fill the void, to seek new experiences, new "drunkenness." He abhors the monotony of his life, which consists of eternal repetition and is therefore entirely predictable: "Twenty-four times a day I turn myself inside out like a glove. Oh, I know myself, I know what I'll be thinking and dreaming in a quarter of an hour, in a week, in a year. God, what sin have I committed that you make me repeat my lesson like a schoolboy over and over again?" (I.iii). Marriage would not offer a solution to his problems, he feels, but would only burden him with an additional routine and boring function: "Get married! That means drinking a well dry. Oh, Shandy, old Shandy, if someone gave me your clock!" (The hero of Laurence Sterne's novel *Tristram Shandy* regularly went to his wife's bed after he wound up the clock once each month.) To escape such an unpleasant prospect, Leonce flees to Italy, and, ironically, to Lena.

The structure of comedy

The tragic hero moves along a linear path toward a conclusion which is final and irreversible. Comedy lacks this finality. It retains the cyclical pattern of the ritual from which it grew. "Comedy is recurrent, always coming around, like ritual, to where it was and ought to be, where we want it to be. Its endings are always beginnings or re-beginnings."[66] Because the rhythm of his life is based on the repetition of such patterns, Leonce claims to be able to predict what he will be thinking and dreaming at any given time in the future. Indeed, the larger cycle of the whole comedy consists of two such repetitions, both ending with expressions of idealistic, utopian anticipation and longing and both marking the conclusion of one development and the beginning of a new one.

In the initial excitement of his new love he may consider Lena to be the ideal woman with whom he can spend the rest of his life in joy and happiness. But given his unchanged and unchanging character and the repetitive or cyclical rhythm of his life, one can scarcely assume that Lena will be more for him than one more note on the "scale of love." After a year with her, he will again wake up, drink a glass of water, get dressed, rub his forehead, and recollect himself. Lena correctly diagnoses his condition after their first meeting when she says: "I believe there are people who are unhappy, incurably so, simply because they *exist*." She stresses the word "incurably" by shifting it out of its normal syntactical position, thus setting it off from the rest of the sentence. In this way she emphasizes a fundamental truth of Leonce's existence, namely, the fact that his unhappy condition is permanent and unchangeable. Leonce's meeting with Lena was a "flight into paradise" (III.iii). His inevitable return to the court is a return to the inescapable comic absurdity of life, where the whole joke is destined to begin again. "Go home now," he tells his subjects in his first act as King, "but don't forget your speeches, sermons, and verses, for tomorrow we will begin the joke again from the beginning in leisure and comfort" (III.iii).

The play ends with an expression of the same sense of dissatisfaction and incompleteness that is both the end and the beginning of each new cycle. Leonce describes to Lena the power they now have to make soldiers, diplomats, or entertainers out of their subjects and to manipulate and play with them as they would with puppets and toys. When none of these options appeals to her, he comes up with something more to her liking: he promises her a land of eternal summer, where time is measured by the rhythm of nature:

> But I know better what you want: we'll have all the clocks smashed, all calendars forbidden, and we'll count hours and moons only by the flower-clock, only by blossom and fruit. And then we'll surround the little country with magnifying mirrors, so there will be no more winter and so we can distill ourselves in summer to the level reached in Ischia and Capri, and we will live the whole year among roses and violets, among oranges and laurel. (III.iii)

Of course Valerio wants to have a say, too, in defining this utopia:

> And I will become Prime Minister, and a decree will be issued that whoever gets calluses on his hands will be placed in protective custody, that whoever works himself sick is criminally punishable, that everyone who boasts of eating his bread in the sweat of his brow will be declared insane and dangerous to society; and then we'll lie down in the shade and ask God for macaroni, melons, and figs, for musical throats, classical bodies, and a comfortable religion.

This apparently beautiful and happy conclusion is deceptive: utopian dreams would be unnecessary if reality itself were, or could be made, beautiful and enjoyable. While Leonce and Valerio know that it is as impossible to find or create a utopia as it is for them to realize their other ideals, they nevertheless feel compelled by their restless discontent and playful bent of mind to repeat their attempts to escape from the real world. Except for the fact that Lena is to join them in the pursuit of their new absurd ideal, nothing has changed.

IV. *LENZ*

Büchner first mentions writing a "novella" about Lenz in response to Gutzkow's eager requests for material for his periodical. (He attempted to dignify the project in a letter to his parents by calling it an "essay" [II.448].) Despite Gutzkow's frequent reminders and requests, Büchner never submitted the novella for publication. After Büchner's death, Minna sent Gutzkow a clean copy of the manuscript, which he published two years later as a "relic" in his *Telegraph für Deutschland*. Gutzkow was more interested in the biographical material contained in the narrative than in its intrinsic merit as a literary work of art. He introduced it with the apologetic explanation that he would have hesitated to print the novella in its fragmentary form were it not for the fact that it contained material about Lenz which would be surprising to his readers. And to Minna he wrote: "Lenz, which I will print in its entirety, is an extremely important contribution to literary history, for until now nothing was known about this contact with Oberlin."[1] But while his primary interest was in the subject matter, he also recognized and admired Büchner's skill and insight: "What descriptions of nature! What portrayal of the soul! How the poet is able to perceive the finest nervous conditions of a temperament, which, at least in things poetic, is related to his own. He empathizes with him in everything, and he penetrates into all his mental and spiritual suffering. We must be astonished at such an anatomy of mental and emotional disturbances."[2]

It is indeed astonishing with what amazing accuracy Büchner depicts the symptoms and development of a mental disorder first isolated and defined some sixty years later by Bleuler and Kraepelin (1896). Büchner's novella has since become recognized by professional psychiatrists for its validity and importance as the first classical study of schizophrenia.[3] As recently as 1965, Gerhard Irle concluded from a careful assessment of Büchner's novella: "The rounded and concise sketch of the pathography of a schizophrenic could just as well have been recorded today as 125 years ago."[4]

J. M. R. Lenz (1751-1792) interrupted his study of theology in Königsberg to accompany two noblemen to Strasbourg, where, under the influence of Herder and Goethe, he became one of the leading representatives of the German Storm and Stress movement. Although richly endowed with genius, intuition, talent, and a unique capacity for understanding the social and intellectual situation of the time, Lenz suffered in his own mind by comparison with his friends and felt compelled by ambition and admiration to compete with and finally to imitate Goethe, not only as a writer, but in his private life as well. After Goethe left Strasbourg and Friederike Brion, the inspiration for his Sesenheim poems, Lenz began to court her himself and wrote love poems enough like his idol's to have at one time been attributed to Goethe.[5] He also imitated Goethe's *Werther* with his own epistolary novel *Der Waldbruder*. Seeking more direct competition, he followed Goethe to Weimar and tried to endear himself to Charlotte von Stein, the new woman in Goethe's life; his behavior was so scandalous that Goethe had him expelled from the duchy (November 1776). Following this rupture in his relationship with Goethe and the death shortly thereafter of Goethe's sister Cornelia, whom Lenz worshiped, the first signs of madness began to appear. After having spent some time in the care of the philanthropist Christoph Kaufmann, whom he had met through Goethe in Weimar, Lenz became restless and anxious to move on. Kaufman sent him to his friend Oberlin, who was pastor in the mountain village of Waldersbach near Strasbourg. The beautifully idyllic setting and Oberlin's friendly hospitality brought some improvement, but soon the process of deterioration resumed. When Lenz began to make attempts on his own life, Oberlin no longer felt capable of coping with him and sent him to Strasbourg. After once again showing some improvement, he was apprenticed to a cobbler, but when the cobbler's son, to whom Lenz had become deeply attached, left on his journeyman travels, Lenz's depression and sense of isolation returned. In a frantic attempt to make human contact Lenz wrote his friends and benefactors a number of heartrending letters, some of which Büchner originally intended to include in his narrative.

Because his condition appeared to be incurable, Lenz's friends wrote his family suggesting they have him return home. When his father refused to finance such a journey, the friends, including Goethe, paid for it themselves. Lenz was never again creatively productive, though he did recover enough to occupy himself in the profession he hated and had condemned in his play *The Tutor*. He eventually ended up in Moscow, where he lived in misery and died alone.

Büchner obtained the factual information for his narrative from Oberlin's daily account of Lenz's actions and behavior during his stay in Waldersbach.[6] A certain affinity coupled with a great capacity for empathy enabled him to penetrate beneath the objectively described phenomena into Lenz's psyche, from the third person into the first. Whereas Oberlin's intention was to make an accurate record of his observations, Büchner's was to reveal from within the condition and suffering of his subject. His creation of the means for accomplishing that end so accurately and convincingly is a remarkable artistic achievement.[7]

The narrative begins succinctly and with detached objectivity. An opening statement of who, what, when and where— "On the twentieth of January Lenz went across the mountains" —is followed by a brief impressionistic description of the setting: "The peaks and high surfaces in snow; running down the valleys gray rocks, green surfaces, boulders, and firs" (I.79).[8] This sentence fragment with its asyndetic series of nouns and noun-phrases presents the larger aspects of the landscape simply and objectively. Büchner then moves or "zooms" in on his subject until, as the addition of adjectives reflecting a definite mood and manner of perceiving indicates, he enters into the mind of his subject, whereupon the setting is described as seen and experienced by Lenz:

It was wet and cold [*nasskalt*]. . . . The branches of the firs hung down heavily in the damp air. Gray clouds moved across the sky, but everything so dense, and then the fog steamed up and passed, heavy and damp, through the brush, so sluggish, so awkward. (I.79)

The adversative conjunction "but" indicates directly the adverse reaction of a perceiving subject to the damp and oppressive heaviness of the setting, and so does the repeated recurrence of "so," which expresses Lenz's rather childlike astonishment or amazement and is typical of his response to the world around him.[9] It recurs almost immediately, for example, in an explicit statement of what has already been implied: "Everything seemed to him so small, so near, so wet."

Penetrating even deeper into Lenz's mind, Büchner indicates with remarkable conciseness and Kafkaesque matter-of-factness the aberrant state of Lenz's psyche: "He felt no fatigue; only sometimes it was unpleasant for him, that he could not walk on his head."[10] Because of the disjunction between his inner world and external reality, Lenz is disoriented with respect to time and space; he is unable to understand, for example, why he cannot cover distances more rapidly: "he did not understand why he took so much time to climb down a slope, to reach a distant point; he thought he should be able to cover it all in a few steps." Even more telling is his wish to dry off the wet earth by placing it behind a stove. Lenz may feel that congruence between his inner world and nature might be restored by a complete reversal in their relationship.

According to R. D. Laing, a person is "schizoid" when the totality of his experience is split in two main ways: "in the first place, there is a rent in his relation with the world and, in the second, there is a disruption of his relation with himself. Such a person is not able to experience himself 'together with' others or 'at home in' the world, but on the contrary, he experiences himself in despairing aloneness and isolation; moreover, he does not experience himself as a complete person but rather as 'split' in various ways, perhaps as a mind more or less tenuously linked to a body, as two or more selves, and so on."[11] In Büchner's narrative the relation between Lenz and the world is so thoroughly and accurately described that it can serve as an indication of Lenz's psychical condition at any given moment. The degree of his intrapersonal disruption corresponds to and depends upon the nature of his relations with his surroundings.

Lenz desparately needs to find stability, clarity, and substantiality in his surroundings. When nature is alive with constant motion, when it continually changes in appearance, or when it loses its clear definition, as in the fog, at dusk, or at night, his anxiety causes him to feel an oppressive pain or tearing in his chest. "At first he felt pressure in his chest when the rocks jumped away [so *wegsprang*], the gray forest shook itself beneath him, and the fog swallowed the forms in one moment and half unveiled their powerful limbs in the next. He felt oppressed; he looked for something, as if for lost dreams, but he found nothing" (I.79). The kinds of activity in nature that cause Lenz's anxiety and the sudden changes in his disposition are described in a very long sentence consisting of two extensive "when"-clauses sandwiched between the two halves of the short main clause: "But often . . . he felt a tear in his chest"; the syntax and sound pattern of the sentence add graphical and aural support to its meaning:

> But often, when the storm hurled the clouds into the valleys, and the fog steamed through the forest, and voices awakened along the rocks, now like distant dying thunder, and then rushing in powerfully as if wanting to celebrate the earth in their wild jubilation, and the clouds came galloping in like wild whinnying horses, and the sunshine came and went between them, drawing its dazzling sword along the snow fields, so that a bright, blinding light cut across the peaks and into the valleys; or when the storm drove the clouds downward, tearing a light blue lake into them, and then the wind died down and hummed upward from deep down in the ravines and from the crests of the firs like a lullaby and the pealing of bells, and a soft red climbed up along the deep blue, and little cloudlets on silver wings drifted by and all the mountain peaks, sharp and solid, glittered and flashed far across the land, he felt a tear in his chest. . . . (I.79)

Such a long and complex sentence might seem peculiarly out of place among the simple sentences which surround it and which predominate throughout the narrative, were it not for the extreme importance of the relationship between Lenz and the natural forces and phenomena it describes. Büchner purposefully uses hypotaxis to indicate the interrelationships and interconnections that exist when Lenz is able to relate to his surroundings, and parataxis to indicate confusion, fragmentation, disjunction, and isolation.

Karl Viëtor has claimed that *Lenz* "begins in the tone of a report," that the "pure epic style carries through to the end," and that it "appears to be stylistically almost without artistic pretensions" and "constructed without technical exertion."[12] If the artist's ability to create the technical means for expressing his meaning and if his sensitivity to the sounds and rhythms of language and his use of imagery and metaphor are any indication of his "artistic pretensions" and "technical exertion," then Viëtor's claim could scarcely be further from the truth. A close analysis of the long sentence just quoted clearly reveals Büchner's poetic sensitivity and his mastery of technique.

The author uses carefully chosen verbs to create a powerful, almost dizzying and decidedly threatening sense of the turbulent motion of nature as experienced by Lenz: "hurled," "steamed," "rushing in powerfully," "galloping in," "cut," "drove," "tearing," "glittered," and "flashed." The sense of motion is enhanced by the adjectives, a large number of which are verbal forms. The sound of the language corresponds to and reinforces the meaning. (Since much of this effect is lost in translation, I must use the original to illustrate this point.) The distant storm is first heard in the soft rumble of the short vowels and soft consonants, *"bald wie fern verhallende Donner,"* before reaching its maximum force in the full *"au"* of *"brausten"*: *"und dann gewaltig heranbrausten."* The beat of horses' hoofs sounds in the alliterative repetition of accented w's: *"die Wolken wie wilde, wiehernde Rosse."* The cutting flashes of sunlight and the final clearing of the scene are expressed with the sharp clarity of short vowels and sibilants, which replace the generally predominating full vowel sounds and soft consonants: *"und alle Berggipfel, scharf und fest, weit über das Land hin glänzten und blitzten."*

The two "when"-clauses are closely parallel to each other in structure, but almost mirror images in content. The first begins: "when the storm hurled the clouds into the valleys," and describes the building up of the storm to a mighty crescendo. The second clause begins like the first: "when the storm drove the clouds downward," but is followed by a descrescendo as the storm subsides. Both clauses describe the activity of the clouds and wind and are full of vivid visual and auditory imagery, and both clauses end with a description of the flashing of sunlight on the mountain peaks and into the valley. The grandiose, flowing motions of nature and the language used to describe them give way to Lenz's hasty, choppy, and compulsive motions, which are described in primarily short and rhythmically unvaried simple sentences. The fluctuations in nature between dark and light, up and down, distant and close, and the abrupt change of focus from the large, flowing motions of nature to the staccato of Lenz's restless activity anticipate and reflect the oscillation between extremes which is typical for Lenz and of schizophrenia in general.[13]

After thinking that he "must draw the storm into himself" and "contain everything in himself," Lenz feels that he actually has expanded and that he covers the earth and extends out into the universe. His response to his new condition is ambivalent, however—"it was a pleasure that hurt him" (I.79-80)—for in escaping the oppressive feeling of being confined and limited, he is in danger of losing his sense of personal identity. As he attempts to resist the one threat, he exposes himself to another: in shutting out the world and withdrawing into himself, the feeling of extreme expansion is replaced by one of extreme contraction. In both cases his relationship to the world is disoriented.

Lenz's disorientation with respect to time, space, and natural laws does not disturb him nearly as much as does the anguish of being alone in the dusk of evening or the dark of night. And where he had previously been disturbed by the presence of motion around him, he is now even more disturbed by its absence. He needs to be aware of his surroundings in order to know that the world actually exists and that he is part of it. Otherwise he has the sensation of being alone in a void: "he became terribly lonely; he was alone, completely alone" (I.80). He feels that a voice speaking to him out of the surrounding void, even his own voice, might reassure him that there is an outside world, or, at least, that he himself exists. But Lenz cannot talk to himself; he scarcely even dares to breathe. For what might his voice sound like in the silence of the void, when just bending his foot sounds like thunder beneath him? He eventually feels his isolated existence in nothingness so intensely that he is seized by a terrible, nameless fear; he rushes down the slope in a frantic attempt to escape the madness he feels pursuing him.

As soon as he hears voices, sees light, and comes into contact with people, he loses his fear and becomes somewhat calmer. The special importance the "peaceful, still faces" in the lighted room have for him is indicated by the fact that they actually appear to him to be the source of light: "it seemed to him as if the light must be coming from them [the faces]; it relieved him." When Lenz reaches Waldbach and Oberlin's parsonage, he is welcomed into a similar "homey room," where the still and peaceful faces again seem to be sources or gathering points of light. The description of the setting calls to mind the canvases of the Dutch masters Büchner admired: the faces stand out from the shadows with varying degrees of intensity, ranging from the brightly lit countenance of the child to the face of the mother, "sitting back in the shadows, calm and like an angel" (I.81).

At first Lenz has difficulty finding words; he speaks in a rapid but tortured manner. Slowly, the fear-induced hypertension, which caused him to twitch around the eyes and mouth, relaxes, and he calms down enough to feel at home and to entertain his hosts by telling them stories about his homeland and by drawing pictures of costumes. But in this situation, too, there is danger, for he becomes so involved with memories out of the past that he again loses contact with the reality of the present: "he was away, far away."

Lenz benefits from contact with people and pleasant surroundings only as long as the actual contact lasts. His experience has no duration for him: he cannot draw from past memories or future hopes and anticipations to sustain him; his condition is determined by the circumstances of the moment. Thus, as soon as he is alone in the dark, empty spaciousness of his own room, the memory of the friendly atmosphere of Oberlin's well-lit room with its tranquil occupants disappears into the formless confusion of his mind "like a shadow, a dream." As reality slips away from him, "unnamable fear" and the feeling that he exists in a void seize him once again, and again he takes flight to escape the threat of madness. This time he finds only blackness, however, since the lights are out and the people in bed. What Lenz cannot see does not exist for him, except as in a dream. That is true even of his own body: "he was a dream to himself. . . . He could no longer find himself" (I.81). By concentrating his attention on thoughts that come into his mind and by continually repeating "Our Father," he struggles to regain contact with reality and with himself.[14]

Such mental efforts may help him concentrate and sustain his inner life, but they cannot help him to establish contact with the outside world. Aid comes from a deeper level of the mind, however, as a still intact "dark instinct" compels him to seek strong physical sensations. Both his own existence and the existence of the world outside him are affirmed by the body's response to self-inflicted pain and the shock of cold water: "the pain began to restore his consciousness."[15] In *Danton's Death* and later in this narrative (I.99) the existence of pain is considered to be the strongest argument against God, and yet it is the price Lenz must pay to restore his consciousness and preserve his sanity.

The first long paragraph ends as Lenz finally finds peace in exhausted sleep. Bergemann's division of this segment into thirteen paragraphs tends to obscure the fact that Büchner considered it to be a unit. From the beginning Lenz is seen to be mad or near madness. He oscillates between terrifying fear and relative calm, but the emphasis is decidedly on the former.

As a new day begins, his condition is considerably improved, which seems to indicate that his new surroundings and the influence of Oberlin have a beneficial effect on him. Once again he is moving through the same landscape as at the beginning of the narrative, but this time he is not alone. The actual appearance of nature has not changed much since the previous day: there are still sparse, dark forests, massive rock formations, impressive mountain peaks, clouds of various kinds and shapes, winds, moving "masses" of light, and flashes of sun. But the mood of the landscape has changed. Nature is stiller now and less threatening: the verbs used to describe it are fewer in number and less violent than in the earlier description. Gone also are the variety of loud noises which accompanied the turbulence of the earlier scene. (It is not possible to determine with certainty to what degree nature is seen through Lenz's eyes as a reflection of his condition and to what degree nature actually helps to determine that condition.) The sight of the "still and sober" people who live in complete harmony with their surroundings also has a healing effect on him.

By far the most important source of peace, however, is Oberlin. Lenz derives comfort and assurance from the older man's strength and fatherly maturity:

> It all had a beneficial and soothing effect on him; often he had to look into Oberlin's eyes, and the powerful peacefulness conveyed to us by nature in repose, in a deep forest, in moonlit, melting summer nights, seemed even nearer to him in those calm eyes, this venerable, sober countenance. (I.82)

But like a very small child, who must see things to know they exist,[16] Lenz must be in the actual presence of Oberlin to feel his influence. Once he is alone again and it begins to grow dark, he is overcome by a peculiar fear. Because his sanity depends on maintaining contact with concrete reality, he would like to chase the sun and stay in its light. At this point the author explicitly states what he already has demonstrated, that Lenz experiences a childlike fear when the objects around him become vague in their outlines and therefore "dreamlike" or unreal: "as the objects slowly became more and more shadowy, everything appeared to him so dreamlike, so repulsive. Anxiety befell him as it does children who sleep in the dark; it seemed to him as if he were blind" (I.82). In a desperate attempt to prevent reality from slipping away, he clings to objects, speaks and sings to himself, or recites passages from Shakespeare. Similar attempts failed earlier, and this time, too, he remains "completely rigid" and "cold, cold." Finally, repeating the action that had helped before, he runs outside. He can see better in the pale evening light than he could in his dark room. The cold water of the fountain helps too. He has the secret hope that he will get sick, because sickness means suffering, and to suffer, as we have seen, means to be aware of one's existence.

Lenz's frenzied attempt to fight off madness is expressed by the frantic quality of the language used to describe it: the tempo increases, the words become generally shorter, the accents stronger, and the rhythm almost iambic. This development culminates in the climactic finality of parallel spondees, a finality made even more definite by the assonance of the four words involved: *"ganz starr"* and *"kalt, kalt":*

Now his terror grew: the nightmare of madness sat down at his feet; the hopeless thought that everything was only his dream spread out before him; he clung to every object; figures swiftly passed him by; he pressed toward them; they were shadows; life drained out of him and his limbs were quite numb [*ganz starr*]. He spoke, he sang, he recited Shakespeare, he grasped at everything that usually had made his blood flow faster, he tried everything, but cold, cold! (I.82-83)[17]

When he regains control of himself by once again plunging into cold water, the tempo of the language slows down to a more normal prose rate.

Such attacks become less and less frequent, however, as Lenz's condition gradually improves. Partly responsible for his improvement is the comfort offered by religion: Oberlin helps the former theology student to gain a new understanding and appreciation of religion and especially of the New Testament. In particular, Oberlin's account of a personal encounter with the deity strengthens Lenz's faith: "this faith, this eternal Heaven on earth, this being in God; now for the first time the Holy Scriptures became clear to him. How close nature came to the people, all in heavenly mysteries; not violently majestic, but still familiar!" Lenz had previously experienced nature, and probably religion too, as "violently majestic." His new relation to both is a more reassuring and soothing "familiarity" or "intimacy."

Hearing the story of Oberlin's personal religious experience prepares Lenz emotionally and psychologically for a similar experience of his own. The propitious moment comes one bright sunny morning, when the beauty and serenity of nature correspond with and intensify Lenz's new feeling of tranquility. The extent of the change that has taken place in him since the beginning can be demonstrated by contrasting the opening description of nature with the way it appears now. Where the sun previously cut through the landscape like a fiery sword, it now "cuts crystals." In contrast to the earlier stormy, dark, heavy landscape with its mighty, thundering, driving winds, everything now is light, calm, and peaceful: "No motion in the air except for a gentle breeze and the rustle of a bird lightly brushing snowflakes from its tail. Everything so quiet . . ."

(I.83). And where the limbs of the trees were heavy and hanging, they now quiver like white feathers in the blue air. The
part of the landscape that can have a disturbing effect on Lenz,
"the uniform, tremendous surfaces and lines," are covered and
hidden from view. The imagery has become delicate and serene. The tempo of the language is slow and flowing, with soft
accents and soft vowel and consonant sounds. The large number of sibilants captures the soft rustling of the birds and
the breeze.

The setting reflects Lenz's emotional state, but it also influences it: "He gradually became comfortable . . . a cozy feeling of Christmas crept over him." As a relief from the dreadful
alienation that prevails in what have become his normal relations with the world, such a moment of peace and harmony
with nature fills him with the kind of festive joy a child feels
at Christmas; it seems to him that his mother should appear
and say that she has given all this to him. In this moment
of heightened awareness, "he felt as though something had
touched him on the forehead: the Essence spoke to him."
Lenz's experience differs from Oberlin's in its vagueness and
apparent lack of Christian overtones: not God or Christ, but
the Essence or Being *(das Wesen)* spoke to him. Nevertheless,
by bringing him into accord with himself and the world, it
contributes substantially to his improvement. He collects himself enough to work on the preparation of a sermon, and his
nights become peaceful.

The day he delivers the sermon could scarcely be more
beautiful in its harmonious blending of sensory impressions.
The sun shines, the sound of ringing bells fills the air, and the
landscape "swims in fragrance": "it was as if everything were
dissolving into a harmonious wave" (I.84). The churchgoers
blend physically with their surroundings, and the "pure, brilliant sound" of their singing voices harmonizes with the ringing
bells. Considering the connections that exist between Lenz and
nature, it might appear that all should be quite well for him
now. But the passage also contains ominous signs. The warmth
and beauty of the day can provide only brief respite from
winter's cold death. The snow has melted and "belated flowers"
are visible amidst the black crosses of the cemetery; the last
vestiges of autumnal life are thus juxtaposed with foreboding
symbols of death. Lenz's situation is similar. Before the mental

death of schizophrenic rigidity and depersonalization sets in, he reaches the deceptive highpoint of his development, a state of euphoria. His catalepsy *(Starrkrampf)* ceases, and he regains the ability common to all normal men of experiencing pain and suffering from within. Being thus freed from dependence on the world outside him for physical sensation and pain, he experiences a feeling of well-being: "his whole agony awakened now and settled in his heart. A sweet feeling of infinite well-being crept over him." All the people of the congregation suffer with Lenz, and it comforts him to be able to help them and to bring their misery into a religious context, to direct it toward heaven. His gospel of suffering culminates in the strophe:

> Let in me the holy pain
> Open wells of misery;
> Suffering shall be my gain,
> Suffering my liturgy.

Büchner was well able to understand the importance of pain for Lenz, because he too had experienced the frightening rigidity and numbness that can cause one to become insensitive to pain and suffering. In the same letter in which he described his reaction to the discovery of fatalism in history, he also wrote: "I do not even have the pleasure of pain and longing. Since I crossed the Rhine bridge, it is as if I were dead inside. Not a single feeling arises in me. I'm an automaton; my soul has been taken" (II.426). Half a century earlier, in a letter not published until after Büchner's death (1857), J. M. R. Lenz also recognizes the positive value of suffering: "My greatest suffering is now caused by my own heart, and the most unbearable condition is nevertheless when I don't suffer at all. Perhaps all happiness here is always just a moment and resting point that one takes in order to plunge oneself into new suffering."[18]

Paradox and ambivalence pervade the description of the intense suffering Lenz experiences following his sermon. Once again he projects his own inner state onto the world and the universe—"To him the universe seemed full of wounds" —which causes him, in turn, to feel "deep, ineffable pain." He also feels the presence of God more directly and intensely than before: "Now, another being: divine, twitching lips bent down

over him and attached themselves to his lips; he went to his
lonely room. He was alone, alone!" (I.84-85). At the beginning
of the narrative, "alone" was repeated to emphasize Lenz's
terrible loneliness. Now he has reached the opposite extreme;
he *wants* to be alone in order to enjoy fully the pleasure of what
appears to be mystical ecstasy: "Then the spring rushed,
streams broke from his eyes; he convulsed inside, his limbs
twitched. It seemed to him as if he would dissolve; his ecstasy
[*Wollust*] would not end."[19]

But even in what appears to be a mystical religious experience, the instability of Lenz's psyche reveals itself in the
exaggeration of his feelings and in the abruptness of the change
from one emotion to another. Oscillation between extremes is
characteristic of his condition, as we have seen, and so is the
fact that his emotions and sensations take on universal validity
for him: a feeling of well-being is "a sweet feeling of *infinite*
well-being;" when he suffers, it seems to him that the whole
universe is "full of wounds"; his pain is "ineffable"; and "his
ecstasy *would not end.*" His religious ecstasy is an expression
of his exaggerated sensation of pleasure, just as his apprehension of a wounded universe is an exaggerated expression of
his suffering.

After having slept through the night in the light of a full
moon, which begins at this point to function symbolically as a
foreshadowing of impending madness, Lenz tells Oberlin in the
morning that his mother has appeared to him. She was dressed
in white and wore a white and a red rose on her bosom. She
emerged from the dark church wall, against which Lenz had
seen a rose bush growing, then sank into a corner where roses
grew slowly over her. Lenz interprets this dream or vision as a
sign that his mother is dead. He does not appear to be especially disturbed, but, considering what she represents for him,
her loss or the sense of her loss is highly significant. Her
presence has been felt in one way or another during his more
peaceful moments. She was doubtless among the "faces and
figures" that came into his memory when he told the Oberlins
about his homeland, and when he experienced a "cozy feeling
of Christmas," he thought that she should appear. In dreaming
now of her death, he unconsciously expresses the fearful presentiment that this source of peace and comfort is irrevocably
lost to him.

Since Oberlin fails to recognize the significance of this loss for Lenz, he does not try to dissuade him. On the contrary, by recounting how a voice had correctly told him of the death of his father, he unwittingly encourages him. Picking up Oberlin's cue, Lenz begins to discuss extrasensory perception. "The simplest, purest nature is most closely connected to what is elemental," he speculates. People who live close to nature and have not developed their intellectual, critical faculties have a stronger "elemental sense," which enables them to be aware of the "peculiar life of every form," whether animate or inanimate, and to be able to absorb every "being in nature" into themselves. Such intimate contact with other forms is possible because of an ineffable harmony in all things. The higher, more sophisticated forms with their larger number of organs perceive complexity and diversity rather than unity and harmony. Lenz does not condemn or criticize the "higher forms," which have possibilities unknown to the simpler forms, but he does think it would yield "a feeling of infinite pleasure" to be able to perceive the inherent harmony of all things.[20] Because such speculation leads Oberlin "too far astray from his simple nature," he interrupts Lenz. But Lenz is compelled by his more complex nature to pursue such matters until their abstraction leads him away from empirical reality into "frightening dreams."

The arrival of Kaufmann and his wife upsets Lenz: he does not want to be reminded of the past, and he sees them as a threat to the peaceful and orderly life he has finally established for himself. The schizophrenic does not like to be defined or labeled, which is why he avoids action. "He must remain always ungraspable, elusive, transcendent."[21] If he can be identified with his acts, he feels helpless and at the mercy of those who can so identify him. Consequently he may attempt to dissociate himself from his past, which imprisons him and makes him vulnerable. Lenz has found a measure of peace with Oberlin, who accepts him as he is. Since he has made some progress under these new conditions, he fears that the intrusion of his past into the present will be disruptive and threatening. By dinnertime, however, he is in such good spirits that he discourses at considerable length on the weaknesses of idealism and the desirability of realism in art. Although carried away by his enthusiasm, he does not encounter the difficulties he did when speculating about nature and the various forms of life. His competence and experience as a writer and critic enable him to speak with assurance and conviction. (While the views he puts forth are Büchner's, they are also compatible in spirit with the aesthetic writings of J. M. R. Lenz.)

With this discourse Lenz reaches the apex of the general trend toward improvement that began with his arrival in Waldbach. A peripety follows, as Kaufmann takes Lenz aside and suggests that he return home and support his father.[22] Kaufmann also tells him he is wasting his life and should work toward some goal. The mere suggestion throws Lenz into a fit of frantic desperation: whereas he had been lucid and self-controlled in his discussion of art, he now becomes agitated, confused, and completely unable to cope with this kind of practical reality. He is repelled and feels threatened by Kaufmann's bourgeois mentality with its emphasis on striving toward future goals. There can be no meaningful future for Lenz if he cannot retain his hold on the present; and to do that he needs the tranquility he has been able to find with Oberlin. How can he be expected to support his father, when he is not even capable of fighting off madness without the help of others? His incredulity and agitation are expressed by the questioning, exclamatory nature of his language; and his attempt to grasp the implications of Kaufmann's suggestion is indicated by his repetition of key words:

"Go away, away! Home? Go mad there? You know I can't bear it anywhere but around here, in these parts. If I couldn't sometimes climb a mountain and see the countryside, and then go down again to the house, through the garden, and look in at the window—I'd go mad! Mad! Leave me in peace! Just a little peace, now that I'm beginning to feel better. Go away? I don't understand that; with those two words the world is ruined. Everyone needs something: if he can rest, what more could he have? Always climbing, struggling, and so eternally throwing away everything the moment brings and always suffering so as to enjoy later, thirsting while clear springs bound across your path. I can bear it now, and I want to stay here. Why? Why? Just because I feel well. What does my father want? Can he give me more? Impossible! Leave me in peace." (I.88-89)

Kaufmann cannot persuade Lenz to leave the Steintal, but he does accomplish something equally disastrous: he persuades Oberlin to accompany him to Switzerland. Lenz is frightened by the prospect of being separated, even temporarily, from the person upon whose calming influence his mental stability depends. Lenz has become as dependent on Oberlin as Büchner's Woyzeck is on Marie: in both cases the disruption of the relationship has fatal consequences.

Not wanting to stay in the house alone, Lenz accompanies the departing Oberlin into the mountains. On the way back he wanders aimlessly over the kind of terrain that disturbed him at the beginning of the narrative. At this point a brief description of the natural setting with its massive and powerful, but rigid and undifferentiated surfaces and lines is enough to signal Lenz's imminent loss of contact with reality: "everything seemed to melt into a single line, like a wave rising and falling between heaven and earth. He felt as if he were lying beside a boundless ocean that gently rose and fell" (I.89-90).

In a situation parallel to, though in many ways the reverse of, his arrival at Oberlin's, Lenz is accepted that night into the house of strangers. Whereas the parsonage was brightly lit, the hut he finds now is almost dark. The Oberlins eagerly welcomed him and made him feel at home; at the hut he must knock repeatedly before he is admitted. At Oberlin's he was soon made the center of interest; here he is given something to eat, shown a place to sleep, and then ignored. Both scenes are painted with Rembrandt's chiaroscuro palette, but this one is much darker and more mysterious. Here, too, a single face catches the full light of the lantern, but this time it is the pale face of a peculiarly withdrawn girl. There are no partially lit faces, and the "angelic" mother in the shadows has been replaced by an old woman who constantly sings in an unpleasant "snarling voice."

The scene is completed by the arrival of a man about whom there is a mysterious, demonically disturbing aura. Unlike Oberlin, who is at peace with himself and a source of peace for others, this man is agitated and disturbed, and his presence causes the girl to become restless too. He calms her down again, but by the magical procedure of applying dried leaves to her hand, rather than by persuasion or personal contact. Like Oberlin, this man, too, has heard a voice in the mountains; but whereas Oberlin's vision was accompanied by a brilliant light, this man saw flashes of lightning over the valleys; and whereas Oberlin felt that God had entered into him in a mystical union, this man fought like Jacob with the unnamed force *(es)* that "attacked" him.

The people of the valley consider the strange man to be a saint and make pilgrimages to him. He is reputed to have the kind of supernatural powers Lenz and Oberlin discussed earlier: "he could see water under the ground and conjure up spirits" (I.91). The girl represents a peculiar form of the disembodiment that threatens Lenz. Her relationship to reality is so tenuous that she does not respond to Lenz's arrival and appears unaware of his presence in the room. She sits up most of the night chanting and talking; with the light of the moon striking her face she looks weird and unearthly. When she finally calms down in the morning, her face expresses "indescribable suffering." By the time Lenz leaves, she is ecstatic again. Religious ecstasy apparently provides her with the means of escaping the pain and suffering of life, just as schizophrenic withdrawal eventually does for Lenz.

Unlike Oberlin, who helps and advises others, these people are isolated and apart from the activities of daily life. Since they make no effort to recognize Lenz's presence among them or to establish any kind of human contact with him, he feels alone with them and welcomes the arrival of others the following morning as if relieved to be in the presence of people again.

This episode is the reverse counterpart of Lenz's stay with Oberlin, and it has an opposite effect on him: "But the past night had made a powerful impression on him. The world had been bright for him, and now he felt a stirring and turmoil around him, as an implacable force was dragging him toward the abyss. He raged now inside himself" (I.91). Lenz must renew his fight against insanity. According to the peculiar rhythm which defines his illness, he again oscillates between extremes, whose poles in this case are exertion and exhaustion, crying and laughing: "The higher he raised himself up, the lower he plunged." Once again he begins to lose contact with reality, and again he throws himself into various activities, but

without the concentration and persistence that would be necessary for any one of them to be meaningful and helpful.

While seeking comfort in the presence of Madame Oberlin,
Lenz hears a maid sing a song that reminds him of the girl
whose fate weighs heavily upon his heart. He now feels compelled to talk about the girl who was never far from his mind.
He seems to think of her as a sweetheart or lover, but she is
really more of a mother-figure. Like Oberlin, the father-figure,
she was able to make him feel as happy and content as a child.
Lenz suffers from the same malady that afflicts most of Büchner's major figures, namely, the suffocating feeling of being
confined or enclosed: "Now everything is so close, so close.
You see, it often seems to me, as if I were hitting against the sky
with my hands; oh, I'm suffocating!" But in the presence of
Friederike,[23] who could sit in a confined place and still be
perfectly happy, Lenz was able to overcome his feeling of
oppression: "she withdrew into herself; she looked for the
narrowest little place in the whole house, and there she sat, as
if her whole happiness were in one small point. And then I felt
like that too" (I.92).

An associative connection is made between the maid's song
and Friederike. Another is made between Friederike and Lenz's
attempt to raise a young girl named Friederike from the dead.
As recorded by Oberlin, Lenz's attempt to perform a miracle
precedes his conversation with Madame Oberlin and consequently also any mention of Friederike. Büchner's change in
the sequence clearly reveals his intention of establishing a
connection between the figures, as if in raising the one, Lenz
also hopes to regain the other.

The attempt to bring the dead girl back to life is also connected with Lenz's renewed religious torment. As Lenz becomes inwardly emptier and colder, he feels the need to
awaken some sort of inner glow. In contrast to the times "when
everything seethed inside him, when his many emotions made
him breathless" (I.93), he now despairs, because he is dead
inside. After his various attempts to revive his inner life and
emotions have failed, he hopes for a miracle and prays that
God will give him a sign. He cannot and will not wait, however,
but intends to force God to reveal Himself by using him as an
instrument to awaken the dead child: "he prayed with all the
misery of despair, as he was weak and unhappy, that God

would give him a sign and restore the child to life." Lenz
identifies with the child's apparent isolation and loneliness; his
fate is connected with hers, since his own salvation is magically
dependent on his success in saving her. He prays and tries to
collect himself before committing his entire being to what he
considers to be the proof of God's existence. A loving, omnipotent God could not forsake him in his desparate need. How
terrible and final it is, then, when Lenz pronounces the words
that had proved their power for Christ—"'Arise and walk!'"—
only to hear them echo soberly from the walls of the room as
if to mock him, while the corpse remains cold. "He collapsed,
half mad, to the floor; then it drove him to his feet, out into
the mountains."

Lenz's failure destroys his last hope. Just as the hut episode
was the counterpart of his arrival at Oberlin's, this scene is
the reverse counterpart of his earlier success with religion.
Whereas the sermon was followed by a mystical apprehension
of God's presence, Lenz's futile attempt to perform a miracle
results in a violent rejection of God. And whereas the earlier
experience made him all the more aware of the beauty and
harmony of nature, he now becomes completely alienated from
it. The cosmos appears foolish and ridiculous to him—"and the
sky was a stupid blue eye in which stood the ludicrous, vacuous
moon"—and his surroundings lose their reality: "everything
was empty and hollow to him." He now turns against God for
having betrayed and abandoned him: "he felt as if he could
thrust a monstrous clenched fist into Heaven and seize God
and drag Him between His clouds; as if he could grind up the
world with his teeth and spit it into the Creator's face; he
cursed, he blasphemed" (I.93-94). Soon the passion of his violent denunciation gives way to the even more terrible emptiness
of despair coupled with the realization that God does not even
exist: "Lenz had to laugh loudly, and with that laughter atheism
seized him and held him securely and calmly and firmly."

The difference between this negative religious experience
and the earlier positive one is also directly manifest in the
natural setting. The sun shone brightly on the unseasonably
clear and beautiful day of the sermon. Now, complete darkness
alternates with weak moonlight to allow only fleeting glimpses
of a hazy, undefined, "disappearing" landscape. Following the

sermon Lenz felt the touch of divine lips; now he feels a triumphant song of Hell in his breast.

Lenz's violent, blasphemous reaction against God is especially dreadful since his own existence depends on the existence of God. His unstable psyche cannot withstand the enormous stress caused by his alienation from nature and God; when the pressure becomes too great, it explodes into the compulsive laughter of despair and madness. The active rebellion lasts only a moment before being replaced by compulsive behavior and schizophrenic passivity. Numbness and insensateness make Lenz forget what had caused his agitation: "He no longer knew what had moved him so much before. He was freezing. He thought he wanted to go to bed now, and he went, cold and unshakable, through the eerie darkness—everything was empty and hollow for him, he had to run and went to bed" (I.94). For the first time, now, he is too far gone to resist or even to care. By morning, however, he has recovered enough to be horrified by his condition of the day before. He realizes that he is standing on the edge of the abyss, but "a mad desire compelled him to look into it again and again and to repeat this torment" (I.94).

Until this point in the narrative Büchner uses Oberlin's report primarily as a source of factual material and as a framework around which to construct his artistic version of Lenz's breakdown. Once he has followed Lenz's development through its various ups and downs until there is no more hope for him— "'But it's all over for me! I have apostatized; I am damned for eternity. I am the eternal Jew'"—little remains to be told. Examples can be multiplied and cycles repeated, but little or nothing of fundamental importance is required to complete the representation of Lenz's mental deterioration. For that reason Büchner begins at this point to borrow more heavily from Oberlin and to lose his interest in reworking the borrowed material. The more Lenz's inner life rigidifies, the less need there is for the author to penetrate into his psyche, and the more adequate is the kind of objective description provided by Oberlin.

When Oberlin returns from Switzerland, it immediately becomes apparent that his attitude toward Lenz has been influenced to such a degree by Kaufmann that he can no longer be of any help. The insight we have been given into the workings of Lenz's mind and the nature of his condition makes us sensitive to the change in Oberlin and enables us to predict what the effect will be on Lenz. At first Oberlin speaks to Lenz only incidentally, while doing other things: "*At the same time* Oberlin walked back and forth in his room. . . . *At the same time* he related. . . . *At the same time* he admonished him. . . ." In taking up Kaufmann's suggestion that Lenz return to his father, he does not try to understand Lenz's situation. He also fails to recognize the depth of Lenz's despair and counters his pleading supplication with religious platitudes.[24] Now, more than ever, Lenz needs and expects comfort and reassurance from Oberlin; and yet now, for the first time, Oberlin's words disturb him: "During the conversation Lenz became extremely agitated; he sighed deeply; tears welled from his eyes; he spoke disjointedly: 'Yes, but I can't bear it. Do you want to drive me away? In you alone is the way to God. But it's all over for me!'"

While despairing of the possibility of finding "divine comfort," Lenz's thoughts suddenly turn again to Friederike. The close association in his mind between her and his mother makes it easy and natural for his thoughts to jump from one to the other. He seems to feel that suffering as great as his must be punishment for some terrible sin, such as murdering the women who loved him and whom he loved.[25] By repenting of and atoning for his sins, he should be able to receive forgiveness. To that end he wants to be punished by Oberlin. When Oberlin refuses to comply, Lenz inflicts punishment upon himself. After "yelling with an empty, hard voice the name Friederike, which he does with extreme rapidity, confusion, and despair," he throws himself repeatedly into the cold water of the fountain.

For the following episode, Büchner departs entirely from his source to introduce a malady which afflicted him personally and from which most of his main figures also suffer: ennui. Oberlin does not mention it as one of Lenz's symptoms, but the experience of boredom is compatible with the nature of Lenz's condition. Once he has lost all faith in God, man, and nature and has given up the struggle to preserve his sanity, nothing remains for him but an empty life in an absurd world. Since all action in such a world is futile and meaningless, the appropriate response is to do nothing at all, or, since that too is unbearable, to make an end of it, either by taking one's own life, as Lenz attempts to do, or by escaping into total madness, as he does.

Lenz decides to stay in bed and do nothing. He now laughs at Oberlin's suggestion that he turn to God, for he has come to believe that God is an illusion in the minds of those people who are naive and fortunate enough to have found such a "comfortable pastime." In recognizing idleness and boredom as the motivational force behind all activity, Lenz, like Danton and Leonce, loses his will to act: "'Indeed, if I were so fortunate, as you, to find such a comfortable pastime, indeed, one could fill his time in that way. Everything out of idleness. For most people pray out of boredom; the others fall in love out of boredom; the third are virtuous, the fourth depraved, and I am nothing at all, nothing at all. I don't even want to kill myself: it is too boring!'" (I.96).

The full extent of Lenz's mental disorientation can be seen by comparing an earlier passage—"But only as long as light was in the valley could he endure it; toward evening a peculiar anxiety befell him; he felt like running after the sun" (I.82)—with the strophe Lenz recites now:

> Oh God, in all your waves of light,
> And in your noonday glowing bright,
> My eyes from watching have grown sore,
> Will night not come for ever more?[26] (I.96)

Having given up the struggle to preserve his sanity, he now actually longs for night, for release into nothingness. The extent of Lenz's degeneration is indicated as much by the mocking, jeering tone of his voice and his choppy, hasty manner of speaking as by what he says. The impression of grotesqueness and madness conveyed by this high-pitched, staccato, jerky language is enhanced by the rodent-like motion described by the verb "to scamper" *(huschen)*. As Oberlin starts to leave, "Lenz scampered after him. . . . he then scampered back into bed." Also significant is the fact that Lenz looks at Oberlin "with eerie [*unheimlichen*] eyes" as he speaks: the adjective "eerie" has frequently been used in the narrative to refer to Lenz's feeling when threatened by fear and madness as well as to those things that disturbed him. It is as if these incomprehensibly disturbing and threatening elements had now taken possession of him, for there is something decidedly "eerie" in Lenz's words and actions in this scene, especially in the incongruity of his tone and manner with the serious nature and deep truth of his remarkably accurate assessment of his problem: "'You see, now something does occur to me. If only I could distinguish whether I'm dreaming or awake: you see, that is very important. Let's look into it.'"

Despite his apathy and insensateness Lenz is still compelled by some unconscious force to fill the inner void: "he had no hate, no love, no hope; a terrible emptiness and yet a torturing restlessness and need to fill it. He had *nothing*. What he did, he did with consciousness, and yet an inner instinct compelled him" (I.98). (This *"nothing"* is one of only three words Büchner italicized. The others are a personal pronoun referring to Friederike and the first mention of Kaufmann's name.) Opposing forces are represented in him by different voices of his now divided personality: "When he was alone he felt so dreadfully lonely that he constantly talked out loud with himself, called out, and then was startled again; and it seemed to him as though a strange voice had spoken to him . . . it was as if he were double, and the one part attempted to save the other and called to itself" (I.97-98). His contact with the world becomes more and more tenuous. Sometimes he is filled with indescribable anguish at not being able to finish a sentence he has begun. Then he feels compelled to repeat over and over the last word he has spoken, as if struggling to collect himself enough to complete his thought, or as if hoping to regain the meaning and substance he feels his words have lost. And by clutching the arm of the person nearest him, he tries to bring himself back to reality.

When he is alone, he becomes totally involved in the new reality he creates in his imagination. He realizes Leonce's wish of being able to become the person he thinks about. He has the desire to manipulate nature and people according to his whims, just as he had wanted to walk on his head or cover distances more rapidly. He apprehends the world, himself, and his actions as being dreamlike. His peculiar abilities are possible because his new reality obeys the laws and logic of dreams: "he entertained himself by standing houses on their roofs, dressing and undressing people, and thinking up the maddest pranks." And where he had previously admired the people who could be moved by the "peculiar life of every form" and who could "take every being in nature into themselves," he is now able to be like a cat, for example, and to exercise peculiar power over a real cat: "she seemed to be spellbound by his gaze; she became terrified; her fur bristled with fright" (I.98).

Lenz's condition appears to be hopeless, but a "powerful instinct for self-preservation" compels him, in his better moments, to continue the fight against madness, a struggle which is no longer limited to the hours of darkness: "Even in the daytime he had these attacks. They were even more terrible then, for otherwise the light had saved him from them." He knows no reality other than his own existence, "as if the world were only a figment of his imagination. . . . He was the eternally damned Satan; alone with his tormenting imaginings" (I.99). Bound up as he is in his own self, his life seems fully consistent and logical to him, whereas the words of others strike him as being inconsistent, since they come from a world to which he no longer belongs.[27] He is cut off from other people and their world by a "gulf of hopeless madness, a madness through eternity."

Lenz's fluctuations continue, though he has become too weak and shattered to carry the upward swing very high. At best he clings to Oberlin, in whom he sees his only hope: "he flung himself into Oberlin's arms; he clung on to him as if he wanted to penetrate into him. He was the only being who was alive for him and through whom life was again revealed to him." But he is not helped by Oberlin's talk of God, since Lenz can find no comfort in a deity who allows such suffering to exist in his creation: "'but I, if I were almighty, you see, if I were like that, I couldn't endure the suffering; I would save, save. I want nothing but rest, rest, just a little rest and to be able to sleep." Like his longing for night and his attempted suicide, Lenz's denial of pain is only a momentary expression of resignation and surrender. In the next moment his attitude changes and he again tries to bring himself back to reality through self-inflicted pain:

> The half-hearted attempts at suicide, which he repeatedly carried out, were not wholly serious. It was not so much a desire for death—for him there was no rest or hope in death. Rather, in moments of the most dreadful anxiety or of the dull repose that borders on nonbeing, it was an attempt to bring him to himself through physical pain. Moments in

which his mind seemed to ride on some sort of insane idea were still the happiest. They did give him some rest, and his wild gaze was not so terrible as the anxiety which longs for salvation and the eternal torment of restlessness! He often beat his head against the wall or inflicted some other violent physical pain on himself. (I.99-100)

Büchner's own attitude toward pain was also ambivalent. He felt sympathy and compassion for those who must suffer, especially for the poor. At times he seemed to agree with his figure Payne in *Danton's Death* who argued that the existence of suffering is proof that there is no God, since an omnipotent, loving God could not allow such misery to exist in His creation. Opposed to this is the statement he is reported to have made shortly before his death: "We do not have too much pain; we have too little of it, for through pain we go to God!" (B.580). And to his fiancée he once wrote: "I do not even have the pleasure of pain and longing" (II.426). He also refers in *Danton's Death* (I.vii) and in *Leonce and Lena* (I.iii) to the Epicurean pleasure one can get from suffering. Büchner's works reflect his search for an explanation as to why man must suffer; they contain answers, but no answer.

Büchner's feeling toward pain and suffering is very close to Kierkegaard's view of despair as a "sickness unto death." Kierkegaard considers despair in the abstract to be an immense advantage: "The possibility of this sickness is man's advantage over the beast, and this advantage distinguishes him far more essentially than the erect posture, for it implies the infinite erectness or loftiness of being spirit." Despair is inherent in man's nature; it is the result of his being a "synthesis of the infinite and finite, of the temporal and eternal, of freedom and necessity," a synthesis originally from God. Kierkegaard's despair, like Büchner's pain and suffering, involves him in paradox and ambivalence: "So then it is an infinite advantage to be able to despair; and yet it is not only the greatest misfortune and misery to be in despair; no, it is perdition." Lenz's malady has a great deal in common with the sickness Kierkegaard describes in detail.[28]

The balance of forces struggling in Lenz's breast is finally upset once and for all; victorious is his desire for peace, not the preserving, comforting peace he has often sought, but the final deathlike stasis of schizophrenia.[29] The unconscious force willing the preservation of his sanity has gradually weakened to the point that it offers only sporadic feeble resistance. Lenz remains in bed because the oppressive weight of his surroundings has increased to the extent that even the air seems tremendously heavy. He does not want to eat and cannot sleep. In the midst of reporting another suicide attempt, the author simply breaks off the narrative. Lenz's struggle is over, his story ended.

A brief description of Lenz's trip to Strasbourg follows a large space in the manuscript, which may indicate that Büchner originally intended to incorporate some more of the material from Oberlin's account (material filling four pages in Lehmann's edition). Lenz is coldly resigned to his fate and completely indifferent to the serene, beautiful, and harmonious landscape through which he travels. The only thing he feels is "dull anxiety" as he stares out the window and sees how his surroundings again begin to lose their definition in the darkness. This "dull anxiety" differs from the "sinister," "indescribable," "unnameable" anxiety he experienced earlier, just as his present indifference and emotional insensitivity differ from his earlier passionate involvement and extreme suffering. After his arrival in Strasbourg Lenz seems quite normal, but inside he is empty and dead.

Büchner realized that art stands above history in its ability to recreate the historical moment, to capture the life of the time, and to create living figures (II.443). By penetrating into the thoughts and emotions of his figures, by discovering hidden connections and relations, and by explaining, justifying, and motivating, the artist can go beyond the historian's description of people and events. With regard to the difference between history and the novel, E. M. Forster writes that history is based on evidence, while a novel is based on evidence plus or minus x, where x represents the temperament of the novelist. "The historian deals with actions and with the characters of men only so far as he can deduce them from their actions." The historian cannot get at the hidden life of a character, for as soon as the hidden life appears in external signs, it has entered the realm of action and is hidden no longer. The novelist, on the contrary, reveals the hidden life at its source. Thus fiction can be even truer than history.[30]

Büchner learned from the reception of *Danton* that the public could not recognize and appreciate the artistic merit of a lifelike, realistic treatment of well known events of recent history. His inclusion in *Lenz* of a discussion of his ideas on aesthetics may have been motivated by the desire to prepare his readers for a new kind of art. Unlike the historical material he used for *Danton,* Oberlin's journal had not yet been published, but Büchner knew that it soon would be. Lenz's discourse on literature is not an indispensable, perhaps not even an integral part of the narrative, but neither is it incongruous. Since Lenz was a writer and critic, it is quite conceivable that he should welcome the chance to discuss his métier. And at this high point in his mental well-being it is plausible that he could do so.

Lenz begins with an attack on idealism in art.[31] God made the world as it should be, he says, and the artist should strive to re-create this God-given reality in his art, since no amount of glorification or idealization can make it any better. The essence of Büchner's artistic creed is tersely summarized in the statement:

> I demand in everything—life, the possibility of existence, and then it's good; we needn't ask then whether it is beautiful or ugly. The feeling that what has been created has life stands above such considerations and is the only criterion in matters of art. (I.86)

The only true representatives of such art are Skakespeare, *Volkslieder,* and sometimes Goethe. Those who attempt to create idealistic figures end up with nothing but wooden puppets. In order to capture nature and life, the artist must be sensitive and empathic: he must be able to get inside his characters, and he must be responsive to the slightest nuances of expression, physical as well as verbal. No social stratum should be eliminated from art; even the lowliest creatures de-

serve to be understood and represented. The artist must love
all men before he can understand each one individually:

> One must love mankind in order to be able to penetrate into
> the peculiar essence of each individual. No one may be con-
> sidered too lowly or too ugly; only then can they be under-
> stood. The least distinguished face makes a deeper impres-
> sion than the mere perception of beauty. And one can cause
> the figures to emerge from themselves without copying any-
> thing into them from outside where no life, no muscles, no
> pulse are felt to swell and throb. (I.87)

Büchner is not advocating naturalism in art, since his primary
concern is not with surface reality, but with the inner physiognomy of his figures, their mental states, thoughts, and internal processes, as well as with their relationships to others and to
their surroundings. Büchner demands that art re-create rather
than attempt to reproduce reality, and that it capture the
essence of reality and life, not just its outward appearance. In
stating that Pygmalion's statue was not able to have children,
Camille expresses a similar unconcern for external appearance
in comparison with the inner life of a work of art. Büchner's art
is expressionistic in that his figures "emerge from within themselves." They create themselves and reveal their thoughts and
feelings through their words, actions, and gestures. What Danton considered to be the impossible prerequisite for understanding another person is possible for the artist, who can
break open the skull of his subject, in effect, and discover what
is in his brain cells.

To illustrate what he considers to be the appropriate structure for realistic art, Lenz describes a scene from life:

> As I was walking yesterday along the valley, I saw two girls
> sitting on a rock. One of them was letting down her hair, the
> other was helping. And her golden hair hung down; and a
> serious, pale face, and yet so young, and the black dress,
> and the other one so carefully attentive. The most beautiful
> and intense paintings of the Old German School scarcely
> give an idea of the scene. Sometimes one would like to be a
> Medusa's head, so as to be able to transform such a group
> into stone and show it to the people. They stood up; the
> beautiful group was destroyed; but as they were descending

between the rocks, another picture was formed. The most beautiful pictures, the most swelling tones group and dissolve. Only one thing remains: an unending beauty that passes from one form to another, eternally visible, changed. (I.87)

Like Camille, who refers to the "glowing, roaring, shining creation that . . . *renews itself every moment*" (I.37, italics added), Lenz views life as consisting of a series of individual moments. As with a sequence of paintings or a progression of musical tones, each unit develops or grows naturally from the preceding one. The painter resembles the head of Medusa in his ability to freeze individual moments into tableaux. Drawing from his memory and imagination, the viewer of such tableaux can feel the mood and atmosphere of the original scenes and can sense or know what has preceded and what will follow the captured moments. Musicians and writers have the advantage of being able to present a whole series of moments, which together form a larger, more comprehensive whole.

That Büchner's ideas on art are closely related to his concept of nature was indicated above. Büchner rejected the teleological explanation of natural phenomena, believing that nature has no goals toward which it is striving, no grand design according to which it unfolds. We do not have hands in order to be able to grasp things, for example, but we grasp things because we have hands (II.292). Similarly, each moment is its own goal and exists for itself. Underlying all existence is a primal law *(ein Urgesetz)* of which each physical entity is a manifestation. According to this law, which Büchner also calls "a law of beauty," the highest and purest forms are produced with the greatest economy of plan and design. Since all existence is a manifestation of this law, all actions and reactions proceed in accordance with it. The result is inevitable harmony in all natural things.[32] The aesthetic correspondence to the teleological view of nature is classical or classicistic art with its linear development toward a goal. Büchner's view of nature demands a form of art in which each segment of the work attains the highest possible degree of autonomy and self-sufficiency, just as each moment in life is complete in itself.

The application to the drama of the episodic or paratactic form was discussed in connection with *Danton's Death*. Its use in prose is not significantly different. The simplest structural level may consist of a series of words or phrases. Parataxis on this level is especially effective for impressionistic descriptions of physical settings; the whole is presented as a simple juxtaposition of its component parts as seen by the narrator or one of his figures: "The peaks and high surfaces in snow; running down the valley gray rock, green surfaces, boulders, and firs" (I.79); "Children at the table, old women, girls, all quiet, peaceful faces" (I.80). Moving up a level, simple sentences or sentence fragments may be strung together paratactically, i.e., without being connected and interrelated by subordinating conjunctions.[33] Paragraphs are similarly arranged to form episodes and episodes to form the narrative in its entirety.[34] Of course excessive use of this form would be artificial and monotonous; Büchner's development as an artist may be defined in terms of his ability to extend the degree of its effective application.

Just as he believes that all phenomena and processes of nature are determined by a single law, which is a law of beauty, Büchner also sees the various arts as fundamentally similar. Lenz describes the succession of life's scenes or moments in terms of painting and music, for example, though his real concern is with reproducing them in literature. His interpretation of two Dutch paintings, on the other hand, reveals a literary perspective. His remarks suggest how the individual segments of Büchner's art should be approached and interpreted.[35]

Lenz prefers Dutch paintings because they are realistic and tell a story. He knows only two pictures that have impressed him "in the same way the New Testament has," he says. The first painting represents a scene from the life of Christ: "Christ and the Disciples from Emmaus." It is impossible to envisage the painting from Lenz's explication, because he describes the scene as he read it in the Bible, not as it is represented in oil: "When one *reads* how the Disciples went out; all of nature lies *in those few words*" (I.88, italics added). Only the physical setting and mood come from the painting: "It is a gloomy evening at twilight, a uniform red streak along the horizon, half dark on the road." What he describes is a series of actions, only one of which could actually be represented in the painting itself. From his knowledge of the event as described in the

Bible, he fills in what immediately preceded and followed the moment actually represented. Thus a single scene suggests a whole series of actions; the whole is contained in one of its parts: "all of nature lies in those few words."

Because the artist and the public share common experiences and knowledge, the artist who works from nature and life or from history can expect the viewer or reader to supply the missing details of his work and to place it in a broader context, just as Lenz draws from his knowledge of the New Testament in order to extend the boundaries of the scene as actually represented. The manner in which the viewer can add to and complete a picture is further illustrated in Lenz's description of the second picture. This time the extrapictorial material is probably based on his own experience. From the representation of a woman sitting by a window and reading a book, Lenz assumes that she was not able to go to church. He even seems to perceive the sound of ringing bells and of hymns coming from the nearby village. The appeal for Lenz of both pictures lies more in the whole complex of mood and the situation they suggest to him than in their intrinsic aesthetic value, more in content than form.

While recent interpreters of *Lenz* have disagreed among themselves about the novella's structure, they have agreed in concluding from their respective arguments that it is a finished or near-finished work, not just the torso or incomplete fragment most earlier critics, beginning with Gutzkow, had considered it to be. My own investigation of the work's structure and of Büchner's views on art leads me to the same conclusion. Some editors have wanted to complete Büchner's work for him by interpolating into the narrative Oberlin's account of what occurred between Lenz's jump from the window and his departure for Strasbourg. The addition of this material is merely repetitive and therefore not only unnecessary, but actually detrimental to the intent and artistic effectiveness of the work.

The critics who have considered the narrative to be incomplete have generally based their judgments on classical aesthetic presuppostions which do not apply to this type of art. Whereas Aristotle taught and his followers rigidly maintained that all parts of a work should be "so closely connected that the transposal or withdrawal of any one of them will disjoint and

dislocate the whole," and that a series of episodes bound together by their concentration on a single individual does not
constitute a unified plot,[36] Büchner learned from Shakespeare
that plot can be episodically constructed around a single individual and that its parts can indeed be transposed and withdrawn and new parts added without necessarily disjointing and
dislocating the whole. The primary criterion for this type of art
is that it present a segment of life which is complete in itself and
aesthetically pleasing. The end may be open, but it must not
leave the feeling that something is missing. And so it is with
Lenz. As J. P. Stern has pointed out, no one "has ever given
any hint of what more could possibly be said when Büchner
reaches the end of Lenz's passion."[37]

V. *WOYZECK*

Construction of the Text

Büchner's finest, most original and most revolutionary play was so far in advance of its own time, so far out of phase with the modes of drama which commanded the stage throughout most of the nineteenth century, that the history of its reception and influence may be said to begin with the regeneration of the German drama in the last decade of the nineteenth century. Its profound influence on the subsequent development of the drama is a truly remarkable achievement for a play that was never completed by its author and that depends for its existence on the ability of editors to discover the author's intention from a rather confusing assortment of barely legible manuscripts. The development from the first constructions, which were really adaptations, to the relatively accurate contemporary editions has taken place through a complex series of steps involving the gradual increase in the public's awareness of the aesthetics of the play's form and the establishment of more valid principles of editing. From my study of the extant material and the editorial procedures adhered to in constructing the texts now available, I am convinced that further improvement can be made. For that reason, and because the multiplicity of existing constructions demands that any serious interpretive or analytical study of the play indicate the text upon which it is based, I will present and defend what I consider to be a valid construction. This can best be accomplished through confrontation with existing editions, especially Lehmann's construction for the historical-critical Hamburg edition. Those readers who do not have some knowledge of the manuscripts or who are not interested in the technical aspects of editing such a text may wish either to skip over this section to the interpretation that follows or to skim through it with an eye to the interpretive material it contains, a substantial portion of which is not repeated later.

Büchner's collected works were first published in 1850 by his brother Ludwig. Since Ludwig had great difficulty in reading his brother's handwriting, and since he was unable to recognize any connection between the individual scenes in what he evidently considered to be only dramatic sketches, he included none of *Woyzeck* in his edition. Another three decades elapsed before *Woyzeck* was first published in 1879 by Karl Emil Franzos. While claiming to give an accurate reading and reproduction of Büchner's manuscripts, Franzos in fact took considerable liberty in supplementing the text with his own additions and in altering the sequence and construction of scenes. His edition also contains numerous misreadings, including the one that has been perpetuated in the title of Alban Berg's opera *Wozzeck*. Despite Franzos's adaptation of the text to the familiar conventions of the classical drama, however, it still remained too modern and incomprehensible to be accepted by the public.

In their search for new artistic forms, their commitment to social reform, and their desire to capture the life and milieu of poor and simple men, dramatists such as Gerhart Hauptmann, Frank Wedekind, Georg Kaiser, and Bertolt Brecht found a kindred spirit in Büchner and a model in his works. Thus it was other artists above all who prepared the way for Büchner's discovery and reception by literary historians and the general public, both by calling attention to him directly and by establishing through the artistic innovations of their works the prerequisites for understanding his. By the time *Woyzeck* was first performed in November 1913—thirty-four years after the appearance of Franzos's edition—Naturalism had already been superceded by Expressionism and Neo-Romanticism; the public had become familiar with the conventions of the episodic drama and had learned to accept serious treatment of themes and types of persons formerly considered too ugly, too lowly, or too offensive to be dignified by inclusion in serious works of art.

Another artist who contributed to the understanding of the form of *Woyzeck* and who helped prepare the way for its reception was Alban Berg. Berg was inspired by a performance of the Franzos text (1914 in Vienna) to use this material for an opera. His *Wozzeck* incorporates fifteen of the twenty-six scenes contained in Franzos's edition. Berg wanted to "give to the theater what is the theater's" by composing music that would serve and fulfill Büchner's "immortal drama." He modestly disclaimed any intention of reforming the opera or of creating an exemplary new form, but the fact remains that he found in a musical idiom the ideal correspondence to the episodic form of drama. Berg's account of the peculiar musical demands of this form is instructive:

> By obeying the urgent demand of giving musically to each of these scenes and each of the musical passages between acts (either in the form of preludes, postludes, bridges, or intermezzi) its own unmistakable countenance as well as roundness and completeness, utilization of everything that guaranteed such a characteristic on the one hand and completeness on the other quite naturally followed: the much discussed utilization of old and new musical forms, including even those which otherwise were used only in absolute music.[1]

Through Berg's *Wozzeck,* which was first performed in December 1925, Büchner's play became internationally known—albeit under Berg's name rather than Büchner's.

The large number of critical studies and new editions published during the twenties and thirties indicate to what extent interest in Büchner's works was increasing. The first editor since Franzos to work directly with the manuscripts was Georg Witkowski (Insel edition of 1920). Witkowski succeeded in separating Büchner's latest manuscript from the sketches and scenes that preceded it, though he did not attempt to discover any order or sequence in the latter. His edition is noteworthy for its purity: since he made no attempt to construct a playable text, there was no cause for him to alter the sequence or content of the scenes or to add material of his own invention. Except for modernizing the orthography, Fritz Bergemann followed a similar policy in his 1922 edition. He was able to go beyond Witkowski, however, in determining the sequence of manuscripts and of scenes within the manuscripts; his findings have been corroborated by the recent investigations of Werner R. Lehmann[2] and Egon Krause.[3] For the second and all subsequent editions of his text, Bergemann departed from his original intention of presenting a historical-critical edition. Instead of reproducing the various stages of the manuscripts in their proper form and sequence, he presented a stage version of the play which he adapted from a construction by the writer Ernst Hardt.[4]

At a time when the episodic drama had conquered the stage, the structural principles of the form could still prove baffling. Considering the arrangement of scenes contained in Büchner's final manuscript to be aesthetically impossible,[5] Bergemann wanted to construct a text that would accord more with the form of the classical drama and with his own aesthetic sensibilities. He not only altered the sequence of scenes, but also changed the content of individual scenes, contaminating them by the addition of material from earlier compositional stages. With some effort the interested reader can reconstruct from Bergemann's description of his procedure the proper sequence of scenes of the final manuscript, but he cannot determine where Bergemann has contaminated within scenes. From the appearance of Bergemann's text until the publication of Lehmann's in 1967, most editions of Büchner's works have either reproduced or been based upon Bergemann's construction.[6] Literary historians have also accepted Bergemann's text without question; to do otherwise would have required painstaking study of Büchner's manuscripts at the Goethe-Schiller Archive in Weimar.

For the exemplary Hamburg edition of *Woyzeck,* Lehmann presents in the order of composition all of the material contained in the manuscripts.[7] Since he is concerned in this printing with achieving clarity and consistency rather than pedantic accuracy, he completes Büchner's abbreviations, standardizes his spelling and rather idiosyncratic use of the apostrophe, and corrects obvious slips of the pen. Except for his reading of a few essentially illegible words and phrases, only his placement of the two scenes "The Professor's Courtyard" and "The Idiot. The Child. Woyzeck" can be considered problematic. Lehmann follows Bergemann in locating these scenes, which stand on a separate sheet of paper and cannot be integrated into any of the larger manuscripts, between the second major group of scenes (H2) and the final manuscript (H4). As Hans Winkler has pointed out, however, and as my discussion will reaffirm, "The Professor's Courtyard" must have been written before the Doctor scene in H2.[8]

For those who wish to obtain more detailed knowledge of what is actually contained in the manuscripts, what spelling Büchner used, for example, where and how he abbreviated, what he crossed out, what he added as an afterthought or revision, and so on, Lehmann has included a more exact reproduction or representation in a section entitled *"Synopse."* (A later volume will also contain notes and variant readings.) By presenting the corresponding scenes of the various manuscripts side by side, the *"Synopse"* also facilitates the comparison of the various stages in the development of individual scenes as well. Once the actual editing has been completed, the difficult task still remains of constructing from the edited material a valid reading and acting text. While no such text can claim to be entirely authentic, it is possible to restrict the range of possibilities and to test the merit and validity of editorial decisions according to sound and generally accepted principles of editing. The author's intention as revealed in the various manuscripts and stages of development also provides an important criterion for determining validity.

The first manuscript (H1) contains 21 scenes and fragments of scenes. It begins with a demonstration in two carnival scenes of the similarity between man and beast. These scenes also provide the setting in which the three figures of the love triangle are brought together. The third scene consists of two sentences which reveal how impressed Margreth (=Marie) is with the fact that Louis (=Woyzeck) had to obey the orders of the manly and impressive Sergeant (=the Drum Major). In the fourth scene Louis reveals through a brief conversation with his friend Andres that he is disturbed because of Margreth. In the following scene Louis discovers Margreth dancing with the Sergeant. From this point on he is tortured by jealousy and despair, obsessed by visions and dreams of a knife, and commanded by ubiquitous voices to kill his unfaithful paramour. The last half of this group of scenes comprises the murder with its surrounding events. (This material must be used to complete the unfinished final manuscript and will be discussed in that connection.) A number of the scenes in the first half of H1 have been crossed out, which indicates that they were revised and incorporated into the final manuscript. Not crossed out are the carnival scenes, three scenes involving Andres and Louis (H1, 8,11, and 13), and a short scene (one and one-half lines) with Louis alone (H1,12). The carnival scenes present a special problem and will be discussed in another context. The remaining scenes represent alternative attempts to reveal Louis' disturbed condition and preoccupation with death. Their inclusion would have been redundant. Constructions which include one or more of these scenes lose some of the concision, tempo, and tension which is the essence of Büchner's art.

Except for the carnival scenes, the long speeches of the Barber in the inn scene, and the Grandmother's fairy tale, most of the material contained in the first group of scenes is a dramatization of the story of love, betrayal, jealousy, and murder Büchner found in his source. In the second stage of composition Büchner adds greater depth, breadth, and universality to what otherwise is little more than a rather banal and sordid tale of personal disaster. From the first scene of the second manuscript (H2,1) it becomes apparent that Woyzeck's psyche is unstable and threatened. His abnormality is indicated by the frightened reactions of Andres and Marie to his peculiar speech and behavior and also by the Doctor's diagnosis. His peculiarity manifests itself in the attempt to explain and thereby come to terms with the mysterious and inexplicable phenomena that disturb and threaten him. He believes that the Freemasons are hollowing out the earth and causing it to tremble underfoot, and that they are also responsible for the fire and noise that fill the sky. These hallucinations seem to indicate that Woyzeck's psyche is abnormal, but their reference to apocalyptic destruction and the Last Judgment also introduces the important and prophetic motif of sin and punishment.

The addition of new characters and episodes in H2 also enlarges the scope of Woyzeck's immediate surroundings. His relationships and confrontations with the other figures provide considerably more insight into his condition and situation—as well as into the nature of man in general—than was possible within the narrower confines of the first manuscript. Woyzeck furnishes living disproof, for example, of the Doctor's claim that man's will is free. Opposed to the Doctor's idealistic glorification of man, which is arrived at through speculation and pseudo-scientific experimentation, is the deterministic and soberingly realistic concept of the human animal that Woyzeck derives from instinct and observation.

In what appears to have been one of the most difficult scenes for Büchner to write, the Captain is also introduced in the second manuscript (H2,7). Büchner made several false starts before he was able to complete this scene, and even then it does not seem to belong. It is closer in style to *Leone and Lena* than to the rest of *Woyzeck,* and it contains material, including some of the ideas from the inn scene of the first manuscript (H1,10), that has little or nothing to do with Woyzeck. It probably owes its existence to Büchner's love of contrasts: it begins with a comic exchange between the Captain and the Doctor and ends with the Captain's devastating allusion to Marie's infidelity.

Along with the introduction of the Doctor and the Captain, the most important contribution of the second manuscript lies in the development of Marie's character and in the expansion of her role. In the first manuscript she appears only in the carnival scenes, for a short monologue immediately thereafter, as seen by Woyzeck through the window at the inn, and in the murder sequence. By the time Woyzeck comes to kill her, she has spoken only 36 words. All we know about her is that she is impressed by the events at the carnival and by the Sergeant. In the second manuscript she appears not only as a sensuous and passionate woman, but also as a loving mother, who is proud of her illegitimate son. Her infidelity to Woyzeck is partially motivated by the fact that Woyzeck has changed: his peculiar behavior disturbs and frightens her. The manuscript ends with a Biblical quotation that anticipates the important scene of the final manuscript in which she expresses her desire to repent and sin no more, a scene which adds considerable depth to her character and gives her fate a tragic dimension.

Lehmann cautiously refers to the manuscript Büchner was working on when he died (H4) as a "preliminary fair copy." Although one cannot be certain what stage of development this manuscript represents, it seems very probable that Büchner looked upon it as the final version. Shortly before his death

Büchner wrote to his fiancée that he would have *Leonce and Lena* and two other plays published in not more than a week (II.464).[9] Since one of those "other" plays would have to have been *Woyzeck,* it must have been very near completion at the time he wrote the letter.[10] The fact that Büchner crossed out scenes in the earlier manuscripts after he had included them in H4 also indicates that H4 was to be the final draft and not a third group of scenes, which together with H1 and H2 would then provide material for a final version. Further evidence for this conclusion is provided by the spaces Büchner left in H4: rather than include a scene with which he was not yet satisfied, and rather than attempt to rewrite a scene that might still prove unacceptable, he preferred to leave a space which could be filled at a later time. A space was left for the carnival scenes, for example, and it seems likely, as we will see, that one was also left for the scene in which the Captain and the Doctor meet on the street.

But even if we were to assume that H4 was not intended as a final manuscript, it would still be indefensible from an editorial point of view to alter the sequence or the content of the scenes of the manuscript which represents Büchner's last word. An edition or construction which makes such alterations must be considered an adaptation.

Because it was not created by the author, Lehmann prints his construction of a "Reading and Acting Text" in the appendix to his first volume. While acknowledging that contamination, i.e., the introduction into the text of material from earlier drafts or the transposition of material within the text, is the cardinal sin of editing, Lehmann rightly maintains that in the case of *Woyzeck* the question is not "whether or not one may be permitted to contaminate, but how and where."[11] Since every contamination results from a decision that is based on the editor's interpretation of the text and his understanding of the work's form and content, each contamination introduces the possibility of an editorial distortion of the text. Consequently, if it can be demonstrated that any particular contamination is not necessary for the construction of an autonomous text, or if the arguments given in support of any particular contamination can be challenged by equally valid counterarguments, the contamination in question should be rejected, since it is the inclusion rather than the omission of such material that must be justified. Lehmann's construction will be seen to contain unnecessary contaminations in each of the four problematic passages.[12]

1. "Fair Booth. Lights. People"

The space left in H4 under the title "Fair Booths. Lights. People" presents the first problem. The existence of the title and space indicates that Büchner intended to include some kind of a carnival scene, but was not yet satisfied with his earlier drafts. It would be plausible to assume that the author's purpose would be better served by constructing a scene from material contained in the earlier manuscripts than by the space, provided that such a scene agrees with the style and content of the authorized text. The fact that Büchner began his work on *Woyzeck* with two carnival scenes indicates how central this material was to his original conception, and the fact that he revised one of those scenes for the second draft and that he left space for the carnival complex in the final manuscript indicates that it remained important to him.

In H1,1 a Barker stands in front of a booth and attempts to attract the interest of the public for the performance inside. The performance itself is presented in the second scene. In his second draft Büchner revised the first scene, but made no attempt to revise the second one. Since the last execution of a scene is generally the one to be preferred, the revised version of the scene outside the booth (H2,3) should be used for the first part of the carnival complex. For the performance inside, there is only one possibility, namely, H1,2. Following the speech of the Barker in H2,3 is some fragmentary material that can be omitted. This consists of a speech by Woyzeck, which Büchner crossed out in the manuscript, and a few exploratory and fragmentary attempts to refer to the grotesque nature of the Barker's performance and to include a student's confession of atheism. (Büchner attempted to introduce similar statements in other places, but they, too, remained fragmentary.)[13] Büchner crossed out the scene H2,4, which also belongs to the carnival complex, after incorporating it into a later scene of the final manuscript (H4,11). The short scene H2,5, on the other hand, can be retained. It connects the two halves of the carnival scene, and, unlike the fragmentary exchange between the Gentleman and the Student or the protracted speech of the Journeyman, the material in H2,5 is integral to the plot: it introduces the play's primary antagonistic force, the Drum Major, and reveals his sexual interest in Marie. It is significant, as we will see, that this triangular relationship should be placed in the animalistic context of the carnival scene.

Although recognizing that H2 goes beyond H1 and that it is stylistically and structurally denser than the earlier version, Lehmann nevertheless contaminates H2,3 by adding material from the superseded scene H1,1, even though his contaminations result, as he himself admits, in the repetition of the same and similar statements. He considers these statements to be of such importance that they should not be sacrificed.[14]

In reference to one of these repetitions Lehmann refers to his "principle of connected or interdependent contamination *(Prinzip der zusammenhängenden Kontamination)*" which demands that the "transplanted" material be transferred along with its immediate context in order to preserve the authenticity of the transplanted material.[15] What he does not wish to sacrifice is the exchange which forms a causal connection between the two halves of this double scene:

Woyzeck. Do you want to?
Marie. All right. That must be a fine show. Look at the man's tassels! And the woman has pants on! (I.411)

Lehmann explains the significance of this exchange as follows: "Marie and Woyzeck, not each separately, but both together, are now definitely and finally drawn as actors into a play at which they had been spectators until now. The play in the play turns back significantly to the play." He considers Marie's word of agreement ("All right [*Meinetwege*]") to be an indication of the "intersection and unification of action and commentary," since she later uses the same word in yielding sexually to the Drum Major. It is a question, then, of preserving the correspondence between Marie's acquiescence in two separate scenes.[16] The use of corresponding themes and motifs is indeed an important formal and structural principle in Büchner's works, but hardly one that can be used to justify such a questionable complex of textual contaminations: there is scarcely a scene or scenic fragment in all of Büchner's manuscripts to which Lehmann's argument could not be applied.

Furthermore, if Lehmann's interpretation of the lines he does not wish to sacrifice were correct — and I fail to see anything in this passage or in what follows to indicate that it is — that would further justify their omission: this play, like all of Büchner's works, is not about togetherness, but about loneliness and isolation. Woyzeck and Marie do not act *together.* The preceding scene has made clear that there is no real understanding between them, no real dialogue, and little compatibility. And they do not *act* either, but are acted upon by the people and forces that use them as instruments: Marie's *"meinetwege"* expresses passive acquiescence. Inside the booth they are as much spectators as they were outside. When Marie does act, it is to *leave* Woyzeck: she climbs into the first row of seats where she can see better, and where she can also be seen better by the very man who will soon be responsible for their permanent separation.[17]

2. *"Street. The Captain. The Doctor"*

The second editorial problem involves the scene in which the Captain and the Doctor meet on the street (H4,9). In this case the problem has been created by editors who have been unwilling to consider the scene H4,9 complete as it stands. Lehmann and most of his predecessors have concluded from the space following this scene that H4,9 is not complete and that Büchner intended to return to it and complete it. But it is equally possible that Büchner left the whole space blank, as he did with H4,3, and that he later inserted a short scene which required less space than he had allowed.[18] It was precisely the meeting between the Captain and the Doctor, the first part of the scene, with which Büchner struggled in the first draft (H2,7). Nothing in the manuscripts indicates that he attempted to revise the second part of the original scene, the part which includes Woyzeck, as he probably would have done, had he intended to include it in his revised version of the scene (H4,9).

Whereas the witty exchange between the Captain and the Doctor in H2,7 only provided a contrasting introduction to a scene in which the main action involved arousing or confirming Woyzeck's suspicion, the scene in H4,9 is, as Ursula Paulus notes, "entirely oriented toward the juxtaposition of the Captain and the Doctor."[19] Their conversation and the scene come to a definite end when the Doctor and the Captain take leave of each other:

Doctor. I bid you farewell, my dear Mr. Drillcock.
Captain. Likewise, dear Mr. Coffinnail. (I.419)

The inclusion of action designed to arouse Woyzeck's jealousy is superfluous at this stage in the development of H4: the Captain's allusion to Marie's infidelity cannot compare with the evidence Woyzeck already has discovered. In H4,4 Woyzeck surprises Marie as she is admiring her new earrings. Her defiant and challenging response to his questioning prevents him from pressing for an explanation of how she got them, but his suspicion is aroused. Seeing the Drum Major with Marie (H4,7) seems to confirm it. Quite certain now that she is betraying him, Woyzeck looks for some external sign of her sin and is amazed at not finding one. This time he does not give up his pursuit of the matter so easily, but the boldly defiant Marie still refuses to confess. Following this scene, only the unequivocal discovery of Marie's infidelity could contribute to the development of the plot and the intensification of the mounting tension, and such a discovery takes place when Woyzeck sees Marie dancing with the Drum Major and hears her urging him on (H4,11). With this scene a dramatic climax and turning point is reached. In the following scene (H4,12) Woyzeck receives the command to kill Marie, which dominates his thoughts and actions until the end. What purpose can the Captain's allusion to Marie's relationship with the Drum Major have after Woyzeck's suspicion has already been aroused by much more persuasive evidence?

Lehmann answers this question as follows: "Suspicion is followed in H2,7 by debasement through the infamy of the word, since the Captain, seconded by the Doctor, confirms and makes obscene comments about the suspicion; this must destroy Woyzeck."[20] Precisely the fact that Woyzeck is destroyed in H2,7 by the Captain's allusion is reason not to include this material in H4, where such a reaction can no longer be convincing or effective. The Captain's words in H2,7 were able to have such an effect on Woyzeck because they were his first indication that Marie was betraying him. The same does not hold true for H4, as we have seen, where Woyzeck has already seen Marie and the Drum Major together. From the standpoint of content and structure, Woyzeck's reaction from H2,7 is no longer congruous with the context of the final manuscript: neither debasement by the infamy of words nor reinforcement of his already strong suspicion could plausibly destroy Woyzeck in the scene H4,9; and the extremity of his response does not fit into the new scheme of developing tension. Woyzeck's destruction in this scene would seem exaggerated, and it would undermine the effect of the much more important inn scene.

The conflict of Woyzeck's manner of expression in H2,7 with the idiom he consistently uses in H4 also speaks against contaminating H4,9 by the inclusion of material from H2,7. In his discussion of the language in *Woyzeck,* Karl Viëtor notes: "The illusion of authenticity and undiminished truth is broken in only a few passages, passages in which the poet himself speaks through his figures." As an example of language that goes beyond Woyzeck's "power of thought and expression," Viëtor quotes part of Woyzeck's speech from H2,7: "You see, such a pretty, hot, gray sky. One could get the desire to drive a wedge into it and to hang oneself from it, just because of the dash between yes—and yes again—and no. Captain, sir, yes and no? Is the no to blame for the yes, or the yes for the no? I will think about it." Viëtor rightly characterizes this as the style of *Leonce and Lena,* just as the line "Every man is an abyss. You get dizzy when you look in" would only be credible in Danton's mouth.[21] Lehmann does not include Viëtor's second example in his construction because it is not authorized material. But neither is the first one.

As the following defense of his contamination of H4,9 and the inclusion of the scene "The Professor's Courtyard" (H3,1) clearly reveals, Lehmann's contaminations are not based on sound editorial procedures, but on his desire to emphasize the play's social criticism: "It would result in a questionable reduction of the play's social criticism if H3,1 and H2,7 were to be suppressed, for Büchner left keys (if not a *passepartout*) in them, as it were, that we must try."[22] While criticizing Bergemann for imposing his own aesthetic preconceptions on the text, Lehmann defends editorial decisions that are meant to support *his* interpretation. Such argumentation leads to the heart of the problem both of constructing a text and of interpreting it, for each of these procedures depends upon the other. To avoid becoming entrapped in a *circulum vitiosus,* one should limit contaminations to those required to construct a playable text and those which, as in the case of the carnival complex, are clearly in keeping with the author's intentions and which do not alter the meaning of the authorized material.

Egon Krause has chosen the alternative of publishing an uncontaminated and therefore unplayable text, not because he questions the editorial validity of constructing a playable text, but because he assumes against overwhelming evidence to the contrary that Woyzeck was not going to kill Marie in the final version. He interprets the introduction of Marie's remorse as an indication that Büchner planned to have her repent and be forgiven by Woyzeck, who supposedly would have been able to resist the forces which were commanding him to kill her.[23] In place of the tragic conclusion which seems inevitable, there would have been a joyful reconciliation and a happy ending. Such an interpretation not only goes against the form and content of all extant material, it also runs counter to Büchner's respect for the reality of life and history and his concept of man and nature.

As indicated above, Büchner began work on his play with a dramatization of the historically given material; in the second stage of composition he filled in the background, developed his characters more fully, and placed the main action in a broader context. To prepare the final manuscript he combined revised scenes from both earlier stages and added some new ones. Of the first nine scenes of H4, five are based on scenes from H2 and one more, the carnival complex, must be constructed from H1 and H2. The remaining three scenes (H4,4-6) are new. Beginning with scene 10, material from H2 finds its way into only two scenes (H4,11 and 16), while the sequence of scenes from H1 is followed exactly, albeit with the addition of some new scenes. H4,10 is a revision of H1,4; H4,11 brings the discovery, which is briefly presented in H1,5; H4,12 is a condensation of H1,6; H4,13 is a revision of H1,7; and H4,14 apparently replaces, or is a substitute for, H1,10, which Büchner crossed out. H4,15 is a new scene: Woyzeck's purchase of a knife clearly indicates the direction in which the action is inevitably moving. (It is not clear in H1 how he gets the knife.) H4,16 is anticipated by the Biblical quotation and responding exclamation of H2,9—"And no deceit was found in his mouth! God Almighty!" (I.165). H4,17, the scene in which Woyzeck

leaves his possessions to Andres, is also new. Büchner crossed
out seven of the nine scenes contained in the second manuscript after he had used them in H4. Not crossed out are H2,3
("Public Square. Booths. Lights"), a scene Büchner no doubt
intended to revise and insert into the space left for it in H4, and
H2,7, which was superseded by H4,9, but which Büchner failed
to cross out. (If H4,9 was added to the space left for it in H4 at a
time when Büchner was otherwise finished with H2, he might
not have bothered to cross out H2,7. Since he would no longer
be working with that manuscript, there was no need for making
such a notation.) This survey of the manuscripts reveals that
all the scenes of H2 were used in one way or another in H4.

Of the twenty-one scenes in the first manuscript, seven (H1,
14-20) can be used to supply the conclusion. Of the remaining
thirteen scenes, seven have been crossed out. The second of
the two carnival scenes (H1,2) contains the only presentation of
the action inside the booth; I have suggested that it be used
together with H2,3, which supersedes H1,1, to fill the space left
for this complex in H4. In one of the remaining four scenes,
H1,12, Woyzeck tries to resist killing Marie by hiding the knife.
The other three contain short dialogues between Woyzeck and
Andres. One of these, H1,13, is superseded by H4,13 and could
have been crossed out. In another, Woyzeck talks about death
in the opaque, metaphorical style that is incompatible with H4.
Finally, only one scene remains unaccounted for, namely H1,8.
This scene may have been eliminated from the final version
because of the obvious connection Woyzeck makes between
the knife from his dream and Marie's infidelity, thus indicating
a higher degree of intention in the murder than is compatible
with the final version.

From the evidence provided by the relationship of H4 to H1
and from the fact that almost all the scenes of the first two
drafts find their way with varying degrees of revision into the
final manuscript, we can assume that Büchner did not change
the basic concept of his play during the various stages of its
composition and that he would have continued to follow the
sequence of scenes in H1 to complete H4. We cannot know to
what extent he would have revised them, but since he considered the work on *Woyzeck* to be nearly completed he probably did not anticipate major problems or extensive revisions.
Indeed, the unrevised scenes are entirely compatible in lan-

guage and style with H4, and since they also continue the development and progression of the play's various motifs and mounting tension, which reaches its climax in the murder scene, they can be included without creating a break or even a seam.

More problematic is the disposition of the two scenes of the manuscript Lehmann calls H3: "The Professor's Courtyard" and "The Idiot. The Child. Woyzeck." Nothing in Büchner's manuscripts indicates whether or not he intended to use them, let alone where. Before including either of these scenes, an editor must be able to demonstrate that such an interpolation does not in any way alter the meaning of the authorized text.

3. *"The Professor's Courtyard"*

Lehmann's inclusion of H3,1, it was noted, is motivated by his desire to strengthen the play's social criticism. Elsewhere Lehmann has claimed that the Doctor's "systematic, scientifically calculated mutilation of Woyzeck's existence, which has its source in society *(im Gesellschaftlichen)*" is a major cause of "Woyzeck's paranoia, hallucinations, and visions and of his alienation from his self and from the world."[24] More specifically, Lehmann regards Woyzeck's diet of peas as the cause for his mental aberrations and consequently as a key without which the "Doctor-Woyzeck scene . . . and perhaps the whole problem of social criticism" would be incomprehensible to us.[25] The inclusion of H3,1 is important and justified, then, according to Lehmann, because it contains additional information about Woyzeck's diet and the effects it has on him.

We have already encountered and rejected this type of circular argumentation, which justifies the inclusion of a scene by an interpretation based on the inclusion of that scene. The substance of this argument is equally untenable: Lehmann would justify the stress he places on Woyzeck's diet by claiming that it is "more strongly and exclusively" emphasized in H4 than in H2, but a comparison of the relevant passages easily refutes such a claim. In H4,8 the Doctor simply asks Woyzeck if he has eaten his peas:

Doctor. Have you already eaten your peas, Woyzeck?

. . . .

Doctor. Do you still do everything as usual? Shave your Captain?
Woyzeck. Yes, sir.
Doctor. Eat your peas?
Woyzeck. Quite regularly, Doctor, sir. My wife gets my food allowance. (I.174-175)

The earlier H2,6, on the other hand, is more detailed and specific:

Doctor. Have you already eaten you peas? Nothing but legumes—*cruciferae.* Don't forget. Next week we will begin with mutton.

. . . .

Doctor. Woyzeck? You'll go to the madhouse. You have a beautiful fixed idea, a priceless *alienatio mentis.* Look at me! What should you do? Eat peas. . . . (I.161-162)

The Doctor's main interest in both scenes is in the diet's effect on the chemical content of Woyzeck's urine. In the development from H2,6 to H4,8, as in the development from the earlier to the later manuscripts in general, the emphasis shifts from Woyzeck's physical to his psychological condition. Furthermore, the specific effects of Woyzeck's diet are not as important as the fact that he hires himself out as a guinea pig in order to earn money for Marie: the Doctor gives him a small wage, and he can save the money allotted him by the military for food. This is only one of a number of means Woyzeck employs to earn money for his family. It is the cumulative effect of all these endeavors that strain and exhaust him and that help to undermine the stability of his psyche.[26] The exaggerated emphasis Woyzeck's diet receives through the unauthorized inclusion of H3,1 may in fact detract from the more important causes of his suffering.

As already noted, H3,1 was probably written before H2,6 and was already superseded by that scene.[27] The Doctor was initially conceived as a caricature of a professor whose idealistic assertions about human freedom and man's exalted rank in the creation Büchner had been subjected to at the University of Giessen. Another model for Büchner's dramatic figure was the famous chemist Justus von Liebig, who was in fact engaged in experiments with soldiers in Giessen involving the influence of diet on the chemical content of urine.[28] Büchner's Doctor developed from a caricature of a specific professor into a representative of the general type of scientist who "combines professional learning with intellectual stupidity, and scientific erudition with human coarseness,"[29] and for whom ideas and theories are more important than the suffering and humiliation of his fellow man.

This figure appears in the beginning of H3,1 in the role of a Professor, who is delivering an absurd and disconnected lecture from a dormer window of his house. In the middle of the scene, just after Woyzeck has caught the cat thrown down to him by the Professor, his title changes from Professor to Doctor and his role shifts accordingly. The Doctor is still somewhat professorial in the latter part of H3,1, but in H2,6 and H4,8 he is no longer presented in his capacity as a teacher, but only as a medical doctor engaged in research, a development which strongly suggests that H3,1 was the first of the three Doctor scenes. The Professor speaks in an abstract, idealistic manner about scientific principles which have nothing to do with medicine. In this part of the scene, Woyzeck's job is to assist him in carrying out his demonstrations. The Doctor, on the other hand, directs his attention to Woyzeck, who serves now as the object of his medical experiments. The Doctor attributes Woyzeck's trembling, irregular pulse, and loss of hair to the fact that he has eaten nothing but peas for three months. This scene contains more details about the Doctor's experiment than any of the later scenes. It is the only one to make an explicit connection between Woyzeck's symptoms and his diet, and it is the only one in which Woyzeck's malady is physiological in nature. In H2,6 and H4,8 the Doctor is interested in the chemical content of Woyzeck's urine and in his pulse, but he does not mention any irregularity.

From the foregoing we may conclude that H3,1 represents a stage of development which is not compatible with the content or style of the later manuscripts. Furthermore, since it cannot be incorporated within the authorized sequence of scenes of H4, it would have to come after the exposition has been completed, the first turning point has passed, and the climax of the play is near. The inclusion at this point of what is essentially expository material is more likely to confuse the spectator and detract from the mounting tension than to add to his understanding of the social causes of Woyzeck's condition.[30]

4. "The Idiot. The Child. Woyzeck"

Unlike H3,1, the scene "The Idiot. The Child. Woyzeck" (H3,2) can be incorporated into a text construction without resulting in redundancy, disruption, or incongruity. It cannot be placed at the end, however, where Lehmann situates it, without destroying the ambiguity of Büchner's open ending and without imposing a conclusion and an interpretation on the play which may well disagree with what the author intended. In Büchner's only rendition of the conclusion, Woyzeck returns to the scene of the murder to get rid of the incriminating evidence. He finds the murder weapon and throws it into the pond, but not far enough. He goes into the pond and throws it still farther out. Even then he fears that it will be found in the summer by divers looking for mussels. It will have become rusty and unrecognizable, to be sure, but he thinks he should have broken it. In this state of confused and anxious vacillation, Woyzeck remembers the blood on his arm and feels compelled to wash it off. The manuscript ends here, leaving us with questions and possibilities rather than answers.

While we cannot know how Büchner would have ended his play, the range of possible and plausible solutions is definitely limited by internal evidence such as foreshadowing, recurring motifs, and consistency. The possibility of assuming that Woyzeck drowns should not be excluded by an editor, for example, since this conclusion is fully compatible with and even suggested by the evidence within the play.[31] In leaving his possessions to Andres, Woyzeck reveals that he anticipates and is preparing for his death. The kind of death suggested by the last scene also accords with his visions of punishment and destruction and with his belief that he is being threatened and pursued by unknown, mysterious forces. The same force that compels him to murder Marie and to eliminate the traces of his deed may also compel him to go further and further into the water. When Woyzeck leaves the inn (H1,17), he is so shaken and confused that he scarcely knows what he is doing. Perhaps the force of retribution or Nemesis uses the mind deranged by fear as an instrument for its own punishment.[32] It is also possible to assume, on the other hand, that he does not drown. All that can be said with certainty is that there is nothing in any of the manuscripts to indicate what might have followed Woyzeck's entry into the pond.

Despite the sound arguments that have been offered to the contrary,[33] Lehmann persists in interpreting the phrase from a child's finger-counting rhyme—"he fell in the water"—as if it referred to Woyzeck, who has just come from the pond and is still wet; and he considers this questionable interpretation to be sufficient justification for placing H3,2 at the end of his construction, thus weakening the open end by eliminating the possibility of assuming that Woyzeck may drown.[34] Here and throughout the play, however, the Fool's words and fragmented quotations do not refer to the actual situation, but contain veiled prophecies or grasp a present situation with supersensual perception.[35] If this scene is placed before the final inn scene (H1,17), it can reinforce the important theme of loneliness and isolation without adding a conclusion that goes beyond what the author wrote and may very well disagree with what he intended, and it can also function as a foreshadowing of Woyzeck's going into the water.[36]

The first manuscript ends with the scene "Court Clerk. Barber. Doctor. Judge" (H1,21). Of the four persons named, only the Court Clerk speaks. The Barber is described, but the scene breaks off before he speaks. The inclusion of such a fragmentary and problematic scene in a text construction would be highly controvertible at best. The inclusion of this particular fragment is especially questionable because its placement at the play's end gives it undue stress. By emphasizing the callous inhumanity and cynicism of the official representatives of society, it tends to alienate the tragic conclusion. Its inclusion in Lehmann's construction is consistent with his desire to emphasize the play's social criticism and can be rejected for the same reasons as his inclusion of H3,1 and his contamination of H4,9 were.

To preserve the authenticity of the material he adds to the play's conclusion, Lehmann feels justified in transposing the street scene (H1,18) from its authorized context to a position following the scene "Woyzeck by a Pond" (H1,20) where it can serve as a bridge between Büchner's concluding scene and the scenes added by Lehmann. Lehmann admits that he has departed from his own working principles in making "this concession to the pragmatic nexus." Besides, he is uncertain about the chronology of the scenes H1,18-20. The compressed writing of

H1,19-20 may indicate, he suggests, that these scenes were later additions to the manuscript and actually belong before H1,18.[37] Of course it is also possible that Büchner simply crowded his writing in order to get these final scenes onto the last sheet of the manuscript. Lehmann also calculates that in its given place the action of H1,18 would take place around midnight, and he cannot imagine that the children would still be up that late. The transposition makes it possible to assume that this occurrence takes place sometime in the morning.[38] The scene is followed in Lehmann's construction by "The Idiot. The Child. Woyzeck," which, consequently, would also have to take place in the morning. Thus, according to Lehmann's transposition and interpolation we would have to assume that Woyzeck has run around wet all night, for it was "evening" when he went into the pond.

From this lengthy technical analysis we may conclude that Büchner's last and greatest play was indeed nearly finished at the time of his death. By comparing Büchner's final manuscript with the preceding manuscripts or collections of scenes, one can discover how the author was using the earlier stages to create the finished work. In constructing a reading and acting text, the author's own procedure should be followed as closely and simply as possible, i.e., with the fewest editorial interventions or contaminations. Since the manuscript was near completion, very little is actually required: (1) construction of a carnival scene to fill the space left under the title "Fair Booth. Lights. People," (2) addition of the conclusion as contained only in the first manuscript, and (3) interpolation of "The Idiot. The Child. Woyzeck" in a place where it can complement without altering the meaning of the whole.

Reading and Acting Text

1. H4, 1 An Open Field. The Town in the Distance.
2. H4, 2 The City. Marie with her Child at the Window.
3. H4, 3 = [H2,3; H2,5; H1,2] Fair Booths. Lights. People.
4. H4, 4 Marie's Room.
5. H4, 5 The Captain. Woyzeck.
6. H4, 6 Marie's Room. Marie. The Drum Major.
7. H4, 7 In the Street. Marie. Woyzeck.
8. H4, 8 At the Doctor's.

Interpretation

On 28 February 1822, Johann Christian Woyzeck was sentenced to death for the murder of his faithless mistress, the widow Johanna Christiane Woost, whom he had stabbed seven times with a broken sword blade mounted on a wooden handle. When Woyzeck's court-appointed lawyer claimed that the defendant was mentally disturbed at the time he committed the murder and could not be held accountable for his action, the court commissioned Hofrat Dr. Clarus to examine Woyzeck and to offer a medical opinion on the question of his sanity and accountability. Clarus found characteristics of moral degeneration, insensitivity to natural feelings, and indifference to the present and the future, but he found nothing to indicate that Woyzeck was not fully accountable for his behavior.

When a private citizen testified that a number of eyewitnesses had assured him that Woyzeck had on several occasions exhibited signs of mental disturbance, the defending lawyer, who had continued his efforts in Woyzeck's behalf up to and beyond the sentencing, succeeded just two days before Woyzeck's scheduled execution in having the case reopened. Denying the defense's request for the appointment of a different expert, the court reappointed Clarus to conduct an examination which would take into account all the factors of Woyzeck's life, general state of health, and mental condition that might have influenced and could help to explain his condition at the time he committed the crime.

Because of the chaos and uncertainty caused by the Napoleonic wars, Woyzeck could not find steady work, either as a wig maker, which was the trade he had learned, or in any of the various odd jobs at which he was skilled. Only mercenaries were in great demand; hence Woyzeck joined a Dutch regiment. The story of his life as a soldier reads like a Baroque novel. While stationed at Stralsund he fell in love with and had a child by a woman identified as "the Wienbergin." Their relationship was interrupted when he was captured by the Swedish and sent to Stockholm, where he joined the Swedish army. As a Swedish soldier he took part in a campaign in Finland against the Russians. He was then transported with the regiment to Germany, where he was disarmed by the French. He joined the Mecklenburg troops, but soon deserted in order to return to his Swedish comrades. Meanwhile Napoleon's star had fallen and the Swedish part of Pomerania had been ceded to Prussia by the Congress of Vienna. Thus Woyzeck's military career came to an end with his release from Prussian service.

Woyzeck's desertion was also motivated by the desire to return to the Wienbergin, whom he loved and wanted to marry. He resumed living with her, but his disappointment over her sexual involvement with other soldiers during his absence eventually caused him to leave her for good. There appears to be a connection between the termination of this relationship and the beginning of his depression and mental disturbances:

> But his whole misfortune was actually due to his having left the *Wienbergin,* since his officers were later willing to help

him get married. Only through the fact that he made no preparations for marriage was his previously good character embittered, since the opportunity was now past and he was not able to make it good again. The thought of his child and of this abandoned person was the only cause of his constant disquiet and of the fact that he was never able to be at peace with himself. He later reprimanded himself for associating with the Woostin, since he really should have married the Wienbergin. For that reason it made him angry when the people said of him that he was a good man, because he felt that he wasn't. (I.509)

Following his dismissal from the army, Woyzeck returned to his native Leipzig, but since the possibility of finding steady employment was worse now than before, he was forced to lead a very irregular life, working at whatever jobs he could get, stealing now and again, begging when necessary, sleeping wherever he could find a place, and drinking too much. He also became the lover of the widow Woost, who, at 46, was five years his senior. When she refused to give up her relationships with other men, mostly soldiers, Woyzeck became very jealous. He repeatedly abused and mistreated her, often quite severely. On one occasion he bloodied her head with fragments of a broken pot, for which he was punished by a short imprisonment. Not long after his release from prison he threw her down a flight of stairs for having danced with a rival. Despite such treatment, the widow did not break off her relationship with him.

Among the voices Woyzeck heard was one commanding him to "Stab the Woostin dead!" While attempting to resist this command, he also obtained a weapon. On the day of the murder he had a broken sword blade mounted to a wooden handle. When he accidentally met the widow, who had lied to him about her plans for the day, he accompanied her home. By the time they reached her house, they were involved in a violent argument. Once again Woyzeck lost control of himself and stabbed her to death. When he was arrested shortly thereafter, he tried to throw the knife away, but he never denied having committed the murder.

Although his investigation uncovered many indications and examples of a disturbed psyche, Dr. Clarus was not persuaded to reverse his opinion. He concluded:

> that *Woyzeck's* alleged hallucinations and other peculiar occurrences must be seen as *deceptions of the senses,* which were caused by disturbances in his circulation and which were aggravated and increased by his superstition and preconceptions into fanciful notions of an objective and supersensual cause; and that there is *no* reason to assume that he found himself in a disturbed state of mind at any time in his life and specifically directly *before, during* and *after* the murder, or that he acted thereby according to a necessary, blind, and instinctive impulse and other than according to common, emotional stimulations. (I.534)

Since Clarus's opinions were being attacked by other specialists, and since Clarus himself did not want to carry the full weight of the responsibility for Woyzeck's execution, the court finally complied with the defense's request to seek the opinion of experts from the medical faculty of the University of Leipzig. When that body found itself in full agreement with Clarus, Woyzeck's fate was decided and on 27 August 1824 he was publicly beheaded. Because of the attacks from disagreeing experts and the considerable public and professional interest Woyzeck's case had attracted, Clarus published the lengthy report of his investigation in a well-known medical journal. This report provided Büchner with the historical source material for his play.

Some years after the original controversy had subsided, the young medical student and political activist took up the matter again, not only to question the validity of Clarus's findings and the court's decision, but to challenge the basic legal, social, and religious assumptions that determine our concept of justice and the methods used in administering it. Where Clarus attempts to *moderate* the sympathy felt by the "educated and compassionate" segment of the public for one of its unfortunate members by appealing to the "inviolable sanctity of the laws" whose responsibility to "throne and hut" alike demands severity in judging where to punish and where to spare, Büchner wanted to *arouse* sympathy and to make the public aware of the injustice of laws which fail to take the peculiar circumstances of the individual into account; whose rigid, cold-blooded enforcement violates the very humanity they are meant to serve; and which clearly favor those who occupy thrones over those who dwell in huts.[39]

And in answer to Clarus's claim that the law demands and can get truth and not feelings from those witnesses and specialists it consults for information and testimony, the skeptical creator of Danton poses the counter-questions: Can one be sure that Woyzeck's "alleged visions and other uncommon occurrences" were only "deceptions of the senses" which were caused by "disorders of his circulation"? And even if they were, would they be any less real? What, after all, is madness? How does one define and determine accountability? Is the "truth" Clarus discovers really more accurate and dependable than the judgment of the feelings which he opposes to truth?

The fundamental concern of Büchner's play is not the guilt of one man and the judgment of a few others, but the legal, social, religious, moral, psychological, and even scientific systems, institutions, and presuppositions of society in general. In the spirit of the dawning scientific age, Büchner gives radically new and modern answers to the old questions concerning the nature of man and his position in society, and these answers give rise, in turn, to new questions. Changes in the concept of man demand corresponding revisions of his moral and legal codes and social institutions to the extent that these are based upon presuppositions about man's nature. While Büchner was too much of a realist and fatalist to believe that art could directly stimulate revolution—and too much of an artist to compromise his works by the inclusion of blatantly tendentious material—he may have considered it possible to prepare for revolutionary change by attempting through his art to change man's attitudes, consciousness, and awareness.

Taking full advantage of the drama's singular potential for informing and affecting the spectator through direct, forceful, and concise presentation, Büchner requires only a few moments to give the spectator more insight into Woyzeck's psyche than Clarus does in his lengthy report. According to the extent that a person's relations to others and to his surroundings deviate from the norms and conventions of the society of which he is a part, he will be considered odd or insane by the "normal" members of that society. Woyzeck's words and hallucinations in the first scene clearly reveal a peculiar and disturbed mental state: Andres is frightened by his friend's mysterious behavior and the peculiar phenomena he describes. This first indication of Woyzeck's abnormality is reinforced in the following scene by Marie's reaction to Woyzeck's account of the same experience. After he has left, she comments: "That man! So weird. He didn't even look at his child. Those thoughts of his will drive him mad." The more she thinks about what she has just witnessed, the more uneasy, anxious, and frightened she becomes: "Why are you so quiet?" she asks her child. Are you scared? It's getting so dark, you'd think you're blind. Usually the street light shines in. I can't stand it. It gives me the creeps. *(She goes out)*." (II).[40]

What Andres and Marie sense and imply through their responses, the Doctor is able to diagnose and name with certainty after he too has heard Woyzeck's account of his experience in the field: "Woyzeck, you've got the most beautiful *aberratio mentalis partialis*. The second type. Beautifully developed. Woyzeck, you're getting a raise. The second type: fixed idea, with generally rational condition" (VIII). Woyzeck's aberrations—his hallucinations and attempts to explain them—seem especially strange and disturbing precisely because of his "generally rational condition."

But while Woyzeck's hallucinations appear to indicate a deranged mind, they are also prophetic. Like the oracles in Greek tragedy or the witches' prophecies in *Macbeth*, they anticipate and foreshadow what is to come. In the first moments of the play a connection between nature, death, and the action of mysterious forces is established. Woyzeck believes that the Free Masons caused the strange death he describes, and, by hollowing out the earth beneath him so he will fall through the earth's crust, they are preparing to get him too.[41] His paranoiac presentiment may be interpreted as a prophetic anticipation of his peculiar death, assuming that he drowns. Furthermore, the forces which Woyzeck calls the Free Masons might be identified with those which later speak to him out of the ground, commanding him to kill Marie.[42]

Even more important and unequivocal is the threatened punishment for sin which is introduced in the second part of the scene through the reference of Woyzeck's hallucinations to the destruction of Sodom and Gomorrah and the apocalyptic events described in the revelations of St. John: "Andres! How bright it is! A fire's shooting through the sky and it's thundering down like trumpets. It's coming closer! Run! Don't look back!" (I). The importance of the sin/punishment motif is clearly indicated by the recurrence at key moments in the play of references and allusions to Woyzeck's visions. The fact that their occurrence exactly coincides with the beginning of Marie's sinful involvement with the Drum Major is not accidental. When describing his experience to Marie, Woyzeck makes cryptic reference to a quotation that could be either from the description of the destruction of Sodom and Gomorrah in Genesis[43] or from Revelations,[44] both of which refer to destruction and punishment following sin: "Marie, it happened again. A lot. Doesn't it say: And behold, smoke arose from the land like smoke from a furnace?" (IV). Thus Marie's anxiety may be caused as much by the threatening connotation of Woyzeck's words as by his peculiar behavior.

When Woyzeck has good reason to believe that Marie has betrayed him, he makes an ominously direct connection between the sin/punishment motif and her offense. After discovering to his amazement and disbelief that her guilt has not marked her physically—to his mind her transgression is of the order of Cain's—he says: "A sin so big and fat. It stinks so much, it should *smoke the angels out of heaven.* You have a red mouth, Marie. No blister on it? Farewell, Marie, you're as beautiful as *sin.* Can *mortal sin* be so beautiful?" (VII. Italics added.) And again, after he discovers her dancing with the Drum Major at the inn, he wonders how God can allow such sin to take place in broad daylight: "Why doesn't God blow out the sun, so everything can roll around together in lechery!" (XI). (In both of the Biblical passages mentioned above, smoke is a sign of destruction and punishment. In Revelations the smoke rises to darken the sun.) Once Woyzeck has become certain of Marie's guilt, the content and focus of his hallucinations shift from the mysteriously prophetic anticipation of sin and punishment to the definite and irresistible compulsion to punish the sinner: he now sees a knife and hears voices commanding him to kill Marie; he himself is to become the instrument of the forces of retribution and punishment. The suggestions of apocalyptic destruction in general and of the destruction of the individual sinner in particular are united in a single image, when Marie's description of the rising moon connects in Woyzeck's mind with his visions and with the knife he felt compelled to purchase:

Marie. How red the moon is rising.[45]
Woyzeck. Like a bloody knife. (XIX)

The sin/punishment motif spans an arch from the first scene through the various stages of discovery to the murder and the last scene. Woyzeck tries to get rid of the bloody knife but he cannot dispose of the red moon, which also remains, or so it seems to him, as an incriminating witness to his crime: "The moon is like a bloody knife! Does the whole world want to blab it out?" (XXV). In spite of the moon's testimony and the fact that the blood on him has already been discovered and witnessed by a number of people at the inn, he nevertheless continues his frantic attempt to conceal the knife and to wash off the blood.

Following the murder, Woyzeck becomes the tortured victim of a tragic paradox similar in nature to the one which torments Büchner's Danton: although he has acted as an instrument of the force or forces that use men like puppets and cause them to "whore, lie, steal, and murder," he nevertheless feels guilty or realizes that he has become guilty from the objective standpoint of the law.[46] Like Danton, Woyzeck is convinced that he has done the right thing and that he has acted as he must: he knows from the Biblical referents of his visions that divine justice exacts the severest penalty for the sin of lechery. And in yielding to what he experiences as the inexorable demands of mysterious external forces, Woyzeck believes himself to be an instrument of divine justice. Marie was black from her sins, and he made her white again (XXIV). He killed her because he must.

Woyzeck and Marie are not destroyed either directly or indirectly by society's villains in the guise of the Captain and the Doctor. Melodrama and the literature of disaster are made of such stuff, but tragedy is not. Büchner purposely sought to stimulate the sterner emotions associated with tragedy rather than the softer emotions, especially sentimentality, upon which melodrama relies. Woyzeck is destroyed by members of his own class, who act as instruments of a force far more universal and ineluctable and therefore more terrifying than those represented by the Captain and the Doctor, and that is the force of nature. The irresistible force which causes Marie to betray Woyzeck is similar in source to the force which compels him to kill her. Fate for Woyzeck, as for Büchner's characters in general, is in nature; it is as inexorable and dreadful as fate in the Greek tragedies.

Because a mistake was made at his creation, man is lacking something, according to Danton (II.i), which prevents him from living in harmony with others or even with himself. The lack of congruity between his reason and his emotions, between his thoughts and his feelings, is a major source of conflict and suffering for Danton, and it is for Woyzeck too. (Büchner may have been familiar with Pascal's discussion of this internal conflict or "civil war" between reason and emotion.) Woyzeck realizes, on the one hand, that men, or at least poor people, act according to their nature, yet he is unable to accept the consequences of this knowledge when it involves the infidelity of the woman he loves. If he were reasonable and consistent, he would have to recognize that Marie follows her nature in yielding to the Drum Major, just as he follows his when he urinates on the wall.

Marie suffers from a similar inner conflict between the demands of her nature and the urging of her conscience, which, like Woyzeck's, has been formed by Christian concepts of good and evil. Because of her greater awareness of the conflict, her attempt to resist her nature, and her feelings of guilt, Marie more nearly conforms to traditional definitions of a tragic figure than Woyzeck does.

Büchner probably discovered Marie's tragic potential as his work on the play progressed. In the first manuscript she is important only as the cause of Woyzeck's suffering and as the object of his wrath. In the second draft she is portrayed with the sympathy and understanding which result, according to Büchner's Lenz, from loving penetration into the individual's unique being (I.87). Büchner proves the effectiveness of such a procedure by moving far beyond his source material to discover in Marie a tragic conflict between the dictates of her conscience and the irresistible demands of her nature, between her desire to be faithful and her stronger need for sexual gratification. In the final manuscript Büchner creates a scene in

which a contrapuntal sequence of Biblical quotations and despairing outcries enables Marie to express with eloquence her
sense of guilt, helplessness, and suffering. The effect of this
scene is considerably enhanced through irony: since Woyzeck
has just purchased the knife with which he intends to kill her,
the spectator knows that it is her last chance to repent.

The first passage she reads: " 'And no deceit was found in his
mouth,' " reminds her of her own deceit and causes her to cry
out in shame: "God Almighty! God Almighty! Don't look at
me" (XVI). Motivated, perhaps, by the hope of finding something more comforting, she leafs on and begins again: " 'And
the Pharisees brought unto him a woman taken in adultery and
set her in their midst. —And Jesus said unto her: Neither do I
condemn thee; go, and sin no more.' " The damning implications of this quotation are even stronger and so is her reaction.
She slaps her hands together and exclaims: "God Almighty!
God Almighty! I can't. Lord God, just give me enough so I can
pray." Apparently sensing her disturbance, the child presses up
to its mother for reassurance. Instead of pleasing her, however,
as it did in the second scene, the sight of the child now gives her
a "stab in the heart" by increasing her feelings of guilt. Marie's
self-identification with the Biblical adultress indicates that she
agrees with Woyzeck in considering their relationship to be
equivalent to marriage, even though it has not received the
"blessing of the Church." Seeing the child reminds her of
the bond she has broken, and that thought causes her to
become apprehensive about Woyzeck's prolonged absence:
"Franz hasn't come! Not yesterday, not today. It's getting hot in
here." Since Marie cannot go her way without sinning, she
would like to imitate the sinful woman who wet Jesus's feet with
her tears, dried them with her hair, and was forgiven because of
her faith.

But of course Büchner is not attempting to exonerate Woyzeck by condemning Marie on the basis of the religious authority both she and Woyzeck have been taught to accept as
divine and absolute. On the contrary, he is no more inclined to
accept judgments based on Judeo-Christian concepts of morality than those based on the laws which that morality underlies, for he considers both to be products of false and idealized
presuppositions about the nature and condition of man. A

corollary to Büchner's discovery that there are no heroes is that there are no villains or sinners either, "since it is in no one's power not to become a dullard or a criminal—since the same conditions would probably make us all the same, and since the conditions lie outside of us" (II.422).

Already in his school essays Büchner rejected judgments which are based on absolutistic and dogmatic codes or which apply the standards accepted in one particular time and context to deeds carried out in another. One cannot judge Cato's heroic suicide, for example, from the standpoint of Christianity (II.26). Insofar as the teachings of Christianity are used to condemn actions which are justifiable from the subjective standpoint of the actor, Büchner writes, those teachings are false or have been misinterpreted (II.20). Of primary importance in judging any act are "the motives and the conditions that caused, accompanied, and determined such a deed," not its effects or consequences (II.11-12). These criteria are based on a scientific awareness of the importance of hereditary and especially environmental factors as determinants of man's actions. The general acceptance and application of such criteria would demand extensive revision of our moral and legal codes and political and social institutions, to the extent, namely, that those codes and institutions are based on outdated beliefs and presuppositions about man.

Thus Büchner opposes all forms of idealism and idealistic glorifications of man. The nature of his opposition may be illustrated by contrasting his scientific viewpoint with a statement by a major representative of German Idealism, Immanuel Kant. Kant wrote that man transcends "the mechanical disposition of his animal existence" because nature has given him "reason and freedom of the will."[47] Büchner believes, on the contrary, that man is determined by his nature and surroundings and that his reason is by no means a strong or reliable attribute of his mental constitution.[48] Take away freedom of will and minimize the role of reason and all that remains of Kant's definition is man's "animal being." To the claim that man can overcome and transcend his animal nature through education, Büchner answers that education, like clothing, is only a thin and superficial veneer, a "ridiculous externality" (II.422-423). In *Woyzeck* Büchner strips off that veneer, as it were, to reveal the naked beast.[49]

The idealistic view of man comes under direct attack in the carnival scene. The Barker ridicules enlightenment and idealist philosophy, for example, by using some of their tenets to demonstrate the very antithesis of what they intend, namely, that there is no basic separation between man and animal. Not only man, but animals, too, are progressing along the path to perfection: "Observe the progress of civilization. Everything progresses: a horse, a monkey, a cannybird!" (III). The higher forms of animals need only to don clothing in order to close the gap between them and the lower forms of man. Dress a monkey like a soldier, and he is one. "The monkey is already a soldier. That's not yet much, to be sure. The lowest level of the human race!" And this is only the beginning. Through their ability to learn tricks, i.e., to be educated, animals reveal that they too have reason—"a beastly reason or rather a very reasonable beastliness"—which is in no way inferior to man's: "They're not beastly stupid individuals like a lot of people." Since "everything is education" and since animals can be educated, they can even reach the highest stages of human development: "Gentlemen, this animal you see here, with its tail on its body and standing on its four hooves, is a member of all learned societies, is a professor at our university, where the students learn from him how to ride and fight." What is more, the learned horse can even think with "double reason."[50] Only in its inability to express itself is the animal inferior to man: "He just can't express himself, can't explain. He's a transformed person!"

The grotesque identification of man and beast displayed in these exhibitions is reinforced by the pun *"Viehsionomik"* (a combination of *"Vieh"* [=beast] and physiognomy) and by the Showman's explanation: "Indeed, this is no beastly stupid animal; this is a person! A human. A beastly human, and yet an animal, *une bête.*" When the horse demonstrates its uninhibited naturalness,[51] the Showman admonishes the spectators to learn from the beast. Attempts to distort or idealize one's nature are harmful and should be avoided: "Observe that the beast is still nature, unideal nature. Learn from him. Ask the doctor—it's extremely injurious. It has been said: Man, be natural. You are made of dust, sand, muck. Do you want to be more than dust, sand, muck?"[52]

While the Showman demonstrates in his "representation"

how animals are like men, the play as a whole demonstrates
how men are like animals. Like clothes and education, virtue
and morality can raise man above the beast, but they too are
luxuries, according to Woyzeck, which only the rich can afford:

> Us poor people. You see, Captain, sir—it's money, money.
> Whoever hasn't got money. What good is morality for some-
> one like that.
>
> . . . .
>
> Yes, Captain, sir: Virtue! I haven't quite figured it out yet.
> You see, us common people, we don't have virtue. We just
> follow our nature. But if I was a gentleman and had a hat and
> a watch and a frock coat and could talk refined, then I'd sure
> want to be virtuous. There must be something beautiful
> about virtue, Captain, sir. But I'm a poor guy. (V)

Woyzeck has his "flesh and blood," or, as he says in explaining
why he urinated on the wall "like a dog," his nature: "But
Doctor, sir, when nature calls" (VIII).

The sexual side of man's animal nature is expressed with
primitive simplicity and directness in the relationship between
Marie and the Drum Major. Both figures are characterized by
pride in their own appearance and by their sexual vitality.
Marie knows that only her poverty prevents her from being
admired and courted like the fine ladies, for she is no less
beautiful than they are: "People like me have only a little
corner in the world and a small piece of mirror; and yet I have
as red a mouth as the grandest ladies with their full-length
mirrors and their handsome gentlemen, who kiss their hands.
I'm just a poor woman" (IV). Like Woyzeck, she sees money as
the determinant of one's social position, attitudes, and behavior. The poor make less of an effort to idealize their natural
or animal drives by pretending they are something other than
what they really are; they do not disguise them behind euphem-
isms or behind the artificial masks of elaborately refined conventions, rites, and formalities. Thus the nature of the at-
traction between Marie and the Drum Major is immediately
apparent from the explicitly animal and sexual terms they use
to describe each other. Marie's initial excitement at seeing him
is conveyed indirectly by the contrast of her more vital simile
with Margret's static one and directly by the latter's comment:

Margret. What a man! Like a tree.
Marie. He stands on his feet like a lion. *(The Drum Major greets them.)*
Margret. Ooh! What friendly eyes, neighbor. (II)

And the Drum Major far outdoes his companion in the explicitness of his response to Marie:

Sergeant. Hold it! Look at her! What a broad!
Drum Major. By God! For reproducing cavalry regiments and for breeding Drum Majors. (III)

Their mating rite follows the basic pattern of such rites as universally performed in the animal world. Marie's answer to the Drum Major's approach and address reveals that she is impressed by his appearance and flattered by his attention: "Go on—let me look at you! Chest broad as a bull's and a beard like a lion's! No other man's like that. I'm the proudest of women" (VI). To further impress and attract her, he struts about in ritual self-display and brags cockily about his manly appearance: "By damn, Marie, you should see me on Sundays, when I wear my plumed helmet and white gloves! The Prince always says: 'By God, there's a real man!'" Marie teases him briefly: "*(mockingly)* Is that so?!" but she is compelled by her passionate desire to invite his further advance: "*(Goes up to him)* Man!" Her exclamation reveals that he is not important to her as a specific person, but as a man, a mate; and he responds in kind: "And you're quite a woman." At this point the first phase of the mating rite ends and the final stage begins: "By God, let's lay up a brood of Drum Majors. Hey?" By now her attempted resistance is futile, the outcome inevitable:

Marie *(irritably)*. Let me go!
Drum Major. Wild animal!
Marie *(violently)*. Just touch me!
Drum Major. Is that the devil in your eyes?
Marie. For all I care. It makes no difference.

When Woyzeck sees Marie dancing with the Drum Major and hears her urging him on, he realizes that the nature which controls man is no different from the nature which determines the actions of the beasts and insects: "Why doesn't God blow out the sun, so everything can roll around together in lechery!

Man and woman, man and beast. They do it in broad daylight, do it on your hands like flies" (XI). This tragic moment of discovery is immediately followed by a Journeyman's parodistic sermon praising God's wisdom and foresight in having created man. The alienating contrast prevents the spectator's response from becoming sentimental, but it also makes idealism's teleological explanation of man's existence appear all the more ridiculous:[53]

> However, when a wanderer, who stands leaning by the stream of time or who answers divine wisdom and addresses himself: Why is man? Why is man?—But verily I say unto you: How could the farmer, the cooper, the cobbler, the doctor live, if God had not created man? How could the tailor live, if God had not implanted the sense of shame in man? How could the soldier live, if God had not armed men with the urge to kill each other?

For his portrayal of Woyzeck and Marie, Büchner penetrates, as he advocated in Lenz, "into the life of the lowliest creatures and reproduces it with its palpitations, its suggestiveness, and the whole fine, scarcely perceptible play of its features," and he causes his figures to emerge from within, where the life is and where the muscles and pulse beat and swell (I.87). Lenz claims that a work of art can be judged only on the basis of whether or not it conveys the feeling that it has life; all other considerations are secondary. Woyzeck and Marie engage our feelings and interest us because they do have life. We can empathize with them and be affected by their fate. That is not true of the Doctor and the Captain, however, since they lack the complexity, the humanity, and the life of their counterparts. As representatives of fixed ideas they engage our intellect rather than our emotions. Because of their grotesquely exaggerated and mechanical behavior they appear to be comic and ridiculous stereotypes or caricatures rather than human beings. The Captain is an unquestioning spokesman for the conventional morality taught by the Church, and the Doctor is totally dehumanized by his monomaniacal concern for medical science. As embodiments of ideas and attitudes, they represent the lifeless, mechanical puppets Büchner considers characteristic of idealistic art; as "idealized nature" they contrast with the flesh-and-blood figures demanded by Büchner's art.

To the extent that they degrade, abuse, and harm Woyzeck, they also serve as vehicles for social criticism. However, interpretations which focus on this aspect of the play's social criticism not only overstress what is of relatively minor and superficial importance, but also fail to do justice to the play's deeper and far more revolutionary content. An analysis of the successive stages of the play's development reveals that Büchner purposely avoided creating a melodramatic conflict between the good man and the villainous representatives of an evil society. In the final manuscript Woyzeck is not excessively threatened or harmed by them: the Captain does not harm him at all, and it is unclear what effect the Doctor's experiment has on him. Rather than filling us with dread or hate, they tend to strike us as grotesque and ludicrous. They do not function as oppressors, but as vehicles for satirizing and ridiculing the narrowness, insufficiency, and rigidity of Christian morality and the callousness of experimental science. Along with the Journeymen, they provide the only comic moments in the play.

Both the Captain and the Doctor appear only twice, once each with Woyzeck and once together. While it is true that Woyzeck must serve and obey his military superior and that he is treated with some condescension, it cannot be said that he is abused or degraded because of his inferior military rank and social status. When Woyzeck absent-mindedly agrees that the wind is from the South-North, the Captain tells him he is terribly dumb, but in the subsequent argument on morality Woyzeck clearly reveals more insight and independent thought than the Captain. The Captain regrets the fact that Woyzeck has no morality, for otherwise he is a "good man." But all he knows about morality is that it is a "good word." Like the Fool with his fragments from fairy tales (XVI), or like King Peter in *Leonce and Lena* with his philosophical terms (I.ii), the Captain repeats phrases and sentences he has heard, but does not understand. He even imitates the dignified manner of his source when pronouncing the borrowed words:

Woyzeck, you're a good man, a good man, but *(with dignity)* Woyzeck, you have no morality! Morality—that is being moral. Do you understand? It's a good word. You have a child without the blessing of the Church, as our Right Reverend Chaplain says. Without the blessing of the Church. I didn't just make it up. (V)

Since the Captain has never thought about the moral code he accepts mechanically, he is confused by Woyzeck's sound defense, which is based on the words of Jesus:

Woyzeck. Captain, sir, the good Lord won't judge the poor worm by whether or not an Amen was spoken before he was made. The Lord said: "Suffer little children to come unto me."
Captain. What's that you say? What kind of a curious answer is that? You thoroughly confuse me with your answer.

When Woyzeck continues his defense with the claim that virtue and morality are luxuries which only the rich can afford, the exhausted Captain ends the discussion. If Woyzeck could meet the Drum Major's challenge as well as he does the Captain's, there would be no tragedy.

Like Danton and Leonce, with whom he has much in common, the Captain is also aware of the absurdity and emptiness of life and can become melancholy at the thought of how many hours of potential boredom he has to fill. Büchner suggests in *Leonce and Lena* that only a fool or an idealist can find a means of creating order from chaos and meaning from absurdity. The Captain finds his answer, or partial answer, in a ready-made moral system.

Much has been written about Woyzeck's inability to express himself, but the Captain is equally inarticulate. He is no more capable of explaining the fear he feels when thinking about eternity than he is of defining morality. Though he is not conscious of it, the arrangement of his words in circular patterns—like the motion of the millwheel and the earth—conveys his meaning better than what he says:

I fear for the world when I think about eternity. Activity, Woyzeck, activity! Eternal, that is eternal, that is eternal. You understand that. But then again it is not eternal, and that is a moment. Yes, a moment. Woyzeck, I shudder when I think that the earth turns around in one day. What a waste of time! What's the purpose of it all? Woyzeck, I can't look at a mill wheel anymore or I become melancholy.

The Captain's desire to engage the preoccupied Woyzeck in conversation is, like Woyzeck's similar effort with Andres in the first scene, an attempt to break out of his isolation and to escape his disturbing thoughts. But like Leonce, the Captain represents a comic, satiric variation on a serious theme. Since he lacks the life and humanity of the serious figures, he is risible rather than pitiable.

Contrasting with the rather complex figure of the Captain is the monomaniacal Doctor. He has become so totally dehumanized by his obsession with scientific facts and theories that he lacks human feelings. He is a caricature of those scientists and scholars who sacrifice the great mass of their brothers to their disdainful egotism, who consider data more important than people, and who will do anything to establish and aggrandize their reputations.[54] He is not interested in the actual goal of his profession, which is to understand man in order to heal him. He cannot recognize or appreciate the humanity of others because he completely lacks it himself. He shows more concern for an experimental animal than for a man, because the animal is less tenacious and therefore more likely to ruin his experiment by dying. "With utmost coldbloodedness" he says to Woyzeck: "God forbid that I should get upset about a man. A man! Now if it were a proteus that easily dies on you!" (VIII). He is callously indifferent to others unless they can serve as objects for scientific observations and experimentation. He is so delighted with the development in "Subject Woyzeck" of a most beautifully developed aberration, for example, that he promises him an increase in pay.

The Doctor's callous attitude toward Woyzeck is only indirectly related to their difference in class: the meeting on the street between the Doctor and the Captain indicates that he regards and treats his social equals in the same way. The Doctor shows no inclination to stop and converse with the Captain until he learns that the latter is suffering from melancholy. This promising news invites a closer look, whereupon the Doctor discovers, to his delight, that the Captain too is an interesting case:

Hm! Puffed up, fat, thick neck, apoplectic constitution. Yes, Captain, you may get an *apoplexia cerebralis*. But you might get it on only one side and just be paralyzed on that side. Or, if all goes well, it may only paralyze your mind, and you will simply vegetate from then on. That just about covers your prospects for the next four weeks. Incidentally, I can assure you that you provide one of the more interesting cases. And if it be God's will that your tongue become partially paralyzed, we'll perform the most immortal experiments. (IX)

The Doctor actually displays greater cruelty and lack of pity in dealing with the Captain than he does with Woyzeck.[55] What distinguishes Woyzeck's situation from the Captain's is the fact that the responsibility Woyzeck has assumed for supporting Marie and their child demands that he accept all available means for earning money, including one as potentially harmful as hiring himself out as a human guinea pig.

The criticism implied in this situation is not directed against an individual or a particular social class, but against the very structure of a society in which a man like Woyzeck cannot sustain a small family without having to drive himself through long days of exhausting and often debasing work. The message of Büchner's *Hessian Courier* recurs here in dramatic form. The laws and the organization of the state are designed by and for the rich to preserve order. But for the poor the existing order means going hungry and being overworked (II.36). The conclusion to be drawn from Woyzeck's situation is the same as that proposed in the political pamphlet: the laws and the organization of the state must be changed in order that the poor may derive greater benefit from their own labor.

In contrast to popular or *"Trivialliteratur,"* "authentic" art is always critical and revolutionary to some extent, since it always attacks and endeavors to change the customary schemes of experience and behavior, to push beyond what has become conventional and established. It attempts, as Dieter Wellershoff writes, "to irritate the reader, to destroy the certainty of his prejudices and accustomed mode of behavior. It makes the apparently familiar unfamiliar, the unequivocal equivocal, the unconscious conscious, and it opens up new possibilities of undergoing experiences, which are perhaps confusing and terrifying, but which break out of the narrowness and abstraction of the routine upon which he depends and relies in daily life."[56] We progress in our experience and understanding of life, just as we do in our quest for knowledge, when confrontation with reality and truth disappoints our expectations, thus obliging us to revise the knowledge and presuppositions upon which those expectations were based. Literature can substitute for actual experience in this process; it can provide a reality through which expectations can be tested and their scope expanded. Literature can preserve actual experience, as history does, but it can also go beyond history to anticipate unrealized possibilities. In this way it can teach us to cope with unfamiliar conditions and problems without exposing us to their dangers. And it can enable us to incorporate foreign modes of thought and behavior into the range of our experience, to become less narrow-minded and, in relation to the social context, less bound by norms.[57]

If the revolutionary potential of art lies in its ability to influence the reader's or viewer's attitudes and consciousness, to change his way of thinking and seeing, and to give him new insight and knowledge, then the socio-political importance of *Woyzeck* lies in its exposure of the injustice inherent in the structure of society and in its questioning and implied rejection of some of the basic assumptions upon which contemporary moral and legal codes and institutions were based. Büchner anticipates in his play the basic change in the concept of justice that began late in the nineteenth century as a reaction against the classical system of criminal justice, a system which such preeminent idealist philosophers as Kant and Hegel had defended. Since this system is based upon the assumption that man's will is free and his actions self-determined, it demands that the punishment fit the crime and that criminals be made to pay for their aberrant behavior. Rejecting the idea of free will, the positivist school of thought maintained that behavior is determined and that criminals must be considered ill or deprived. According to this view, criminal or delinquent behavior is merely a symptom of an underlying maladjustment, which may be psychological, biological, or social in origin. Instead of fitting the punishment to the crime, the positivists maintained that the treatment should fit the criminal and should attempt to cure him.

Also revolutionary in Büchner's play is the fact that for the first time in the history of drama a figure from the lowest stratum of society is not only made the hero of a serious play, but is even endowed with the dignity and stature demanded by tragedy. If the theatergoer can be moved to regard Woyzeck with sympathy, insight, and understanding, his attitudes toward members of Woyzeck's class may be permanently affected.

What the bourgeois tragedy was for the rise in importance of the middle class—and it has been said that Lillo's *London Merchant* was as revolutionary as the Jacobins—*Woyzeck* might have been for the emergence of the proletariat as a political and economic force,[58] not by dealing directly or profoundly with the miserable conditions and problems of that class, as Gerhart Hauptmann does in *The Weavers,* for example, but by making one of its members the object of serious and sympathetic consideration. When contrasted with the reception and influence of the *London Merchant,* the example of *Woyzeck* would seem to indicate that the revolutionary work of literature can do little to effect change until the time and circumstances are right. The fact that *Woyzeck* was not published until more than forty years after it was written does not explain its tardy reception, for even after its publication in 1879 it attracted little attention until the political and social situation and the art of the Naturalists, Expressionists and others began to catch up to it.

Form

No dramatist since Shakespeare has used the open or episodic form of drama with greater skill and effectiveness than Büchner does in *Woyzeck.* Büchner had as little use for the classical, Aristotelian dramatic form with its linear, causal plot development and its complex arrangement of independent parts according to principles of logic and rank, as he had sympathy for the idealistic, teleological, and hierarchical *Weltbild* which finds its proper medium in such a dramatic form. Unlike the idealists, who tend to view the moment in terms of the past and the future, Büchner considered each moment to be important in its own right; life consists of a series of such individual moments, each of which is complete in itself and its own reason for being. The succession of moments is not determined by a divine will or a rationally conceived world spirit, but by the laws of nature; life and history do not develop according to some grand scheme or design, which gives each event purpose and meaning, but according to the inherent physical, biological, and psychological patterns and processes, which are their own meaning and purpose. By re-presenting such moments as they actually occurred or might have occurred, the author should attempt, in Büchner's opinion, to recreate the events he wishes to present and to capture the life of his figures and of the time in which they lived.

According to Büchner's Lenz the literary work of art should consist of a sequence of petrified moments or episodes from life. Of course the artist need not, and in a larger work cannot, present a sequence of contiguous moments. He must select those which are especially charged with meaning, tension, and action or those which effectively stretch beyond their own borders to imply what preceded and suggest what will follow, just as Büchner's Lenz sees an entire story in a painting, and not just the moment actually represented. Thus the episodic play demands the active participation of the spectator in filling in the background and connecting material from the hints and allusions contained in the various episodes.

In *Woyzeck* the paratactic structure is fully and consistently developed. This form is especially suitable for presenting a fragmented world, a world in which clearly defined relationships are lacking and in which the individual is isolated and alone. The play contains very few complex sentences, and only a small number of those involve subordinate relationships.[59] Similarly, the speeches do not interlock and interconnect to form true dialogue or a "continuum of conversation."[60] The figures often strive to converse and communicate, but they seldom succeed in overcoming the distance which separates them.

In the first scene, for example, Woyzeck and his friend Andres talk to each other, but they do not communicate. Since Andres does not hear and see what Woyzeck does, he cannot understand what Woyzeck is trying to say. (Comparison of the finished scene with the first draft, in which Andres does hear the sounds, reveals that Büchner purposely reduced the amount of communication and community in the later version.) Andres even whistles and sings in order not to hear his friend's strange talk. Later, when Woyzeck is tortured by anguish and when he disposes of his possessions, Andres thinks he has a fever.

Likewise, in Woyzeck's first meeting with Marie, which was discussed above, Marie has the role of a spectator rather than a partner, as she merely responds to his account with her exclamations. As a further example of conversation with minimal communication and as an illustration of how dialogue is formed from the paratactic arrangement of distinct, loosely connected conversational units, the exchange immediately preceding the murder may be cited.[61] Woyzeck's failure to visit Marie for two days has made her nervous and apprehensive; his sudden appearance after the Grandmother's tale and the peculiar manner in which he leads her away increase her fear and uncertainty:

> **Woyzeck.** Marie!
> **Marie** *(startled)*. What do you want?
> **Woyzeck.** Marie, let's go. It's time.
> **Marie.** Where to?
> **Woyzeck.** How should I know? (XVIII)

The murder scene itself begins with Marie's observations: "So, the town's over that way. It's dark." The ominous tenor of Woyzeck's peculiar reply heightens the tension and increases Marie's apprehension. She cannot understand, as the spectator does, the hidden meaning of his statements, but she does sense from the peculiarity of his behavior and speech that he is severely disturbed and that she is threatened:

> **Woyzeck.** You must stay awhile. Come sit down.
> **Marie.** But I have to go.
> **Woyzeck.** You won't get sore feet from walking.
> **Marie.** What's gotten into you?!

The theme of the dialogue shifts several times, but the suggestion of impending disaster remains throughout as a unifying mood. A new unit begins when Woyzeck questions Marie about the past and future of their relationship:

Woyzeck. Do you know how long it's been now, Marie?
Marie. Two years on Pentecost.
Woyzeck. Do you also know how long it's going to be?
Marie. I must go make supper.

Woyzeck's monologic response to Marie's nervous reply constitutes a new unit:

Are you freezing, Marie? And yet you're warm. How hot your lips are! Hot—hot whore's breath. But still I'd give heaven to kiss them once more.

When you're cold, you don't freeze any more. You won't freeze in the morning dew.

Two more short segments precede the murder, and the murder itself constitutes a final one.

The episodes in *Woyzeck* are basically of two types, those which form a part of the central action and those which contribute little or nothing to the development of the plot or to delineation of character, but which provide a new perspective, furnish some form of comment on the action, or add a universal dimension to the particular action of the central plot. To the latter category belong the carnival scene, the meeting between the Doctor and the Captain, the Grandmother's tale, the speeches of the Journeymen, and some of the songs. The poor orphan in the Grandmother's tale, for example, is analogous to Woyzeck and his child. Having lost its father and mother, the child looks all over the earth for human companionship, but everything is dead. The child extends its search for life into the universe, only to discover that the moon is nothing but a piece of rotten wood; the sun, a dead sunflower; and the stars, dead insects stuck on twigs. Upon its return to earth, it finds that the earth has become an overturned chamber pot: "And then it sat down and cried. And it sits there still and is all alone" (XVIII).

Büchner employs the form and conventions of the fairy tale to express hyperbolically one of the basic motifs of the play and of his works as a whole; in its loneliness and isolation the child represents not only Woyzeck and Woyzeck's child, but also Danton, Leonce, Lenz, and man in general. It learns what Woyzeck discovers at the inn and what Danton expresses at the beginning of *Danton's Death:* "We know little of each other. We are thick-skinned. We stretch out our hands toward each other, but the effort is futile. We only rub off the coarse leather against each other—*we are very lonely.*" (I.1. Italics added.) Where the fairy tale and the parable traditionally presuppose an ordered universe and a generally accepted, sacred system of beliefs, Büchner's inverted, nihilistic fairy tale presumes a chaotic and absurd world in which there are no positive values and no hope. In making a general statement about man and the world, this episode stands apart from the central action; but while it does not further the plot, it does contribute significantly to the mood of the play and to the intensification of its dramatic impact. When the silence that must follow the relating of such a tale is broken by Woyzeck, who has come to kill Marie, the expressiveness of their simple dialogue is so intensified by the context that a tension similar to that reached at the climax of a Greek tragedy is achieved.[62]

Besides creating atmosphere, the carnival scene extends beyond the immediate plot to provide realistic criteria for judging or understanding the behavior of the figures of the play and of man in general. Like the carnival scene, the songs not only create atmosphere, but also provide comment on the action. And by relating the experiences of Marie and Woyzeck to the fundamental themes of folk songs, they also help to establsh the play's universal validity.[63] The position of the scenes or episodes of this type is not determined by their function in the development of the central action, but by their contribution to specific moments of that action.

Whether it be words in a sentence, sentences in a paragraph, or scenes in a play, the sequence of parts in a literary work is as much a determinant of meaning and effect as are the parts themselves. Thus, contrary to the claims of some critics and the practice of many directors, neither the position of the purely episodic scenes nor the sequence of scenes constituting the main action can be altered without changing the work's intended meaning and effect.[64] In *Woyzeck* the sequence of events which begin with Woyzeck's suspicion of Marie's disloyalty and culminate in the murder constitute a basic framework in relation to which the other scenes fall naturally into place. Given with this sequence is a continual and dramatically effective increase of intensity and tension.

At the end of the first scene Andres hears the drumming

which opens the second scene; and at the end of the latter
Woyzeck stops on his way back from the field to talk briefly
with Marie. In the final draft of the second scene Büchner
omits Woyzeck's reference to the carnival, thus eliminating the
only direct connection between the second and third scenes.
The location of the carnival scene is nevertheless unequivocally determined by the sequence of Marie's increasing involvement with the Drum Major. In the second scene they
greet each other; at the carnival the Drum Major gets another
look at Marie and expresses the desire to mate with her; between the third and fourth scenes a meeting takes place in
which Marie receives the earrings that arouse Woyzeck's suspicion in scene four.

While the scenes in which Woyzeck is with the Captain and
the Doctor do not fit into any such scheme, one can recognize
the structural and contextual reasons for their placement. Both
of these episodes follow scenes in which Woyzeck's suspicion is
aroused. By revealing after each step in the development of
Marie's relationship with the Drum Major how the loyal Woyzeck drives himself and suffers humiliation in order to support
his family, they provide ironic comment on those betrayal
scenes and intensify their impact. (Woyzeck's mechanical responses and lack of attention in the first part of the scene with
the Captain express his disturbed preoccupation with Marie's
peculiar behavior.)

The only scene whose location cannot readily be determined
by considering its relationship to its immediate surroundings
and its function in the context of the whole is the one in
which the Captain and the Doctor meet on the street. Perhaps
its position can be explained by the author's penchant for
using contrasts to set off important occurrences and to intensify dramatic effects. This scene provides a moment of pause
and relaxed tension just before Woyzeck's suspicion becomes
certainty.

As a relatively short literary form meant for performance,
the drama must be extremely concentrated, and concentration
demands unity of impression.[65] The theoreticians of the neo-
classical drama considered rigid adherence to the dramatic
rules derived from Aristotle to be the *sine qua non* for creating
such a unified impression. Of course the dogmatic application

of these rules may result in the creation of improbable and
unbelievable situations and events, but their complete abandonment has revenged itself on many a would-be Shakespeare,
for a play's effectiveness may indeed be enhanced by the judi-
cious and reasonable observance of the unities of time, place,
and especially action.

But there are subtler, more organic, and for the episodic play
more effective ways of achieving unity of impression. Primary
among these is the repetition and variation of words, phrases,
images, themes, and rhythms. The interconnections and inter-
relations between motifs and motif-complexes bind the parts
together into a unified whole. Through their recurrence, the
motifs also extend the scope of their meaning and accumulate
strength and intensity of expression.

Each major figure in the play can be associated with and
characterized by specific motifs or motif-complexes. We have
already considered the importance of animal imagery as an
expression of Marie's sensual nature and erotic vitality, and we
have seen how similar motifs, oriented more towards breeding,
recur in the speeches of her partner, the Drum Major. Both
figures are characterized by the primitive or animal level of
their sexuality. Characteristic for the Captain's "complacent,
conventional sentimentality"[66] is his repetition of the stock
phrase "a good man," which occurs twelve times in two scenes.
His melancholy lethargy and antipathy to haste and motion are
expressed in his repeated admonitions to Woyzeck and the
Doctor to slow down.

The repetition of words and motifs may also be used to
demonstrate the compulsive nature of man's thoughts and behavior. That is clearly the case with the Doctor and the Captain, but also with Woyzeck, whose preoccupation or obsession
is revealed by such words and phrases as "go on," "knife," and
"stab dead" (or "stab"), and by such contrasting word pairs as
"warm/cold," "hot/freezing," and "life/death."[67] All of these
relate to the sin/punishment motif associated with Woyzeck's
visions. After Woyzeck discovers Marie's infidelity, he concludes that all life is lechery; and he considers the words with
which Marie encourages the Drum Major to be a direct expression of the heat of her lechery: "That woman is hot, hot!—Go
on, go on" (XI). But what is hot with sin will be made cold by
the resulting punishment: the words which stand for Marie's

lechery become transformed in Woyzeck's mind into the rhythmically similar phrase "stab dead."[68] The relationships between these various motifs is clearly indicated in the speech that precedes the murder:

> Are you freezing, Marie? And yet you're warm. How hot your lips are! Hot—hot whore's breath. But still I'd give heaven to kiss them once more.
>
> When you're cold, you don't freeze any more. You won't freeze in the morning dew. (XIX)

Following the murder, Woyzeck tells Kate that she is hot and that she too will become cold. At the same time he admits: "I'm hot, hot" (XX), thus indicating that he too has become guilty. That the heat of sin will be made cold by punishment is a compelling thought in Woyzeck's mind and may serve here as a foreshadowing of his own fate.

Closely associated with this complex are the motifs "red," and "blood."[69] Red is the color of flesh and blood, and of sensuality and sin. Red also signifies beauty when used in reference to Marie's mouth: "and yet I have as red a mouth as the grandest ladies," Marie says (IV). When looking for the blemish that he thinks should mar the beauty that has become sinful, Woyzeck also equates Marie's red mouth with beauty: "You have a red mouth, Marie. No blister on it? Farewell, Marie, you're as beautiful as sin. Can mortal sin be so beautiful?" (VII). The verse Woyzeck finds in his mother's Bible implies by association a connection between pain and suffering, blood, and the color red: "As your body, Lord, was red and sore [wund], / Let my heart be for evermore" (XVII). The same complex of motifs recurs just prior to the murder: when Marie observes: "How red the moon is rising," Woyzeck associates the red color of the moon with blood and with the instrument for inflicting wounds that he is about to use: "Like a bloody knife" (XIX).

"Red" and "blood" are connected again when Kate discovers blood on Woyzeck's hand: "Red! Blood!" (XXII), and when Woyzeck returns to Marie's corpse: "What's that red string around your neck?" Once again he associates "red" and "blood" with sin, and perhaps also with the gift Marie received from the Drum Major: "Who gave you that necklace in payment for your sins?" (XXIV). Marie's sin exacts as retribution the very beauty and vitality that was its cause: "You were black from them [her sins], black! Have I made you white now?" Blood, beauty, suffering, and sin are all connected through the color red, and Marie loses them all when Woyzeck sheds her blood and makes her pale. But in assuming the role of judge and executioner, Woyzeck becomes bloody and guilty himself. There is no need for the author to present what is obvious, the fact, namely, that only death can free Woyzeck from the compulsive desire to cleanse himself from his own guilt. As the play ends, he is engaged in the futile attempt to wash off the bloody spots which mark and betray him.

Besides binding the parts together to create a unified impression, the recurring motifs also provide a means for achieving maximal concentration and force of expression. As words and phrases accumulate special nuances of meaning from the various contexts in which they occur, their capability of arousing specific emotional responses becomes heightened. Whenever Woyzeck repeats the phrase "go on," for example, we recall the circumstances in which he first heard it, and we realize that it obsesses him and that it is closely connected in his mind with the phrase "stab dead." This enrichment of key words and phrases allows the simple speech of Büchner's figures to become naively eloquent and ironic. By supercharging his language in this way, Büchner regains some of the poetic quality, concentration, and elevation that is typical of fine verse but rare in prose.

Where the language is simple and sometimes vague, nonverbal communication becomes all the more important.[70] As the words, phrases, sentence fragments, and simple sentences emerge or explode from deep within the speakers, they demand and shape the clarifying accompaniment of gesture. Büchner occasionally uses stage instructions to describe the physical action which accompanies and complements the dialogue and fills the frequent pauses, but most often the requisite gestures and facial expressions are contained implicitly in the language itself.

Any passage which does not involve the Doctor and the Captain could be cited as an example of how Büchner achieves maximal expression from minimal means. Especially compact and dense is a short passage from the final inn scene (XXII), which recapitulates in scarcely more than a dozen words a number of the play's major motifs. The exchange begins when Kate asks Woyzeck, who has just come from the scene of the murder: "But what do you have on your hand?" Her tone of voice and physical reaction express astonishment accompanied by some degree of suspicion and accusation. This remark forces Woyzeck to become aware of the reality of his situation and to fear that his guilt will be discovered. Frightened bewilderment and self-incriminating defensiveness can be heard in his reply: "Me? Me?" The moment of discovery with its accompanying horror, accusation, disgust, and demand of an explanation is revealed in Kate's exclamation: "Red! Blood!" Still confused and baffled, Woyzeck turns her exclamation into a question, which is immediately followed by a verification: "Blood? Blood." Meanwhile a crowd has gathered; Kate's observation is affirmed and her reaction reinforced by the Innkeeper's response: "Uuh blood."[71] Woyzeck collects himself enough to offer an explanation, but not enough to make it plausible. Seeing himself cornered and threatened, he covers his hasty escape with a frantic barrage of questions and exclamations: "Damn it, what do you want? It's none of your business! Make way! Or the first one—damn it! Do you think I killed someone? Am I a murderer? Why are you gaping? Look at yourselves! Make way there! *(He runs out.)*" Gesture, tone, and action are so clearly contained or suggested by Büchner's dialogue that specific stage instructions are unnecessary. This short exchange is no less effective than an eloquent monologue would be in providing insight into the state of Woyzeck's psyche.

Whether he attempts to philosophize, or whether he stammers in frightened confusion, Woyzeck's language always conveys far more than he is able to express consciously. Whether it is forced out with conscious effort, or whether it bursts forth on its own, it is always filled with life. It is language so charged with emotion and filled with meaning that it overcomes the artificial barriers that seem to separate the speaker from the spectator. Büchner accomplishes in his art what Danton considers to be impossible in life, but what Lenz demands of the artist: his love of mankind enables him to penetrate into the peculiar being of an individual and to share his insight and knowledge with the reader or spectator.

CONCLUSION

Büchner lived in a time of transition. Most of his contemporaries suffered under the burden described by Karl Immermann in his novel *The Epigones* (1835): the great classical age of German culture had come to an end with the death of Beethoven in 1827, Hegel in 1831, and Goethe in 1832, and the artists and thinkers of the new generation felt the onus of having to compete or at least bear comparison with their incomparable predecessors as they attempted to discover, express, and help to create the spirit of the new era, to detect and record the nature and power of the forces which were transforming their world. While lesser talents either resigned themselves to their lot as imitators or wasted their energy in futile attacks on the giants, Büchner became a true heir and successor. With sure instinct he created from forms borrowed from the past, especially from Shakespeare and Goethe, the artistic means for accomplishing the task his generation faced. The Weimar Classicists had brought a great period of development to a golden conclusion; Büchner helped to lay the artistic foundation for a new era. Then, after a beginning more remarkable in its promise than Schiller's or even Goethe's, he was dead at twenty-three. One cannot help but wonder what course German and European literature might have taken, had he lived longer. Those who mourned his passing knew that great potential died with him, but they could not know from their perspective either how great that potential was or how much he had actually accomplished.

At the dawning of the age of science and industry he combined a scientist's gift for observation and analysis and his penchant for questioning traditional beliefs and assumptions with a poet's intuitive sensitivity and perceptiveness, and he devoted his genius to the age-old quest for knowledge about man's nature and his role in society. He began in *Danton's Death* and *Leonce and Lena* with his own variations on the contemporary theme of the Romantic *Weltschmerzler,* but in *Woyzeck* he reached conclusions similar to those later formulated by Charles Darwin. No matter how well dressed or educated he may be, man can never escape the fact that he is an animal and that he is subject to similar urges, drives, and instincts, and to the same laws of nature as the other animals. He is both blessed and cursed by his highly developed mind, blessed in terms of the "progress" it has enabled him to make, cursed because it alienates him from nature. All of Büchner's major figures suffer from the possession of mind. Danton's will-to-act is paralyzed and his will-to-live destroyed by the discovery that he is not the master of his deeds, but a tool of forces he cannot control; and he is tormented by the awareness that he cannot truly know or be known by another person. Woyzeck is shattered by the discovery of Marie's animality, and his self-destructive crime is the compulsive act of an obsessed mind. Büchner's account of the mental breakdown of the Storm and Stress poet and dramatist J. M. R. Lenz has gained recognition as a classical pathography of schizophrenia.

Büchner's political and social philosophy was equally in advance of his time. His rejection of idealistic assumptions about man as a self-determining being led him to question the legal, social, and moral institutions and codes which are based upon such assumptions. He abhorred with democratic fervor all forms of aristocracy and believed that the state should guarantee the physical well-being and the civil rights, including the right to pursue pleasure and happiness, of all the people. Büchner had no sympathy for the nationalism of such German philosophers as Fichte and Hegel, nor could he endorse the elitist political goals of the Young Germans and the students' fraternities (*Burschenschaften*). In a country in which the Industrial Revolution was just beginning, he was one of the first to embrace and actively fight for the realization of the socialistic goals advocated by radical thinkers in the more industrialized countries of France and England. But while he stood for revolution and the establishment of a republic, he rejected the French Revolution for having strengthened the middle class at the expense of the poor.

In his belief that criminal or delinquent behavior is merely a symptom of an underlying illness, deprivation, or maladjustment, he anticipated a basic change in the concept of justice that began late in the nineteenth century. Like later reformers, he suggests or infers that those administering justice consider the motivations and circumstances of the crime and the condition of the criminal and that they substitute treatment and cure for punishment.

With his departure from the Enlightenment's faith in man's ability to know all things and from the classicist's trust in the capacity of language to express all thoughts and feelings, Büchner anticipated major attitudes and concerns of our time. Long before Wedekind and the playwrights of the absurd, Büchner's figures were speaking past each other. Equally modern is his representation of man as a beast, a puppet, or an automaton (cf. Wedekind, Brecht, and the Theater of the Absurd). The feeling that there is no real distinction between life and death, the absence of any metaphysical dimension, and the importance of the grotesque and the surreal—these are but a few of the many points of contact between Büchner and writers of our century. Büchner's works also anticipate most modern dramatic forms and styles: the Naturalists, the Expressionists, Brecht and his followers, and the playwrights of the absurd all admired him as a model and kindred spirit; his incorporation of documentary material into his works prefigures not only the Documentary Theater of recent years, but also the collage technique, which was developed by writers and artists associated with the likewise politically committed Dada movement; and the episodic structure he defended and employed has become the predominant dramatic form of our time.

The seminal nature of Büchner's works and the fact that their reception and influence have run parallel with the development of the modern drama from Naturalism to the present time suggest that Büchner anticipated the change of consciousness and perception which began in the 1880's and which is most obviously manifest in the paintings of the Post-Impressionists. Büchner's rejection of the classical, hierarchical, hypotactic dramatic structure is comparable to the Post-Impressionists' abandonment of linear and aerial perspective, which had been the primary determinant of pictorial order since the Renaissance; and his utilization, especially in *Woyzeck,* of the paratactic or episodic structure with its manifold interrelationships of relatively autonomous parts and its reliance on motifs and motif-complexes (recurring words, phrases, images, themes, and rhythms) to create unity of impression is analogous to the Post-Impressionists' purification and simplified employment of the basic elements of their medium (the two-dimensional plane of the canvas, line, color, shape, and composition). Büchner occupies a place with these painters and their counterparts in the other arts and genres as one of the great precursors of modern art.

APPENDIXES

A. THE RECEPTION OF BÜCHNER'S PLAYS IN THE THEATER

From the time of the Storm and Stress movement with its veneration for Shakespeare and its cult of the genius, it has not been uncommon for German dramatists to disregard the exigencies of the contemporary theater and, taking Shakespeare as their model, to write either for the Elizabethan stage, for an ideal theater which was yet to be developed, or for no stage at all. *Faust II* is sometimes staged in elaborate productions, but even in severely cut versions it is not a work for the theater. Heinrich von Kleist's *Penthesilea* is possibly the greatest tragedy in the German language, but it is by no means the most stageworthy. And though he died in 1836, Christian Dietrich Grabbe seems to have written his historical plays for the cinema. Büchner's plays, too, were out of phase with the theater of his time, but they have repeatedly demonstrated their dramatic and theatrical qualities in numerous performances in the past sixty years.

The history of performance of Büchner's plays began with a presentaion in 1885 of *Leonce and Lena* by a group of young artists in the context of a private garden party in Munich. The purpose of the event was to introduce an almost unknown text to some forty or fifty invited guests. Frequent interruptions for beer and sausage may not have contributed much to the continuity of the performance, but they did assure the success of the evening.

A matinee performance of *Danton's Death* in 1902 by the *Neue Freie Volksbühne* of Berlin was the first public, or semipublic, production of one of Büchner's plays. While well received by the audience, the performance was severely attacked by the critics for its technical deficiencies: one reviewer doubted whether this product of a "morbidly excited youth" could even be considered a drama.[1] By the time *Danton* was performed again in connection with the celebration of the centennial of Büchner's birth, successful performances of *Leonce and Lena* in Vienna and Düsseldorf had begun to establish the author's reputation. On 8 November 1913 *Danton's Death* was given its first truly public performance, albeit in a severely cut version, and *Woyzeck* its premier performance in the *Residenz Theater* in Munich. The main technical difficulty of the earlier performance was overcome here through the use of a revolving stage, which made it possible to change scenes without slowing the tempo and disturbing the rhythm upon which successful performance depends. A more basic flaw in the staging revealed a fact about the play that was purposely taken advantage of in subsequent performances: since the role of the complex and multifaceted Danton is much more difficult to play well than that of his fanatically monomaniacal counterpart, Robespierre easily may emerge as the predominant figure, in which case Büchner's and Danton's rejection of the French Revolution is overshadowed by Robespierre's affirmation.

The surprise of the evening in Munich was *Woyzeck*. In the short time that elapsed between the writing of *Danton* and *Woyzeck,* Büchner's intuitive talent and genius for the theatrical aspects of drama developed to a remarkable degree for someone who had no practical theatrical experience and who had probably not even seen many plays performed.[2] The deeply moved audience discovered that *Woyzeck* definitely was written for the stage. As one critic observed: "Only on stage can the complete magic of these hurried sentences be realized."[3]

Seventy-six years after Büchner's death the theater was finally ready for his plays. The public was now able to understand and respond to both the naturalistic and expressionistic elements in his art. Albert Steinrück, whose success as Woyzeck later gained him the role in Berlin, Vienna and elsewhere, successfully combined the best of both movements: he captured and conveyed the life of the creature he represented while also discovering the expressive characteristics of the play's concentrated language and implied gesture. And the public, to whom Büchner's name was not yet generally known, often responded as it would to the latest insult being hurled at it by the literary avant-garde. When *Woyzeck* was performed in Vienna, for example, the conservative Viennese audience hissed disapproval for what evidently was taken to be the work of a contemporary dramatist of the same ilk as Wedekind. (This was the performance attended by Alban Berg, who also may have noted the similarity. In any case, he used texts by both authors for his two famous operas, *Wozzeck* and *Lulu*.) As late as 1927 the "still very backward public of the Schiller Theater in Berlin" reacted in a similar fashion.[4]

While the avant-garde lauded Büchner as a predecessor and kindred spirit, those opposed to contemporary developments in the arts rejected him. And while the socialists celebrated him as one of the first revolutionary advocates of democracy and the rights of man, conservatives and reactionaries attacked him. A major representative of the avant-garde in the arts and in politics was Max Reinhardt, the first and greatest of a new breed of absolutist directors. Because of the importance in Büchner's works of what is unspoken, his plays require the skills of a director who can bring out their latent energies and subtle meanings. On the other hand, they may also suffer from the distortions of meaning that result from a false emphasis or one-sided interpretation, from the imposition of the director's own personality, or from the introduction of incompatible elements, especially those designed to adapt them to a modern or contemporary context. Reinhardt's great production of *Danton* in 1916 in Berlin established Büchners reputation once and for all and secured a solid place for him in the German theater, but it also established a precedent for overinterpretation and misinterpretation. Reinhardt's *Danton* was expressionistic, ecstatic, and prorevolutionary. Whereas Büchner introduces the people of Paris into the play to make his picture of the historical moment more complete and because they represent the raw power that assures the predominance of the person or party who controls them, Reinhardt allowed the "powerful life of the ecstatically agitated people" to overshadow both the thoughts and personal conflicts of the main figures and the conflict between the two diametrically opposed philosophies of life and politics they represent.[5] The prorevolutionary tendency of the performance was further accented by the fact that the actor playing Danton was not able to fill out his difficult role, while those playing Robespierre and St. Just were—though not without some relapses into a declamatory style of acting. Reinhardt's *Danton* was imitated for some time to come.

While Reinhardt's prorevolutionary *Danton* was received without protest, a performance in 1918 of the rather harmless comedy *Leonce and Lena* caused a small scandal in Mannheim, where Büchner's comic treatment of petty princes and his satire of absolutism in postage-stamp principalities was seen as an attack against the monarchy.[6] Büchner was denounced in the press and from the pulpit. A pastor known for his sermons on Goethe and his defense of Ibsen stormed against *Leonce and Lena* in his Sunday sermon and again by means of an open letter to a local newspaper. This extreme reaction may be explained in part by the fact that the revolutionary atmosphere of the postwar years made people nervous and afraid. Some thought Büchner was a radical contemporary playwright, others knew him as the author of the revolutionary *Hessian Courier* and *Danton's Death*. Furthermore, the director, perhaps following Reinhardt's lead, had purposely stressed the play's satirical and parodistic elements.

A restaging in 1920 of Viktor Barnowsky's earlier Berlin production of *Woyzeck* provides a striking example of the important role the historical moment and the public's preconceptions play in the reception of a drama or any work of art. Now that Büchner's political orientation had become known, *Woyzeck* was seen primarily as a modern social play, a proletarian tragedy. Büchner was compared in the press with Gerhart Hauptmann, socialist author of *The Weavers*. A critic writing for the social democratic publication *Vorwärts* managed to combine an attack of the right-wing Kapp *Putsch* with his review.

Reinhardt's *Woyzeck* of the following year gave Berlin what the critic Julius Bab considered to be the "most valuable evening of the whole season."[7] A revolving stage enabled Reinhardt to avoid the disruptive pauses between scenes which otherwise interrupt the play's rhythm and detract from its effectiveness. He successfully integrated the play's naturalistic and expressionistic elements in such a way as to capture the life of the figures and yet to suggest at the same time that they are of symbolic and universal significance. In contrast to his

Danton, Reinhardt's *Woyzeck* contained no political, revolutionary tendency. Woyzeck was presented as a suffering man and as the archetype of all suffering men. His fate was not felt to be less tragic because of his passivity: on the contrary, Julius Hart, an early exponent of Naturalism, found a "dying Christ more tragic than a dying Achilles, the tragedy of a good man bitterer than that of a hero."[8] Hart's comparison of Klöpfer's interpretation of the title role with Steinrück's by then standard interpretation clearly identifies the innovative contribution of Reinhardt's production: "As far as I can recall, there was also in Steinrück's performance a dangerous and threatening force, a rebellion and revolution, and the red flags waved. Eugen Klöpfer's suffering Job, groaning in misery and flailed by despair, seems to me to grasp more penetratingly and intimately Georg Büchner's man, who is rooted, finally, only in love and pity, and for whom even a French Revolution does not mean liberation and deliverance. . . . "[9] With its emphasis on mood and atmosphere and on the symbolic importance of the suffering hero, this production was no doubt somewhat too abstract and muted, but Reinhardt and Klöpfer did discover and reveal to the public an important dimension of the figure of Woyzeck.[10] (Witkowski's much improved new construction of the text was used for this performance.)

As the people began to recover from the turbulence of the revolutionary postwar years, they demanded theater performances that would not disturb the new peace and quiet of their daily lives. Nevertheless, Büchner's plays not only continued to hold the stage in this period of literary reaction, they actually profited from the shift in the theater from an ecstatic, abstract, expressionistic style back toward naturalism, as well as from the discovery of their nonpolitical content. Whereas Reinhardt exaggerated the role of the ecstatic, revolutionary masses in his staging of *Danton*, a Cologne production of 1921 focused on the play's major figures. It is difficult to compare the effectiveness of the two productions, however, since the Cologne performance was weakened by major changes in the text: the sequence of the scenes was altered in order to facilitate technical production in the absence of a revolving stage, and the text was bowdlerized, hence obscured, in order not to offend the religious sensibilities of the Cologne public.

The reviews of performances of *Woyzeck* in Mannheim (September 1922) and Cologne (May 1923) reveal more about the attitudes of the critics and the public than about the productions themselves. Objection was raised to the performance of social-revolutionary works which may have had some relevance in their own time and perhaps indirectly also in the revolutionary postwar years, but not in the contemporary situation. A critic of the Mannheim performance attributed *Woyzeck's* popularity with directors to the fact that the importance in the play of nonverbal elements offers rich possibilities for the director to exercise his own creative impulses, a welcome opportunity, indeed, at a time in which direction had become an end in itself.[11]

During the mid-twenties, a period of political reaction, *Leonce and Lena,* the least political of Büchner's plays, was the one most frequently performed, usually with puppets, or in a manner suggestive of puppet plays, and with emphasis on the fairy tale content and atmosphere. But even this play offended some people, such as the critic in Cologne who did not like being told "that human life is filth . . . for how can we dare to give a value judgment of a process that is a complete enigma to us."[12] This critic's evaluation would probably have been different, had he seen one of the other productions which ranged from the delicate, refined, and romanticized staging by Gustaf Gründgens in Hamburg (with Gründgens playing Leonce) to the entirely unromantic, exaggeratedly Biedermeier staging by Robert George in Dresden.

Especially noteworthy was a performance in which this seemingly harmless comedy became the cause of a major scandal and bitter controversy. The occasion was the sesquicentennial celebration of the founding of the *Burgtheater* in Vienna. The festival performance began with a one act play written for the occasion by Auernheimer ("At the cradle of the *Burgtheater*"), a play in which the Emperor Franz Josef was duly praised. That such a piece should be followed by Büchner's comedy with its ridicule and derision of a simple-minded monarch struck the public as being more than mere coincidence, especially since the performance tended to emphasize the parodistic passages. The addition of contemporary music composed for the event enhanced the impression of the play's modernity and supported the public's suspicion that it had been especially selected and performed to ridicule the Imperial and

Monarchical period of the *Burgtheater* and perhaps the old Empire itself. The restlessness of the audience steadily increased until pandemonium broke out. Those screaming the loudest were finally silenced, and the performance was completed. The closing curtain set off a mixed chorus of hearty applause and high-pressure hissing.

The battle continued in the press: attempts were made to determine who was to blame for the fiasco, who had started the uproar. Was it monarchists looking for the opportunity to express their predilections? Was it a literarily uneducated element of the public who considered Büchner to be a modern revolutionary writer? Or was it people who simply objected to the tactless and unfortunate juxtaposition in the programing? The *Arbeiterzeitung* (*Workers' Newspaper*) made fun of the monarchists, who thought that Büchner was an "impudent, modern Jew, who presumed, in the Republic and in the theater which belonged to the Republic, . . . to ridicule the monarchy a little."[13] A writer for the *Neue Wiener Journal* was disgusted with the unwarranted cry of "Jewish impudence" which had been heard coming from the audience on the evening of the performance. One writer claimed that the disturbance had been planned in advance, another that it was the spontaneous outburst of simple people who had no appetite for the lack of tact, feeling, and taste displayed by the direction. Still another considered the song composed for King Peter's Council, "Hail to You in Your Conqueror's Laurels," to be a disguised version of the Prussian Hymn; he assumed, therefore, that the parody was directed at the Prussians rather than at the Viennese and that the joke was on the Viennese public for having missed the point.

With the economic crisis of the late twenties, Germany's short period of relative quiet and political stability came to an end. The Weimar Republic's experiment with democracy was not succeeding well; revolutionary stirrings were felt on both extremes of the political spectrum. As it usually does at such times, the theater became both a forum for dealing with immediate problems and a vehicle for protest.

Since *Danton's Death* could easily be made to serve these ends, it was again frequently staged. In 1929 it was performed in four major cities: Dresden, Berlin, Vienna, and Munich.

Each of these productions took considerable liberty in altering the text so as to give the play a prorevolutionary interpretation. The performances in Berlin and Dresden represented Danton and his friends as villains, Robespierre and the people as heroes. The lyrical and reflective passages, which are of central importance for Büchner's play, were either cut or completely overwhelmed by the noise and ecstasy of the Revolution. The performances in Vienna and Munich, both under the direction of Reinhardt, were richer and more varied. Reinhardt was too much the master of mood and atmosphere to forego the opportunities provided by Büchner's text. As in his earlier productions, he overstressed the role of the people and displayed his unequaled ability to move and use crowds. To support his prorevolutionary intention he added passages from Romain Rolland's *Danton*.

Because of the association of Büchner's plays with the political left, the possibility of their survival in the theater following the National Socialists' seizure of power in 1933 was uncertain and had to be cautiously tested. The first significant staging of one of his plays under the new regime was Hilpert's combined production at the *Berliner Volksbühne* of *Leonce and Lena* and Heinrich von Kleist's *Broken Jug* (February 1934). Despite the director's attempt to bring out the satire and caricature in Büchner's play, it could not withstand the contrast with Kleist's more colorful and robust comedy. For various reasons, not least of which was the association of Büchner's name with communistic and socialistic causes and with the expressionistic drama, the reaction of the press was unfavorable: one writer announced that, whereas Kleist still lived, Büchner was now dead and buried.[14]

Such a pronouncement from the government-controlled press had to be taken as a warning; consequently Büchner's plays disappeared from the repertory until 1937, the centennial of his death, when Peter Stanchina produced *Woyzeck* in Frankfort. Cleansed of all revolutionary implications and social criticism, this performance focused on the private fate and suffering of an individual. At least one critic recognized the important new dimension revealed by this change of emphasis. By not reducing the play to a single tendencious formula, Stanchina's *Woyzeck* made "the drama of an individual . . . transparent, so that the whole world can be felt in it."[15]

The success of this production with the public and critics alike helped to prepare the way for other performances of Büchner's works. Noteworthy among these was Otto Falckenberg's *Danton* (Munich, 1937), which was characterized by its historical realism, its complete elimination of any revolutionary tendency, and its emphasis on Danton as a profoundly tragic figure. Again the public approved.[16] Gustaf Gründgen's staging of the same play two years later in Berlin went even further than Falckenberg's in toning down the voice of the masses and the demagogic speeches and in allowing the more poetic aspects of the work to emerge from beneath the noise and turmoil that otherwise overpowered them. But Gründgens went too far; his one-sided interpretation upset the balance of diverse and contrasting elements which is an essential part of Büchner's art. Despite, or perhaps because of, their excessive caution, Falckenberg and Gründgens came closer than previous directors to realizing the author's intention, since they did not cut, add to, or otherwise alter the text. The result was a shift in emphasis from the revolutionary masses and their present leaders to the suffering of individuals and of mankind.

When performance of Büchner's plays was resumed after the war, politically tendentious stagings met with little success except in East Germany, where such an interpretation is the standard one, and on university campuses. Erwin Piscator's prorevolutionary *Danton* of 1956, for example, was rejected by the Berlin public. Then, in the wake of the student protests of the 60's, when an author's theater was again replaced by a director's theater, and when even the classical plays by Goethe and Schiller were made into vehicles of social criticism, politically tendentious productions of Büchner's plays naturally became *de rigueur* and continue to be so to the present time.

Performances of Büchner's plays outside Germany have not deviated significantly from the German ones. Büchner's early reception in this country was connected with German immigrants, the most recent of whom had emigrated for political reasons. Following the publication of Franzos's edition of Büchner's works in 1879, *The Hessian Courier* was extensively reprinted by the socialists in Germany. Side by side with the writings of Karl Marx and Ferdinand Lasalle, it became a household work on socialism and was consequently con-

demned by the Imperial Government.[17] The same was true of
Danton's Death: in 1891 an editor was arrested and jailed for
printing it. It was as a socialist writer that Büchner was first
introduced to this country: *Danton's Death* was published as
one of a series of pamphlets in the "Socialistic Library."[18] Büchner's reputation as a political writer determined the bias of
performances here as it did in Germany; in fact, Reinhardt's
Danton, with the same cast as for the Viennese performance of
1929, was staged in New York in 1928. The audience and critics
were impressed by the director's skillful use of crowds: "he is
without a peer in managing supernumeraries so that they are no
haphazard stragglers, but a living entity with real emotions and
an aggregate will. In the present production his results are the
more remarkable when one remembers that his squalling rab-
ble is an American mob, with only a week or so of rehearsals
behind it and having little idea of the German in which it is
harangued."[19]

Büchner's works were not translated into English until 1927.
A performance in English of *Danton's Death* directed by Orson
Welles in 1939 was similar to contemporary German interpretations in its emphasis on mood and its subordination of the role
of the people. This production suffered from a comparatively
weak Danton, since Welles, who would have been ideal for the
part, was too overburdened to take on the title role himself.
(He played St. Just.) Robespierre, on the other hand, was
played by Vladimir Sokoloff, an excellent actor who had
played the same part for Reinhardt.[20] This production also
suffered, as most public performances of Büchner's works in
this country have, from the tradition of the strong director,
whose aim is not to interpret the play, but to impose his own
ideas on it and to use it as a vehicle for displaying his ability to
create striking theatrical effects. This was also the case with the
staging of *Danton's Death* in 1965 for the festive grand opening
of the Vivian Beaumont Theater in New York's Lincoln Center
for the Performing Arts. The incongruity of the play with the
occasion and setting also contributed to the failure of this
production.[21] In this country Büchner's plays have their greatest success on university campuses, where the author's intended meaning generally takes precedence over spectacle and
entertainment.

B. *WOYZECK:* A READING AND ACTING TEXT

Translated by David G. Richards

I. AN OPEN FIELD. THE TOWN IN THE DISTANCE.
Woyzeck *and* **Andres** *are cutting sticks in the bushes.*

Woyzeck. Yes, Andres, the streak across the grass there—that's where the head rolls at night. Once someone picked it up. He thought it was a hedgehog. Three days and three nights and he was lying in a wooden box. *(Quietly)* Andres, it was the Freemasons. I've got it! The Freemasons! Quiet!

Andres *(singing).* Rabbits nibbling shoots,
　　　　　　　　　Ate up the green, green grass . . .

Woyzeck. Quiet! Something's moving!

Andres.　　　　　Ate up the green, green grass
　　　　　　　　Right down to the roots.

Woyzeck. Something's moving behind me, under me. *(He stamps on the ground.)* Hollow! Do you hear? It's all hollow down there. The Freemasons!

Andres. I'm afraid.

Woyzeck. Strange how still it is. Makes you want to hold your breath. Andres!

Andres. What?

Woyzeck. Say something! *(Stares in the distance.)* Andres! How bright it is! A fire's shooting through the sky and it's thundering down like trumpets. It's coming closer! Run! Don't look back! *(Pulls him into the bushes.)*

Andres *(after a pause).* Woyzeck! Do you still hear it?

Woyzeck. Quiet. Everything quiet. Like the world was dead.

Andres. Do you hear? They're drumming. We've got to go.

II.   THE CITY.

> **Marie** *with her* **Child** *at the window.* **Margret.**
> *A drum corp led by the* **Drum Major** *marches by.*

Marie *(rocking her* **Child** *in her arms).* Hey, boy! Ta, ra, ra, ra. Ye hear? There they come.

Margret. What a man! Like a tree.

Marie. He stands on his feet like a lion.

> *(The* **Drum Major** *greets them.)*

Margret. Ooh, what friendly eyes, neighbor. That's a surprise, coming from you.

Marie *(sings).* Soldiers are such handsome guys . . .

Margret. Your eyes are still shining.

Marie. So what? Take your eyes to the Jew and have them polished. Maybe then they'd shine enough to be sold as buttons.

Margret. What's that? You? You? Look here, Mrs. Virgin, I'm a respectable person. But you? You can stare through seven pairs of leather pants.

Marie. Tramp! *(She slams the window.)* Come, little lad. What's it to them. You're just a poor whore's baby, and you make your mother happy with your illegitimate face.
(Sings)   Dear girl, why are you so sad?
    Because your child has no dad?
    Who cares if some think it wrong?
    I'll fill the night with my song.
    Heio popeio, my son, hurray!
    Who cares what the people may say?

    Hansel, harness your six horses fine,
    And be sure to feed them on time.
    Oats they won't eat for you,
    Water will never do.
    It must be cool white wine, hurray!
    It must be cool white wine.

> *(A knock at the window)*

Marie. Who's there? Is it you, Franz? Come in!

Woyzeck. Can't. Must go to roll call.

Marie. What's the matter, Franz?

Woyzeck *(mysteriously).* Marie, it happened again. A lot. Doesn't it say: And behold, smoke arose from the land like smoke from a furnace?

Marie. Franz!

Woyzeck. It followed me all the way back to town. What'll come of it.

Marie. Franz!

Woyzeck. I must go. *(He leaves.)*

Marie. That man! So weird. He didn't even look at his child. Those thoughts of his will drive him mad. Why are you so quiet, son? Are you scared? It's getting so dark, you'd think you're blind. Usually the street light shines in. I can't stand it. It gives me the creeps. *(She goes out.)*

III.   FAIR BOOTHS. LIGHTS. PEOPLE.

Old Man *(sings while a* **Child** *dances).*

> Everything on earth must end,
> Thus death awaits us all.
> On that you can depend.

Woyzeck. Hey! Hopla! Poor man, old man! Poor child! Young child! Joy and sorrow! Hey, Marie, shall we . . . ? Beautiful world!

Barker *(in front of a booth).* Ladies and Gentlemen. Here you can see the astronomical horse and the little cannybird. They are the favorites of all European potentates and members of all learned societies. They tell the people everything: how old, how many children, what sicknesses. Shoots a pistol. Stands on one leg. It's all education. They only have beastly reason, or rather a very reasonable beastliness. They're not beastly stupid individuals like many people—the respected audience excluded. Enter! It will now take place. The presentation. The commencement of the commencement will immediately begin.

Observe the progress of civilization. Everything progresses: a horse, a monkey, a cannybird! The monkey is already a soldier. That's not yet much, to be sure. The lowest level of the human race.

Sergeant. Drum Major.

Sergeant. Hold it! Look at her! What a broad.

Drum Major. By God! For reproducing cavalry regiments and for breeding Drum Majors.

Sergeant. Look how she carries her head. You'd think that black hair would pull her down with its weight. And those eyes, black . . .

Drum Major. It's like looking into a well or down a chimney. Come on! After her!

Marie. What lights!

Woyzeck. Hey, what a night!

Inside the booth.

Showman. Show your talent! Show your beastly rationality. Put human society to shame. Gentlemen, this animal you see here, with its tail on its body and standing on its four hoofs, is a member of all learned societies, is a professor at our university, where the students learn from him how to ride and fight. That was simple reason. Think now with double reason. What do you do when you think with double reason? Is there a jackass there in the learned society? *(The horse nods.)* Now do you see the double reason? That is beast-iognomy.* Indeed, this is no beastly stupid individual; this is a person. A human. A beastly human, and yet an animal, *une bête. (The horse behaves improperly.)* That's it, put society to shame. Observe that the beast is still nature, unideal nature! Learn from him. Ask the doctor—it's extremely injurious. It has been said: Man, be natural. You are made of dust, sand, muck. Do you want to be more than dust, sand, muck? Look at that reason. He can add, even though he can't count on his fingers. Why? He just can't express himself, can't explain. He's a transformed person. Tell the gentlemen what time it is. Which of you gentlemen and ladies has a watch? A watch?

Sergeant. A watch! *(Deliberately and ostentatiously taking a watch from his pocket.)* There you are, Sir.

---

*The German word is *Viehsionomik,* a neologism formed by combining *Vieh* (cattle, beast) with *Physionomik* (Physiognomy). The pronunciation of the two words *Viehsionomik* and *Physionomik* differs only slightly in the first vowel sound.

Marie. That I must see. *(She climbs into the first row. The* **Sergeant** *helps her.)*

IV. MARIE'S ROOM.

Marie *sitting with her* **Child** *on her lap, holding a piece of mirror.*

Marie *(looking into the mirror).* How the stones sparkle! I wonder what kind they are? What did he say? —Sleep, son! Close your eyes. Tight. *(The* **Child** *covers his eyes with his hands.)* Tighter. That's it. Now stay that way, or he'll fetch you. *(She sings.)*

> Hurry, girl, and lock up tight.
> A gypsy boy will come tonight.
> He will take you by the hand
> And lead you into gypsy land.

(Looking into the mirror again.) It must be gold! People like me have only a little corner in the world and a small piece of mirror; and yet I have as red a mouth as the grandest ladies with their full-length mirrors and their handsome gentlemen, who kiss their hands. I'm just a poor woman. —*(The* **Child** *sits up.)* Quiet, child! Close your eyes! There's the Sandman. He's running across the wall. *(She flashes with the mirror.)* Close your eyes or he'll throw sand in them and blind you.

*(***Woyzeck*** enters behind her. She starts and covers her ears.)*

Woyzeck. What've you got?

Marie. Nothin'!

Woyzeck. It's shining under your fingers.

Marie. A little earring. I found it.

Woyzeck. I've never found anything like that. Two at once.

Marie. Am I a whore?

Woyzeck. It's all right, Marie. —How the child sleeps. Reach under his arm; the chair is pressing him. His forehead is covered with shiny drops. Everything under the sun is work. Sweat, even in sleep. Us poor people! Here's some more money, Marie. My pay and something from the Captain.

Marie. God bless you for it, Franz.

Woyzeck. I must go. See you tonight, Marie. So long.

Marie *(alone, after a pause).* I really am a whore. I could stab myself.—Oh! What a world! Everything goes to the devil, man and woman.

V. THE CAPTAIN. WOYZECK.
The **Captain** *in a chair,* **Woyzeck** *shaving him.*

Captain. Slow down, Woyzeck, slow down! One thing at a time. You're making me dizzy. What'll I do with the ten minutes you save by finishing too early today? Just think, Woyzeck, you still have a good thirty years to live. Thirty years! That makes 360 months! And days! Hours! Minutes! What are you going to do with that horrible stretch of time? Portion it out, Woyzeck.

Woyzeck. Yes sir, Captain.

Captain. I fear for the world, when I think about eternity. Activity, Woyzeck, activity! Eternal, that is eternal, that is eternal. You understand that. But then again it is not eternal, and that is a moment. Yes, a moment. Woyzeck, I shudder when I think that the earth turns around in one day. What a waste of time! What's the purpose of it all? Woyzeck, I can't look at a mill wheel anymore, or I become melancholy.

Woyzeck. Yes sir, Captain.

Captain. Woyzeck, you always look so disturbed. A good man doesn't do that. A good man who has a good conscience.— Why don't you say something, Woyzeck. How's the weather today?

Woyzeck. Bad, Captain, sir, bad: wind!

Captain. I feel it already. There's something very fast out there. Such a wind affects me the same way a mouse does. *(Slyly)* I think it's coming from the south-north.

Woyzeck. Yes sir, Captain.

Captain. Ha! Ha! Ha! South-north! HA! HA! HA! Oh, you're stupid! Dreadfully stupid! *(Moved)* Woyzeck, you're a good man, a good man, but *(with dignity)* Woyzeck, you have no morality! Morality—that is being moral. Do you understand? It's a good word. You have a child without the blessing of the Church, as our Right Reverend Chaplain says. Without the blessing of the Church. I didn't just make it up.

Woyzeck. Captain, sir, the good Lord won't judge the poor worm by whether or not an Amen was spoken before he was made. The Lord said: "Suffer little children to come unto me."

Captain. What's that you say? What kind of curious answer is that? You thoroughly confuse me with your answer. I don't mean him, I mean you, you.

Woyzeck. Us poor people. You see, Captain, sir, it's money, money. Whoever hasn't got money. What good is morality for someone like that? A person's also got his flesh and blood. People like us are wretched in this world and in the next. I think if we ever got into heaven, we'd have to help make thunder.

Captain. Woyzeck, you have no virtue; you are not a virtuous man. Flesh and blood? When I am lying at the window, after is has rained, and I follow the white stockings as they bound across the streets—damn it, Woyzeck, then I feel love. I, too, have flesh and blood. But, Woyzeck: virtue! Virtue! How else should I kill time? I always say to myself: You are a virtuous man, *(moved)* a good man, a good man.

Woyzeck. Yes, Captain, sir: Virtue! I haven't quite figured it out yet. You see, us common people, we don't have virtue. We just follow our nature. But if I was a gentleman and had a hat and a watch and a frock coat and could talk refined, then I'd sure want to be virtuous. There must be something beautiful about virtue, Captain, sir. But I'm a poor guy.

Captain. Good, Woyzeck. You're a good man, a good man. But you think too much. That's ruinous. You always look so driven. Our discussion has completely exhausted me. Go now and don't run so fast. Slowly, nice and slowly down the street.

VI.   MARIE'S ROOM.

Marie. Drum Major.

Drum Major. Marie!

Marie *(looking at him, expressively)*. Go on—let me look at you! Chest broad as a bull's and a beard like a lion's! No other man's like that. I'm the proudest of women.

Drum Major. By damn, Marie, you should see me on Sunday, when I wear my plumed helmet and white gloves! The Prince always says: "By God, you're quite a man!"

Marie *(mockingly).* Is that so?! *(Goes up to him.)* Man!

Drum Major. And you're quite a woman. By God, let's lay up a brood of drum majors. Hey? *(He embraces her.)*

Marie *(irritably).* Let me go!

Drum Major. Wild animal!

Marie *(violently).* Just touch me!

Drum Major. Is that the devil in your eyes?

Marie. For all I care. It makes no difference.

VII.   IN THE STREET.

Marie. Woyzeck.

Woyzeck *(looks fixedly at her, shakes his head).* Hm! I see nothing. I see nothing. Oh, I should be able to see it. I should be able to grasp it with my fists.

Marie *(frightened).* What's the matter, Franz? You're raving, Franz.

Woyzeck. A sin so big and so fat. It stinks so much, it should smoke the angels out of heaven. You have a red mouth, Marie. No blister on it? Farewell, Marie, you're as beautiful as sin. Can mortal sin be so beautiful?

Marie. Franz, you have a fever.

Woyzeck. Damn it! — Is that where he stood? Like this? Like this?

Marie. Because the day is long and the world old, lots of people can stand in one place — one after the other.

Woyzeck. I saw him!

Marie. You can see a lot, if you have two eyes and aren't blind and the sun is shining.

Woyzeck. With these eyes!

Marie *(boldly).* What of it!

VIII.   AT THE DOCTOR'S.

Woyzeck. The Doctor.

Doctor. What's that I saw, Woyzeck? A man of his word.

Woyzeck. What do you mean, Doctor, sir.

Doctor. I saw it, Woyzeck. You pissed on the street. You pissed on the wall like a dog. And I give you two groschen a day. That's bad, Woyzeck. The world's going bad, very bad.

Woyzeck. But Doctor, sir, when nature calls.

Doctor. Nature calls! Nature calls! Have I not proved that the *musculus contrictor vesicae* is subject to the will? Nature! Woyzeck, man is free. In man individuality is exalted into freedom. Not able to hold your water! *(Shakes his head, puts his hands behind his back, and paces back and forth.)* Have you already eaten your peas, Woyzeck? There will be a revolution in science. I'm blowing it sky-high. Urea, 0.10, ammonium hypochlorate, hyperprotoxide.

Woyzeck, don't you have to piss again? Go on in there and try.

Woyzeck. I can't, Doctor, sir.

Doctor *(with emotion).* But you can piss on the wall! I have it in writing, the contract in hand. I saw it, saw it with my own eyes. I was just sticking my nose out the window and letting in the sun's rays, in order to examine the process of sneezing. *(Goes toward him.)* No, Woyzeck, I'm not angry. Anger is unhealthy; it is unscientific. I'm calm, perfectly calm. My pulse is beating its customary sixty, and I'm speaking to you with utmost cold-bloodedness. God forbid that I should get upset about a man. A man! Now if it were a proteus that easily dies on you! But you shouldn't have pissed on the wall. —

Woyzeck. You see, Doctor, frequently a person has such a character, such a constitution. —But with nature it's something different. You see, with nature *(he snaps his fingers)* it's like that. How should I say it—for example . . .

Doctor. Woyzeck, you're philosophizing again.

Woyzeck *(confidingly).* Doctor, have you seen anything of double nature? When the sun is at midday and it seems as if the world were bursting into flames, a terrible voice spoke to me!

Doctor. Woyzeck, you have an *aberratio*.

Woyzeck *(puts his finger to his nose).* The toadstools, Doctor. That, that's where it is. Have you ever seen in what kinds of figures the toadstools grow on the ground? Whoever could read that.

Doctor. Woyzeck, you've got the most beautiful *aberratio mentalis partialis*. The second type. Beautifully developed. Woyzeck, you're getting a raise. The second type: fixed idea, with generally rational condition. Do you still do everything as usual? Shave your Captain?

Woyzeck. Yes, sir.

Doctor. Eat your peas?

Woyzeck. Quite regularly, Doctor, sir. My wife gets my allowance for food.

Doctor. Carry out your orders?

Woyzeck. Yes, sir.

Doctor. You're an interesting case. Subject Woyzeck, you get a raise. Behave yourself. Show me your pulse. Yes.

IX.   STREET.

Captain. Doctor. *The* **Captain** *comes panting along the street, stops, pants, looks around.*

Captain. Doctor, the horses make me terribly afraid; when I think that the poor beasts have to go on foot. Don't run like that. Don't paddle like that with your cane in the air. You're chasing after death. A good man who has a good conscience doesn't walk so fast. A good man . . . *(He catches the* **Doctor** *by the coat.)* Doctor, permit me to save a human life. You're rushing . . .

Doctor, I'm so melancholy. There is something fanciful about me. I always have to cry when I see my coat hanging on the wall. There it hangs.

Doctor. Hm! Puffed up, fat, thick neck, apoplectic constitution. Yes, Captain, you may be getting *apoplexia cerebralis*. But you might get it on only one side and just be paralyzed on that side. Or, if all goes well, it may only paralyze your mind, and you will simply vegetate from then on. That just about covers your prospects for the next four weeks. Incidentally, I can assure you that you provide one of the more interesting cases. And if it be God's will that your tongue become partially paralyzed, we'll perform the most immortal experiments.

Captain. Doctor, don't frighten me. People have died of fright, of pure, sheer fright. —I can already see the people now with their hats in their hands. But they will say: He was a good man, a good man. —You devil's coffinnail!

Doctor *(holding out his hat)*. What is this, Captain? This is hollowhead!

Captain *(holds out his glove)*. What is this, Doctor? This is empty-handed.

Doctor. I bid you farewell, my dear Mr. Drillcock.

Captain. Likewise, dear Mr. Coffinnail.

X. THE GUARDHOUSE.

Woyzeck. Andres.

Andres *(sings)*.   The hostess has a pretty maid.
                         She's in her garden night and day;
                         She sits there in the garden . . .

Woyzeck. Andres!

Andres. Huh?

Woyzeck. Nice weather.

Andres. Sunny Sunday weather. There's music outside town. A while ago the broads went out there. Everybody's hot. Such excitement!

Woyzeck *(restlessly)*. Dancing, Andres, they're dancing?!

Andres. At the Horse and the Star.

Woyzeck. Dancing! Dancing!

Andres. For all I care.
            She sits there in the garden.
            She stays there till the clock strikes twelve
            And watches all the gua-ardsmen.

Woyzeck. Andres, I can't calm down.

Andres. Fool!

Woyzeck. I've got to go out. It won't stop spinning in my head. Dancing! Dancing! What hot hands they have. Damn it, Andres!

Andres. What do you want?

Woyzeck. I've got to go.

Andres. With that whore.

Woyzeck. I've got to get out. It's so hot in here.

XI.   THE INN.

> *The windows are open. Dancing.*
> *Benches in front of the inn. Journeymen.*

First Journeyman.   I have on a shirt that is not mine
                           My soul, it stinks of brandywine . . .

Second Journeyman. Brother, shall I in friendship knock a hole in nature for you? Onward! I want to knock a hole in nature. I'm quite a guy, too, you know; I want to kill every flea on his body.

First Journeyman. My soul, my soul, it stinks of brandywine. Even money falls into decay. Forget-me-not! How beautiful this world is! Brother, I must cry a rain barrel full. I wish our noses were bottles, and we could pour them down each other's throats.

Others *(in chorus).*

> A hunter from the Rhine
> Rode once through a forest green,
> Hallee, hallo, how merry is the hunting life.
> A hunting we will go.
> A hunting we will go.

> *(***Woyzeck*** stands at the window. **Marie** and the*
> ***Drum Major*** *dance by without noticing him.)*

Marie *(dancing by).* Go on! Go on!

Woyzeck *(chocking).* Go on! —Go on! *(He starts up violently and sinks back on the bench.)* Go on, go on. *(Pounding his fist into his open hand.)* Roll around! Wallow! Why doesn't God blow out the sun, so everything can roll around together in lechery! Man and woman, man and beast! They do it in broad daylight, do it on your hands like flies. —Woman. —That woman is hot, hot! —Go on, go on. *(Starts up.)* That scoundrel! The way he paws her, gropes around on her body. He — he's got her like I did at first.

First Journeyman *(preaching from a table).* However, when a wanderer, who stands leaning by the stream of time or who answers divine wisdom and addresses himself: Why is man? Why is Man?—But verily I say unto you: How could the farmer, the cooper, the cobbler, the doctor live, if God had not created man? How could the tailor live, if God had not implanted the sense of shame in man? How could the soldier live, if God had not armed men with the urge to kill each other? Therefore doubt ye not. Yea, Yea! It is lovely and fine, but everything earthly is vain—even money falls into decay. —In conclusion, my beloved followers, let us now piss crosswise so that a Jew will die.

XII.   OPEN FIELD.

Woyzeck. Go on! Go on! Quiet! Musik! *(Bends toward the ground.)* Ha! What? What's that you say? Louder! Louder! —Stab, stab the bitch dead? Stab, stab the bitch dead. Should I? Must I? Do I hear it there too? Does the wind say it too? Do I always hear it going on? Go on! Stab dead! Dead!

XIII.   NIGHT.

Andres *and* Woyzeck *in a bed.*

Woyzeck *(shaking Andres).* Andres! Andres! I can't sleep. When I close my eyes, it keeps spinning, and I hear the fiddles: go on, go on! And then it speaks from the wall. Don't you hear anything?

Andres. Sure. Let them Dance! God protect us, Amen. *(Falls asleep again.)*

Woyzeck. It keeps saying: Stab! Stab! And it slices between my eyes like a knife.

Andres. You should drink some schnapps with powder in it. That cuts the fever.

XIV.   THE INN.

Drum Major. Woyzeck. People.

Drum Major. I'm a man! *(He pounds his chest.)* A man, I say. Who wants to start something? Whoever's no drunken God

Almighty better keep away from me. I'll pound his nose up his ass. I'll . . . *(to* **Woyzeck***)* You there, drink up! A man must drink. I wish the world was schnapps, schnapps.

Woyzeck *(whistles).*

Drum Major. Scoundrel, shall I pull your tongue out of your throat and wrap it around your waist? *(They wrestle.* **Woyzeck** *loses.)* Shall I leave you as much breath as an old woman's fart? Shall I?

Woyzeck *(sits down on the bench, trembling from exhaustion.)*

Drum Major. Let the scoundrel whistle till he's blue in the face. Ha!

> Brandywine is life for me!
> Brandy gives me courage!

A Man. He really let him have it.

Another. He's bleeding.

Woyzeck. One thing after the other.

XV.   PAWNSHOP.

Woyzeck. The Jew.

Woyzeck. The pistol costs too much.

Jew. So buy it or don't buy it. What'll it be?

Woyzeck. How much is the knife?

Jew. It's strong and straight. Want to cut your throat with it? Well, so what? I'll give it to you as cheap as anybody. You'll get your death cheap, but not for nothing. So what? You'll get an economical death.

Woyzeck. This can cut more than bread.

Jew. Two groschen.

Woyzeck. There! *(He goes out.)*

Jew. There! Like it were nothing! And yet it's money! The dog!

XVI.   MARIE'S ROOM.

Marie. The Fool.

Marie *(leafing in the Bible).* "And no deceit was found in his mouth." God Almighty! God Almighty! Don't look at me. *(Leafs again.)* "And the Pharisees brought unto him a woman taken in adultery and set her in their midst. —And Jesus said unto her: Neither do I condemn thee; go, and sin no more!" *(Strikes her hands together.)* God Almighty! God Almighty! I can't. Lord God, just give me enough so I can pray. *(The* **Child** *presses up against her.)* The child gives me a stab in the heart. Carl! It struts in the sunlight!

Fool *(lying down, telling himself fairy tales on his fingers).* This one has the golden crown—His Majesty, the King. Tomorrow I'm going to fetch the Queen's child. Blood-sausage says: Come Liversausage! *(He takes the* **Child** *and quiets down.)*

Marie. Franz hasn't come! Not yesterday, not today. It's getting hot in here. *(She opens the window.)*

"And stood at his feet weeping, and began to wash his feet with tears, and did wipe them with the hairs of her head, and kissed his feet, and annointed them with ointment." *(Striking her breast.)* Everything dead! Savior, Savior, I would like to anoint Your feet.

XVII. THE BARRACKS.

Andres. Woyzeck *rummaging through his belongings.*

Woyzeck. Andres, this jacket is not part of the uniform. You can use it, Andres. The crucifix is my sister's, and the ring. I also have a picture of a Saint, with two hearts and beautiful gold. It was in my mother's Bible, and it says:

> Let suffering be my reward;
> Through suffering I praise the Lord.
>
> As your body, Lord, was red and sore,
> Let my heart be for evermore.

My mother only feels now when the sun shines on her hands. It doesn't matter.

Andres *(blankly answers to everything).* Sure.

Woyzeck *(pulls out a paper).* Friedrich Johann Franz Woyzeck. Soldier. Fusilier in the Second Regiment, Second Battallion, Fourth Company. Born on the Feast of the Annunciation. Today I am thirty years, seven months, and twelve days old.

Andres. Franz, you'd better go to the infirmary. Poor guy, you should drink schnapps with powder in it. That kills the fever.

Woyzeck. Yes, Andres, when the carpenter makes his wooden box, nobody knows who will lie in it.

XVIII.   IN FRONT OF THE HOUSE DOOR.

Marie *with young* **Girls. Grandmother.** *Then* **Woyzeck.**

Girls.   The sun shines bright at Candlemas;
         The grain is in full bloom.
         They marched together down the street
         They marched along in pairs.
         The pipers marched in front;
         The fiddlers came behind.
         The socks they wore were red . . .

First Child. That's not pretty.

Second Child. You're never satisfied!

Third Child. Why did you start first?

First Child. Why?

Second Child. Because!

Third Child. But why because?

Second Child. Someone must sing. —

First Child. Marie, *you* sing for us.

Marie. Come, you little scamps.
         Ringel, ringel rosary. King Herod . . .
    Grandmother, tell a story.

Grandmother. Once upon a time there was a poor child, and it had no father and mother. Everyone was dead and there was nobody left in the whole world. Everything dead. And it wandered around and whined day and night. And because there was nobody left on earth, it wanted to go to heaven. And the moon looked down so friendly. And when it finally got to the moon, it was a piece of rotten wood. And then it went to the sun. And when it got to the sun, it was a dead sunflower. And when it got to the stars, they were little gold flies—stuck up there as if caught in a spider's web. And when it wanted to go back to the earth, the earth was an over-turned chamber pot. And it was all alone. And then it sat down and cried. And it sits there still and is all alone.

Woyzeck. Marie!

Marie *(startled)*. What do you want?

Woyzeck. Marie, let's go. It's time.

Marie. Where to?

Woyzeck. How should I know?

XIX.   EVENING. THE TOWN IN THE DISTANCE.
Marie *and* **Woyzeck.**

Marie. So the town's over that way. It's dark.

Woyzeck. You must stay awhile. Come sit down.

Marie. But I have to go.

Woyzeck. You won't get sore feet from walking.

Marie. What's gotten into you?!

Woyzeck. Do you know how long it's been now, Marie?

Marie. Two years on Pentecost.

Woyzeck. Do you also know how long it's going to be?

Marie. I must go make supper.

Woyzeck. Are you freezing, Marie? And yet you're warm. How hot your lips are! Hot—hot whore's breath. But still I'd give heaven to kiss them once more.
When you're cold, you don't freeze any more. You won't freeze in the morning dew.

Marie. What are you saying?

Woyzeck. Nothing. *(Silence)*

Marie. How red the moon is rising.

Woyzeck. Like a bloody knife.

Marie. What's on your mind? Franz, you're so pale. Stop Franz! For God's sake! He-Help!

Woyzeck. Take that, and that! Can't you die? There! There! Ha! She's still twitching. Not yet? Not yet? Still not yet? *(He keeps on stabbing.)* Are you dead? Dead! Dead! *(People approach. He drops the knife and runs away.)*

XX.   PEOPLE APPROACH.

First Person. Wait!

Second Person. Do you hear? Quiet! Over there!

First Person. Uuh! There! What a sound!

Second Person. It's the water. It's calling. Nobody has drowned for a long time. Let's go! It's not good to hear that.

First Person. Uuh, there it is again. Like a person dying.

Second Person. It's eerie. So misty. Fog everywhere. Gray. And the beetles humming like cracked bells. Let's go!

First Person. No, it's too clear, too loud. Up there! Come on.

XXI.   THE IDIOT. THE CHILD. WOYZECK.

Carl *(holding the* **Child** *on his knees and playing a finger game).* He fell in the water; he fell in the water, ho, he fell in the water.

Woyzeck. Son! Christian!

Carl *(looking at him fixedly).* He fell in the water.

Woyzeck *(attempts to caress the* **Child** *who turns away and screams).* God Almighty!

Carl. This one fell in the water.

Woyzeck. Christian, you're to get a hobby-horse. There, there. *(The* **Child** *resists. To* **Carl***)* Here, buy the lad a hobby-horse.

Carl *(looks at him blankly).*

Woyzeck. Hop! Hop! Horse.

Carl *(jubilantly).* Hop! Hop! Horse! Horse! *(Runs off with the* **Child***.)*

XXII.   THE INN.

Woyzeck. Dance, all of you! Sweat and stink! He'll get you all someday.

> The hostess has a pretty maid.
> She's in her garden night and day;
> She sits there in the garden.
> She stays there till the clock strikes twelve
> And watches all the guardsmen.

(He dances.) Enough Kate! Sit down! I'm hot, hot. *(He takes off his jacket.)* That's the way it is: the devil fetches one and lets the other go. Kate, you're hot! Why is that? Kate, you too will grow cold. Be reasonable. Can't you sing something?

Kate.   To Swabia I've never gone;

Nor flowing gowns do I put on.
For flowing gowns and pointed shoes
A servant girl should never choose.

Woyzeck. No! No shoes. One can go to hell without shoes.

Kate.   Oh phooey, my dear, I don't like your tone;
                 So keep your money and sleep alone.

Woyzeck. Yes, indeed! I don't want to make myself bloody.

Kate. But what do you have on your hand?

Woyzeck. Me? Me?

Kate. Red! Blood! *(People gather around them.)*

Woyzeck. Blood? Blood.

Innkeeper. Uuh blood!

Woyzeck. I think I cut myself, here on my right hand.

Innkeeper. Then how did it get on your elbow?

Woyzeck. I wiped it off.

Innkeeper. What? With your right hand on your right elbow?
You're talented.

Fool. And then the giant said: I smell, I smell, I smell human
flesh. Pooh! It stinks already!

Woyzeck. Damn it, what do you want? It's none of your business! Make way! Or the first one—damn it! Do you think I
killed someone? Am I a murderer? Why are you gaping?
Look at yourselves! Make way there! *(He runs out.)*

XXIII. STREET.

Children.

First Child. Let's go! Marie!

Second Child. What's up?

First Child. Don't you know? Everybody's gone out already.
There's a body out there!

Second Child. Where?

First Child. In the woods, near the red cross.

Second Child. Hurry, so we can still see something. They'll
soon take it away.

XXIV.   EVENING. THE CITY IN THE DISTANCE.

Woyzeck *alone.*

Woyzeck. The knife? Where's the knife? I left it here. It'll give me away! Closer! Still closer! What kind of a place is this. What's that I hear? Something's moving. Quiet. There, close by. Marie? Ha, Marie! Quiet. Everything quiet! Why are you so pale, Marie? What's that red string around your neck? Who gave you that necklace in payment for your sins? You were black from them, black! Have I made you white now? Why does your black hair hang so wild? Didn't you braid it today? Something's lying there! Cold. Wet. Still. Away from this place! The knife, the knife! Do I have it? Ah! People. —There. *(He runs off.)*

XXV.   WOYZECK BY A POND.

Woyzeck. There, in it goes! *(He throws the knife into the pond.)* It sinks into the dark water like a stone! The moon is like a bloody knife! Does the whole world want to blab it out? No, it's too close. When they swim . . . *(He goes into the pond and throws it further out.)* There now. But in the summer, when they go diving for mussels . . . Bah! It'll get rusty. Who'd recognize it. —If only I'd broken it. Am I still bloody? I must wash myself. There's a spot; and there's another.

NOTES

Preface

1. Walter Höllerer, "Büchner, 'Dantons Tod,'" in *Das deutsche Drama vom Barock bis zur Gegenwart: Interpretationen,* ed. Benno von Wiese (Düsseldorf: August Bagel Verlag, 1958), 2:65-66.

2. Antonin Artaud, *The Theater and Its Double* (New York: Grove Press, 1958), pp. 89, 99-100.

3. "*Dantons Tod* renews the possibilities of political drama. *Leonce und Lena* is a dream-play, a fusion of irony and heart's abandon that is still in advance of the modern theatre. *Woyzeck* is not only the historical source of "expressionism"; it poses in a new way the entire problem of modern tragedy. *Lenz* carries the devices of the narrative to the verge of surrealism." George Steiner, *The Death of Tragedy* (New York: Hill & Wang, 1963), pp. 271-272.

I. Georg Büchner: 1813-1837

1. References are to Werner R. Lehmann's Hamburg edition of Büchner's works: *Georg Büchner. Sämtliche Werke und Briefe. Historisch-kritische Ausgabe mit Kommentar,* vol. 1: *Dichtungen und Übersetzungen mit Dokumentationen zur Stoffgeschichte;* vol. 2: *Vermischte Schriften und Briefe;* vols. 3 and 4 announced (Hamburg: Christian Wegner Verlag, [1967—]). The translations are my own. Unless otherwise indicated, the italics throughout this chapter are Büchner's.

2. "Prolegomena zu einer historisch-kritischen Büchner-Ausgabe," in *Gratulatio. Festschrift für Christian Wegner zum 70. Geburtstag* (Hamburg: Christian Wegner Verlag, 1963), pp. 197-213.

3. See Fritz Bergemann, ed., *Georg Büchner: Werke und Briefe,* 7th ed. (Wiesbaden: Insel-Verlag, 1958), pp. 555-557. Subsequent quotations from this edition of Büchner's works will be indicated by the letter B followed by the page reference.

4. Perillus or Perilaos, a Greek sculptor, is said to have cast a metal steer for the tyrant Phalaris of Agrigento. The tyrant had his victims placed inside the steer and a small fire lit underneath. The screams of the slowly dying men

sounded like the steer's bellowing. According to the legend, Perilaos himself was the first victim. Cf. Heinz Fischer, *Georg Büchner: Untersuchungen und Marginalien,* Studien zur Germanistik, Anglistik und Komparatistik, no. 14 (Bonn: H. Bouvier Verlag, 1972), p. 97.

5. In view of the fact that Büchner's letter on fatalism is considered by Lehmann to have been written after 10 March 1834 rather than in November 1833, as Bergemann assumed, the deterministic statement contained in a letter from February 1834 is of special interest: "*I do not despise anyone,* since it is in no one's power not to become a dullard or a criminal—since the same conditions would probably make us all the same, and since the conditions lie outside us. *Reason,* moreover, is only a very small part of our mental being, and education is only a fortuitous form of it" (II.422). Since this letter already reflects Büchner's discovery and changed attitude, the crisis Büchner describes in the later letter to his fiancée must have occurred quite a while before the letter was written and may have preceded or accompanied his physical breakdown. On the other hand, Lehmann's dating may be incorrect.

6. Wilhelm Grimm described the contemporary situation in Germany as follows: "Freedom was gradually reduced to a degree that cannot even be imagined by someone who did not actually experience it. Every frankness, let alone freedom, of speech was suppressed. The police, public and secret, regular and volunteer, penetrated all relationships and poisoned the trust of social life. All the pillars upon which the existence of a people rests, religiosity, justice, respect for morality and law, were overthrown or forcefully shaken. Only one thing was preserved: every resistance to the expressed will, whether direct or indirect, was a crime." (Quoted in Hans Magnus Enzensberger, *Georg Büchner. Ludwig Weidig. Der Hessische Landbote: Texte, Briefe, Prozessakten* [Frankfurt am Main: Insel-Verlag, 1965], p. 40.) In looking back from the year 1847, Friedrich Engels described the power structure of the time as follows: "Whereas the bourgeoisie had become powerful enough in France and England to overthrow, and raise itself into the position of, the ruling class in the state, the German bourgeoisie has not yet had such power. It has had a certain influence on the governments, but in all cases where their respective interests collide, its interests must give way to those of the landed aristocracy. Whereas in France and England the cities control the country, in Germany the country controls the city, agriculture predominates over commerce and industry.... The cause of this is the fact that civilization in Germany is not as far advanced. In those countries commerce and industry are the decisive means of support for the masses, whereas with us it is agriculture." (Quoted in Enzensberger, p. 38.) For more information on the political and social conditions of the time, the reader may be referred to Enzensberger's interesting collection of documents, to Karl Viëtor's fine discussions of the situation in Germany: *Georg Büchner. Politik, Dichtung, Wissenschaft* (Berne: Francke Verlag, 1949), pp. 30-72; and *Georg Büchner als Politiker,* 2nd ed. (Berne: Francke Verlag, 1950), and to Hans Mayer's broader presentation of the contemporary situation and events in Europe: *Georg Büchner und seine Zeit,* 2nd ed. (Wiesbaden: Limes Verlag, 1960), pp. 69-181, 208-256.

7. Viëtor, *Politik, Dichtung, Wissenschaft,* p. 92.

8. Ibid., p. 75.

9. Cf. Enzensberger, p. 123.

10. Becker was later sentenced to nine years in prison for his part in the preparation and distribution of *The Hessian Courier,* which was denounced by the government as "highly treasonous" and "unquestionably revolutionary." Amnestied in 1839, he emigrated to Switzerland and then to America, where he died in 1871.

11. I have restricted my discussion of the *Courier* to the parts generally assumed to have been written by Büchner. As indicated, Weidig added Biblical support to Büchner's arguments, and where Büchner mentioned the sham constitutions, Weidig included detailed information illustrating the meaninglessness of the Hessian constitution. He launched a direct and bitter attack against Ludwig I of Bavaria, whom he called a "monster," a "blasphemer," a "pig," and a "wolf." He also emphasized the idea of the unified Germany that could grow out of the Hessian revolution, which, he assumed, would spread to the other parts of Germany. Unlike Büchner, he did not attack the liberal bourgeoisie.

12. Quoted in Ernst Johann, *Georg Büchner in Selbstzeugnissen und Bilddokumenten,* Rowohlt Monographien, no. 18 (Hamburg: Rowohlt, 1958), p. 71.

13. Enzensberger, pp. 124-125.

14. Büchner and Weidig attempted to free Minnigerode from prison, but he was so severely weakened by the mistreatment of a cruel investigation that he could not carry out his part of the scheme.

15. Gutzkow's account of his reaction upon receiving Büchner's letter and manuscript is also of interest: "It was in the last days of February 1835 . . . that I had a group of older and younger fellow artists and friends of truth at my place. . . . Shortly before the meeting of the expected guests, I received from Darmstadt a manuscript and a letter, whose strange and disquieting content enticed me to read passages of the former. It was a play: *Danton's Death.* One could see how quickly it had been dashed off. . . . The scenes, the words followed each other rapidly and impetuously. It was the anxious language of someone being pursued, who had to take care of something quickly and then look for safety in flight. But this haste did not prevent the genius from demonstrating his extraordinary talent in short, sharp outlines. . . . The first scenes I read guaranteed him that very evening the accommodating, friendly interest of the bookseller Sauerländer." (Quoted in Johann, p. 104.)

16. Georg Büchner, *Sämtliche Werke und Briefe,* ed. Fritz Bergemann (Leipzig: Insel-Verlag, 1922), p. 608. The preface to *Leonce and Lena* consists of two questions, Alfieri's "E la Fama?" and Gozzi's "E la Fame?" which probably reflect the same polarity in answer to the question: Why do I write? See Jürgen Schröder, *Georg Büchners 'Leonce und Lena'. Eine verkehrte Komödie* (Munich-Allach: Wilhelm Fink Verlag, 1966), p. 194. In art as in life, real considerations, such as hunger, take precedence over the ideal and the abstract, such as fame.

17. *Lorenz Oken und Georg Büchner* (Zurich, 1936), quoted in Johann, p. 148.

18. The specific relationship of Büchner's aesthetics to his philosophical and scientific thinking will be discussed in more detail below, especially in connection with his remarks on literature in *Lenz*.

19. A student who had attended his course later wrote that "Büchner's presentation was not exactly brilliant, but fluent, clear, and succinct. He seemed anxious to avoid rhetorical embellishment . . . but what made these lectures especially valuable and so fascinating for the listeners were the repeated references to the meaning of the individual parts of the organs and to their comparison with those of the higher animals, whereby Büchner wisely knew how to keep his distance from the exaggerations of the so-called natural-philosophical [*natur-philosophische*] school (Oken, Carus, etc); it was also the extremely factual, vividly illustrative demonstrations with fresh preparations that Büchner . . . had for the most part to prepare himself. . . . Both these elements, the constant reference to the importance of the parts and the graphic demonstrations with fresh preparations truly stimulated the liveliest interest of the listeners. In my eight years of study . . . I have attended many courses, but I know of none which has remained so alive in my memory as this torso of Büchner's lectures on the comparative anatomy of fish and amphibians" (B.572-573).

20. Wilhelm Schulz, who was with Büchner when he died, wrote in an obituary notice in the *Züricher Zeitung* (23 February 1837) that Büchner apparently had a premonition of his early death. In his journal, which has not been preserved, he compared the condition of his soul to a fall evening and concluded: "I feel no nausea, no disgust; but I am tired, very tired. May the Lord give me rest!" (B.586).

21. Several of Büchner's literary figures cite the existence of pain and suffering as proof that there is no God (I.48) or that God is a sadist who enjoys seeing his creatures suffer (I.71-72, 98). The obvious discrepancy between the death-bed utterance and the recurring theme of the artistic works has lead some writers to consider the former to be a fabrication or a misunderstanding. The second part of the statement, on the other hand, certainly is in accord with Büchner's view of man and almost reproduces a line from *Woyzeck* (I.412). Did the nearness of death cause Büchner to change his attitude toward suffering and God? The unanswerable question which intrigues the biographer has little significance for the interpreter and the critic.

II. *Danton's Death*

1. Compare Büchner's assessment of the French Revolution in the latter part of *The Hessian Courier* (II.46-50). Büchner's general appraisal of the Revolution and many of his statements concerning the inequity of the laws and distribution of wealth and privilege and the self-serving inhumanity of the rich and educated are remarkably similar to those expressed by "Gracchus" Babeuf in his defense at Vendôme (February-May 1797) and elsewhere. Perhaps Büchner was familiar with the ideas of this early communist.

2. "The place should be safe—for my memory, but not for me. The grave gives me more security. At least it secures *forgetting* for me! It kills my

memory. There, however [in Paris], my memory lives and kills me. I or it? The answer is easy. (*He stands up and turns back*.) "I'm flirting with death. It is quite pleasant to ogle it from a distance through the lorgnon. Actually I must laugh at the whole matter. There is a feeling of permanence in me that says it will be tomorrow as it is today, and everything the day after tomorrow and beyond will be like now. It is all empty commotion! They want to frighten me. They won't dare" (II.iv).

References following quotations from *Danton* are to act and scene. Where no reference is given, the quotation is from the scene last cited. The translations are my own.

3. In his discussion of the "open drama" Volker Klotz notes the frequent occurrence of the open window as the means through which the outer world penetrates into the room or inner world of a person and acts upon him. Referring first to the scene where Danton is by the window he writes: "Here the world of Paris at night enters through the window into Danton's lonesome room and provokes his pangs of conscience. The room is the private space of the individual; it separates him from his fellow players, who reside in their own rooms. But the opponent, the world, breaks in through the window; the lonely person communicates with it. A counterpart to this scene is I.vi, in which Robespierre, alone in the dark room, goes to the window and feeds his monologue from impressions received from outside, an outside which recognizes metaphor as an independent, living, and effective force: 'The night snores above the earth and tosses in its riotous dream.'" *Geschlossene und offene Form im Drama,* Literatur als Kunst (Munich: Hanser, 1960), p. 134.

Similar examples are plentiful in *Danton's Death:* Marion looks out the window and sees her drowned lover being carried away. This causes the only "break in her being" she has ever experienced (I.v). The sensual world breaks in upon the young girls looking out of their windows when they witness copulating animals (I.v). Danton goes to a window to contemplate death and to send his thanks through the night to Julie for her promise to die with him (IV.iii); and Julie looks out of the window while waiting for the poison she has taken to end her life (IV.vi). It is significant that, with the exception of Lacroix's vulgar description of the girls learning about sexual life by looking out their windows, all the above scenes involve a confrontation with death and are poetic and lyrical.

4. See Matthew 18.7.

5. See Clemens Heselhaus, "Die Nemesis-Tragödie: Fiesko-Wallenstein-Demetrius," *Der Deutschunterricht,* vol. 4, no. 5 (1952): 44-59.

6. The historical Thomas Paine was not an atheist, as Büchner portrays him, but a deist.

7. Büchner agrees with Schopenhauer, with whose philosophy he may have been familiar, in the importance he attributes to suffering and in the solution he postulates for escaping it. Schopenhauer sees no other salvation from suffering than in the negation of the will-to-life, which means the abrogation of the *principium individuationis* or entrance into nothingness, the Buddhist's nirvana. For a detailed discussion of similarities between Büchner and Schopenhauer see Ingrid Krauss, *Studien über Schopenhauer und den Pessimismus in der deutschen Literatur des 19. Jahrhunderts* (Berne: Verlag Paul Haupt, 1931), pp. 28-104.

8. Lena in Büchner's *Leonce and Lena* expresses a similar view of the world: "My God, my God, is it true, then, that we must save ourselves with our pain? Is it true that the world is a crucified savior, the sun his crown of thorns, and the stars the nails and spears in his feet and loins?" (I.iv).

9. The song to which Camille refers is probably Schubart's "Der ewige Jude," in which Ahasverus cries "Ha! not to be able to die! not to be able to die!" Goethe, Platen, Chamisso, Arnim and others of the time also wrote about the wandering, "eternal" Jew. See Josef Jansen, ed., *Erläuterungen und Dokumente: Georg Büchner. Dantons Tod* (Stuttgart: Reclam, 1970), p. 39.

10. Cf. Büchner's letter from around 10 March 1834 (II.424-425), which was cited above, p. 11.

11. Both Gerhart Baumann (*Georg Büchner: Die dramatische Ausdruckswelt* [Göttingen: Vandenhoeck und Ruprecht, 1961], pp. 82-83) and Helmut Krapp (*Der Dialog bei Georg Büchner,* Literatur als Kunst [Darmstadt: Gentner, 1958], pp. 68-69) consider this statement to be inconsistent with Danton's earlier description of the world as the death of the void from which it was created. While Danton does often contradict himself, his remarks on nihilism are fully consistent with each other. Since the creation destroyed the void, it stands to reason that one cannot become part of the non-existent void—not even in death. The body is matter and therefore indestructible. Even after death it remains as part of the chaos of the world. When Danton says that nothingness is *"der zu gebärende Weltgott,"* he is not prophesying the birth of such a God, as has been interpreted, but designating the kind of God he would like to see come into existence, i.e., the god which *should* (or *ought to*) *be* born, not the god which is *yet to be* or that *will be* born. The interchangeable use of the designations "God" and "gods" does not constitute a contradiction, as Baumann would have it, since both of these words are used metaphorically to name what is unknown and ineffable, the force or forces which are superordinate to man and which act upon and through him to accomplish its or their purposes. It is the force Danton refers to when he asks: "Who spoke the *must*? Who? What is it in us that whores, lies, steals, and murders?" (II.v). The contradiction that does exist, and here Baumann is quite right, is between this nihilistic outlook and the affirmation of life expressed earlier by Camille in his reference to the "creation that . . . renews itself every moment" (II.iii).

12. The response of the Third Citizen provides a dramatically concentrated and graphic parallel to the last section of the *Courier,* in which Büchner describes the failure of the French Revolution: "**Third Citizen.** They have no blood in their veins except what they have sucked out of us. They told us: kill the aristocrats; they are wolves! We hanged the aristocrats on the lanterns. They said the Veto [King] eats your bread. We killed the Veto. They said the Girondists are starving you. We guillotined the Girondists. But they stripped the corpses, and we are still running on naked legs and freezing. Let's peel the skin from their thighs and make ourselves pants from it. Let's melt their fat and lard our soup with it. Away! Kill those with no holes in their coats!" (I.i).

13. See Kenneth Burke, *A Grammar of Motives* (Berkeley: University of California Press, 1969), p. 9.

14. See Wolfgang Martens, "Ideologie und Verzweiflung. Religiöse Motive in Büchner's Revolutionsdrama," *Euphorion* 54 (1960): 90-96. For an interesting comparison between the philosophical positions represented by Danton and Robespierre and the remarkably similar contrast between Epicureanism and Stoicism discussed by Pascal in his *Pensées* see Erwin Kobel, *Georg Büchner, Das dichterische Werk* (Berlin: Walter de Gruyter, 1974), pp. 48-94.

15. In *The Heavenly City of the Eighteenth-Century Philosophers* (New Haven: Yale University Press, 1932) Carl L. Becker points out that the philosophy and politics of eighteenth-century Enlightenment simply substitutes new ideas and concepts for the old Christian ones, thereby maintaining beliefs that were basically parallel to and even identical with the ones they had supposedly overthrown. Rousseau, Robespierre's model, was one of the leading thinkers in this movement. Becker writes: "The utopian dream of perfection, that necessary compensation for the limitations and frustrations of the present state, having been long identified with the golden age of the Garden of Eden or life eternal in the Heavenly City of God, and then by the sophisticated transferred to remote or imagined lands (the moon or Atlantis or Nowhere, Tahiti or Pennsylvania or Peking), was at last projected into the life of man on earth and identified with the desired and hoped-for regeneration of society" (p. 139). And: "Not until our own time have historians been sufficiently detached from religions to understand that the Revolution, in its later stages especially, took on the character of a religious crusade" (p. 155). Büchner anticipates these historians in having recognized the religious nature of the Revolution.

16. The historical Julie remarried and was still alive at the time Büchner wrote his play.

17. The reference may be to Marcus Junius Brutus rather than to the legendary Lucius Junius Brutus. Marcus Brutus was the consul designate who took part in the assassination of Caesar and had to flee Rome. His wife Porcia, whom he left behind, committed suicide.

18. For a discussion of the use of cynicism and wit as a defensive mechanism see Martin Grotjahn, *Beyond Laughter: Humor and the Subconscious* (New York: McGraw-Hill, 1966), pp. 63-65.

19. Compare Büchner's account of how he "almost killed" the judge Georgi through the "polite scorn" of his wit. See II.431-432, and p. 22 above.

20. "**Robespierre** *(reads).* 'This bloody Messiah Robespierre on his hill of Calvary between the two thieves Couthon and Collot: he sacrifices there and is not sacrificed. The Praying Sisters of the Guillotine stand at his feet like Mary and the Magdalene. Saint-Just, like John, is near to his heart and acquaints the Convention with the apocalyptic revelations of the master. He carries his head like a monstrance.'
Saint-Just. I'll make him carry his like St. Denis.

Robespierre *(continues to read).* 'Are we to believe that the Messiah's clean dress-coat is France's shroud and that the thin fingers which twitch about on the tribune are blades for the guillotine?
And you Barrère, who has said that coins would be minted on the Place de la Révolution. But—I don't want to stir up the old sack. He is a widow who has already had half a dozen men and has helped to bury them all. Who can

do anything about it? That is his gift. He can recognize a moribund face six months before death. After all, who wants to sit with corpses and smell their stench?' " (I.vi).

Couthon and Collot were Robespierre's henchmen. "The old sack" is a play on Barrère's family name de Vieuzac. St. Denis is a national saint of France who was martyred in the third century. After being decapitated on the Montmartre, he supposedly carried his head in his hand to the suburb now named for him.

21. "Something else can be noted when studying witty men at close range: how sick at heart most of them are underneath their witty defenses. They are hostile, lonely, often unloving and unloved; they feel near to tears and suffering; often they avoid disaster only by drinking, which leads to new complications" (Grotjahn, p. 47).

22. Saint-Just points out with pride that his words have had the power to kill: "Everyone may have his merits, but no one, neither an individual nor a smaller or larger class of individuals, may have privileges because of them. Every part of that sentence applied in reality has killed people. July 14, August 10, and May 31 are its punctuation marks. It needed four years to be carried out in the material world, and under normal circumstances it would have required a century and would have been punctuated by generations. Is it so astounding that the stream of the Revolution throws out its corpses with every sedimentation [*Absatz*, which also means paragraph], with every new turn?" (II.vii). The new turn which follows the execution of the Dantonists throws out Saint-Just's corpse along with those of the other members of Robespierre's faction. Compare also Barrère's statement: "Yes, go Saint-Just and construct your sentences in which every comma is a blow of the saber, and every period a chopped-off head" (III.vi).

23. Richard Thieberger, *La mort de Danton de Georg Büchner et ses sources* (Paris: Presses universitaires de France, 1953), p. 36.

24. See Reinhard Roche, "Stilus demagogicus: Beobachtungen an Robespierres Rede im Jacobinerklub. (Georg Büchner 'Dantons Tod')," *Wirkendes Wort* 14 (1964): 244-254.

25. Cf. Krapp, pp. 140-145.

26. The contrast in language between the high style and the low, the rhetorical and the lyrical, the idealistic and the realistic is discussed above. Within each of these categories there is also considerable variety. For example, Helmut Krapp identifies three main categories of rhetorical speech: "the programmatic dialogue," "the polemic dialogue," and the "logical deduction." Subcategories of the programmatic dialogue are the "program style" itself, as in the development by Danton's friends of their political program, and the "epigrammatic reduction," as in the epigrammatic remarks immediately preceding that statement. The inflammatory speeches of the First and Third Citizens in the second scene of the first act exemplify the polemic dialogue. The resemblance between these speeches and Büchner's polemical political pamphlet is noted above. The pure form of logical deduction is found above all in Saint-Just's speech to the National Convention (II.vii). (See Krapp, pp. 29-44.)

27. He may also have been inspired by Hamlet's instruction to the players.

28. Danton is talking about the nihilistic laughter of despair: it is the same laughter that seizes Lenz when he loses his last hope of preserving his sanity and is possessed by atheism, the laughter Büchner explains in a letter to his parents (II.423).

29. For a detailed analysis of the characteristics peculiar to each of these forms see the excellent study by Volker Klotz referred to above, n. 3.

30. A survey of the reception of Büchner's plays in the theater is appended to the present study.

III. *Leonce and Lena*

1. See Ingeborg Strudthoff, *Die Rezeption Georg Büchners durch das deutsche Theater,* Theater und Drama, vol. 19 (Berlin-Dahlem: Colloquium Verlag, 1957), p. 17.

2. Paul Landau, Introduction to *Gesammelte Schriften,* by Georg Büchner (Berlin: Paul Cassirer, 1909), 1:126-127.

3. Herbert Anton, "Die 'mimische Manier' in Büchners 'Leonce und Lena,'" in *Das deutsche Lustspiel,* ed. Hans Steffen (Göttingen: Vandenhoeck und Ruprecht, 1968), p. 227. Anton describes a dialectical process in which Büchner occupies a key position as mediator between the modernism of the nineteenth century and the modernism of the twentieth century. Wolfgang Kayser agrees that the Romantic comedy reached a high point with *Leonce and Lena.* See "'Grotesk! Grotesk!—Büchners Woyzeck," in *Das Groteske in Malerei und Dichtung* (Hamburg: Rowohlt, 1960), p. 75.

4. Günter Waldmann, "Georg Büchners Lustspiel 'Leonce und Lena' als realistische Selbstreductio ad absurdum des Romantisch-Idealistischen," *Pädagogische Provinz* 13 (1959): 348.

5. Wilhelm Hausenstein, Introduction to *Gesammelte Werke,* by Georg Büchner (Leipzig: Insel-Verlag, 1916), p. x.

6. Franz Schonauer, "Das Drama und die Geschichte: Versuch über Georg Büchner," *Deutsche Rundschau* 87 (1960): 546.

7. Friedrich Gundolf, "Georg Büchner. Ein Vortrag," in *Romantiker* (Berlin-Wilmersdorf: H. Keller, 1930), 1:390.

8. Armin Renker, *Georg Büchner und das Lustspiel der Romantik: Eine Studie über 'Leonce und Lena,'* Germanische Studien, vol. 34 (Berlin: Emil Ebering, 1924), p. 6.

9. Gonthier-Louis Fink, "Leonce et Lena. Comédie et réalisme chez Büchner," *Etudes Germaniques* 16 (1961): 223.

10. Renker, p. 35.

11. Ernst Leopold Stahl reportedly used that designation in a small essay that appeared in a publication of the Bochum Civic Theater. My source is Gustav Beckers, *Georg Büchners 'Leonce und Lena.' Ein Lustspiel der Langeweile* (Heidelberg: Carl Winter, 1961), p. 165.

12. Wolfgang Martens, review of *Georg Büchners 'Leonce und Lena.' Ein Lustspiel der Langeweile,* by Gustav Beckers, in *Euphorion* 58 (1964): 326.

13. George Steiner, *The Death of Tragedy* (New York: Hill & Wang, 1963), p. 271; Ernst Johann, *Georg Büchner in Selbstzeugnissen und Bilddokumenten,* Rowohlt Monographien, no. 18 (Hamburg: Rowohlt, 1958), p. 113;

Günther Penzoldt, *Georg Büchner, Friedrichs Dramatiker des Welttheaters,* vol. 9 (Velber bei Hannover: Erhard Friedrich, 1965), p. 34.

14. Herbert Samuel Lindenberger, *Georg Büchner* (Carbondale: Southern Illinois Press, 1964), p. 58.

15. Mario Carlo Abutille, *Angst und Zynismus bei Georg Büchner,* Basler Studien zur deutschen Sprache und Literatur, no. 40 (Berne: Francke Verlag, 1969), p. 78.

16. Jürgen Schröder, *Georg Büchners 'Leonce und Lena'. Eine verkehrte Komödie* (Munich-Allach: Wilhelm Fink Verlag, 1966), as subtitle.

17. Beckers, p. 182.

18. Helmut Krapp, *Der Dialog bei Georg Büchner,* Literatur als Kunst (Darmstadt: Gentner, 1958), p. 151.

19. Karl S. Guthke, *Geschichte und Poetik der deutschen Tragikomödie* (Göttingen: Vandenhoeck und Ruprecht, 1961), pp. 185-188. According to Guthke, Büchner creates a tragicomic atmosphere by presenting "the tragic in the garb of a comic manner of expression" (p. 187). Inherent in this definition is the questionable presupposition that the subject matter of a work of art exists independent of its presentation in a particular work. I would maintain that the subject matter and mode of expression cannot be separated: if the "manner of expression" is comic, the play is a comedy.

20. Wolfgang Hildesheimer, "Über Georg Büchner: Eine Rede," in *Interpretationen: James Joyce, Georg Büchner, Zwei Frankfurter Vorlesungen* (Frankfurt am Main: Insel-Verlag, 1969), p. 37. Hildesheimer also calls the play "a romantic fairy-tale-play" (p. 50).

21. Walter Müller-Seidel, Afterword to *Leonce und Lena,* by Georg Büchner, in *Klassische Deutsche Dichtung,* edited by Fritz Martini and Walter Müller-Seidel, vol. 17: *Lustspiele* (Freiburg i. Br.: Herder, 1962), p. 728. After noting this designation, which "paradoxically" has been used for the play, Müller-Seidel adds that *Leonce and Lena* resists all such attempts at classification.

22. Ronald Hauser, "Georg Büchner's *Leonce und Lena,*" *Monatshefte für deutschen Unterricht* 53 (1961): 346.

23. Hausenstein, p. xxix.

24. Erwin Scheuer, *Akt und Szene in der offenen Form des Dramas dargestellt an den Dramen Georg Büchners* (Berlin: Emil Ebering, 1929), p. 69.

25. Renker, p. 14.

26. E.D. Hirsch, *Validity in Interpretation* (New Haven: Yale University Press, 1967), p. 86.

27. One of the few critics to depart from this approach is Herbert Anton, who begins his fine article "Die 'mimische Manier' in Büchners *Leonce und Lena*" with the following critique: "With care and at great length Büchner scholarship has pursued motives which could account for the seriousness of the comedy. The symbolical levels and genera of the style which relativize it were scarcely considered. The comedy had to bear witness to the *tragic existence* of its creator, a *revolutionary* and *pessimist.* It was taken seriously as an allegory of melancholy, boredom, and *taedium vitae* and viewed as a *camera obscura* of grotesque characterization. The main figure, Prince Leonce, fared no better. As a *problematic nature* he stands in a long series of

problematic natures, beginning with Werther and continuing into the twentieth century. As an *aesthetic person* Leonce is lonely and proves to be at the same time a *modern Hamlet,* who is overtaken by life. Such a great force of interpretations is opposed by the delicacy of the comedy, which seems to claim its own right . . . " (p. 225).

28. See above, pp. 65-67.

29. For a different interpretation see Schröder, pp. 180-182.

30. Walter Kerr, *Tragedy and Comedy* (New York: Simon and Schuster, 1967), p. 17. When Kerr set out to write a book about comedy, he found he could not do it without writing a great deal about tragedy too. Comedy could not be defined on its own terms, he discovered, but only in its relation to tragedy.

31. Elder Olson, *The Theory of Comedy* (Bloomington: Indiana University Press, 1968), p. 23.

32. See Olson, pp. 13-14.

33. Friedrich Schlegel, *Prosaische Jugendschriften,* ed. J. Minor (Vienna, 1882), 2:189.

34. Büchner shares with his heroes their disillusionment and loss of faith in ideals, but he differs from them in his conclusion. Less than a month after describing how disturbed he was to learn that man is determined, he wrote his friend August Stöber: "I laugh at my foolishness and think that fundamentally there are nothing but empty nuts to crack. But one must ride on some sort of donkey under the sun, so I saddle mine in God's name" (II. 421-422). The reference is probably to *Don Quixote.* The alternative to death (Danton) or madness (Lenz) is to engage in some form of activity, regardless of how meaningless it may be. Büchner followed this alternate course with fierce determination and dedication.

35. Allardyce Nicoll cites degradation, incongruity, automatism, and the sense of liberation as primary sources of laughter, with incongruity undoubtedly being the greatest. See *The Theory of Drama* (New York: Benjamin Blom, 1966), pp. 196-199.

36. As with *Danton,* the passages from *Leonce and Lena* are located by act and scene, and the translations are my own.

37. Leonce's statement may have been influenced by Hamlet's suggestion to Guildenstern that his madness is feigned and designed to deceive: "I am but mad north-north-west. When the wind is southerly, I know a hawk from a handsaw" (II.ii). Goethe's *Dichtung und Wahrheit* may be another source. In discussing the connection of *Werther* to the nausea toward life which was widespread at that time, Goethe quotes a gardener as having called out in annoyance: "Must I always see these rain clouds moving from west to east!" (*Hamburger Ausgabe,* 6th ed., Vol. 9, p. 578). In the same paragraph Goethe mentions an Englishman who was so tired of getting dressed and undressed every day that he hanged himself. Büchner's Danton expresses a similar feeling (II.i), as did Büchner himself in a letter to his brother (II.460).

38. In his book-length study of Büchner's "comedy of boredom," Beckers sides with the Tutor in taking Leonce's boredom and melancholy seriously: "Leonce's life, which is paralyzed by boredom, is also darkened by his melancholy, for above the emptied landscape of the bored soul the cloud

[blackness] of melancholy has risen" (p. 58; the brackets are Becker's).

39. When Woyzeck agrees mechanically with everything the Captain says, the Captain exposes him in a similar fashion. Referring to the wind, he says: "I think it's coming from the south-north." When Woyzeck agrees as before, the Captain ridicules him for his stupidity (scene V).

40. Especially in *Woyzeck* Büchner succeeds in capturing the life of his major figures while at the same time giving the impression that they are puppets.

41. See Renker for a detailed comparison of *Leonce and Lena* with the Romantic plays from which Büchner borrowed (pp. 80-119) and for a discussion of the Romantic aspects of Büchner's comedy.

42. For a discussion of the "topos of outdoing" see Ernst Robert Curtius, *European Literature and the Latin Middle Ages* (New York: Harper Torchbooks, 1963), pp. 162-165; and Anton, pp. 226-227.

43. Cf. Karl Viëtor, *Georg Büchner: Politik, Dichtung, Wissenschaft* (Berne: Francke Verlag, 1949), pp. 182-183.

44. Cf. Renker, pp. 29, 69, and Peter Schmid, *Georg Büchner. Versuch über die tragische Existenz* (Berne: Paul Haupt Verlag, 1940), p. 21-22.

45. For the prototypal example of the author-director in Romantic comedy, compare the role of the "Poet" in Ludwig Tieck's *Der gestiefelte Kater*. In Tieck's play an actor in the guise of the author-director attempts to explain the play to the fictive audience, which is confused by the failure of the play-within-a-play to remain entirely on its own level of illusion. Cf. also the use of direct address, asides, soliloquies, and plays-within-plays in the Elizabethan drama, the primary source of the Romantic comedy.

46. Anton writes of this passage: "He [Valerio] takes over the introduction and solution of the intrigue, whose seriousness is excluded from the beginning by the fact that Valerio develops it from the hyperbolically extravagant *theatrum mundi* metaphor of the comedy and announces it as *play with a play*. For in the same moment in which Valerio demands a queen for the king and jack, Lena enters and Valerio can proclaim with hypocritical surprise: 'By God, there she is' " (p. 231).

47. Valerio's actual use of these analogies was in reference to one of the small countries through which they passed: "Here we are again on the border; that country is like an onion, nothing but layers, or like boxes placed one inside the other—in the biggest is nothing but boxes and in the littlest is nothing at all" (II.i); but they could be used to describe his identity, too, as Ibsen used the onion as a symbol for Peer Gynt.

48. My discussion of the symbolic meaning of the mirror is based on August Langen's article "Zur Geschichte des Spiegelsymbols in der deutschen Dichtung," *Germanisch-romanische Monatsschrift* 28 (1940): 269-280. Cf. also M.H. Abrams, *The Mirror and The Lamp* (1953; rpt. New York: Norton, 1958), esp. pp. 21-26, 30-46.

49. Langen, p. 273.

50. The symbol of the broken mirror also goes back to mystical literature: "For the mystic, every piece of the [broken] mirror is a self-contained totality; each contains God in his fullness and infinity. The shattering does not mean destruction, but, on the contrary, an emanation of life in all directions." Langen, pp. 274-275.

51. Quoted by Langen, p. 277.

52. Henri Bergson, "Laughter," in *Comedy*, ed. Wylie Sypher (New York: Doubleday & Co., 1956), especially pp. 61-84.

53. Danton, too, considers the maximum life span of man to be fifty or sixty years. Arguing for an early death, he says: "It is very good that the life span is somewhat shortened.... Life becomes an epigram. That is good. Who has enough breath and spirit for an epic in fifty or sixty cantos?" (II.i).

54. Cf. Johan Huizinga, *Homo Ludens: A Study of the Play Element in Culture* (Boston: Beacon, 1966), pp. 30-31.

55. Bergson, p. 117.

56. Bergson, p. 79.

57. Friedrich Schiller, *Sämtliche Werke: Säkular-Ausgabe* (Stuttgart: J. G. Cotta'sche Buchhandlung Nachfolger, 1904), 12: 193-197.

58. Nicoll, pp. 190-191.

59. Michael Hamburger writes that Büchner's "caricature of the metaphysical monarch, King Peter in *Leonce und Lena,* makes the connection between idealism in philosophy and the tendency of the Germans to excuse every vicious practice on the grounds of their genuine devotion to abstract ideas." "Büchner," in *Reason and Energy: Studies in German Literature* (New York: Grove Press, 1957), p. 196.

60. Cf. Henry J. Schmidt, *Satire, Caricature and Perspective in the Works of Georg Büchner,* Stanford Studies in Germanics and Slavics, no. 8 (The Hague: Mouton, 1970), pp. 67-68.

61. See Hans Mayer, "Prinz Leonce und Doktor Faust," in *Zur deutschen Klassik und Romantik* (Pfullingen: Neske, 1963), pp. 306-314.

62. See Krapp, pp. 152-153.

63. See Waldmann, p. 343. As has been suggested above, the inner state of Büchner's major figures usually reveals itself through their respective responses to nature.

64. James L. Calderwood and Harold E. Toliver, "Introduction to Comedy," in *Perspectives on Drama,* ed. James L. Calderwood and Harold E. Toliver (New York: Oxford University Press, 1968), p. 164.

65. In this he resembles Danton, who has similar feelings with regard to women, or, as Lacroix explains it, with regard to beauty: "He's just gathering up the Medicean Venus, piece by piece, from all the grisettes of the Palais Royal. He is making a mosaic, as he says. Heaven knows with which part he is now. It is a pity that nature cut beauty into pieces, as Medea did her brother, and immersed those fragments in different bodies" (I.iv).

66. Calderwood and Toliver, pp. 171-172. As is the case with Leonce, comic characters generally do not develop, but remain unchanged and therefore likely to repeat themselves indefinitely.

IV. *Lenz*

1. Quoted by Werner R. Lehmann, "Prolegomena zu einer historisch-kritischen Büchner Ausgabe," in *Gratulatio. Festschrift für Christian Wegner zum 70. Geburtstag* (Hamburg: Christian Wegner Verlag, 1963), p. 74.

2. Quoted by Karl Viëtor, *Georg Büchner: Politik, Dichtung, Wissenschaft* (Berne: Francke Verlag, 1949), p. 171.

3. When R. Weichbrodt failed to mention Büchner's novella in a pathography of "The Poet Lenz" published in 1921, W. Mayer responded by calling attention to Büchner's important study. In 1938 Walter Moos used Büchner's study as the foundation for another pathography of Lenz: "Büchner's 'Lenz,'" *Archiv für Neurologie und Psychiatrie* 42 (1938): 97-114. See Gerhard Irle, "Büchners Lenz. Eine frühe Schizophreniestudie," in *Der psychiatrische Roman* (Stuttgart: Hippokrates, 1965), pp. 73-83, for a review of the contribution Büchner's study has made to psychiatric literature.

4. Irle, p. 82. Irle also quotes W. Mayer's evaluation of the authenticity of Büchner's description: "The way he [Lenz] . . . becomes more abrupt and peculiar in all his expressions, finally revealing to us the well-known form of schizophrenic dissociation, is written by the poet with such extraordinary emotional penetration and empathy, that I would like to advise everyone interested in the problem of comprehensible connections in schizophrenia to read this masterpiece" (p. 77).

5. The authorship of some of these poems is still uncertain.

6. Oberlin's journal and a number of Lenz's unpublished letters were placed at Büchner's disposal by his Strasbourg friends August and Adolph Stöber, whose father, Ehrenfried Stöber, had published a biography of Oberlin, *Vie de Frédéric Oberlin,* in 1831 (see Ernst Johann, *Georg Büchner in Selbstzeugnissen und Bilddokumenten,* Rowohlt Monographien, no. 18 [Hamburg: Rowohlt, 1958], p. 132). Oberlin's journal and some of Lenz's letters were later published by August Stöber in *Der Dichter Lenz und Friederieke von Sesenheim* (Basel, 1842).

7. According to Irle, it is the language and form of expression which allows even the non-specialist to understand Lenz's inner state. "By the time one reaches the end of Büchner's novella, one is inclined to doubt the thesis pertaining to the fundamental impossibility of empathizing with the schizophrenic experience. Not because motivations are elucidated, because an anxious, abstruse mode of experience is followed to its roots, or because of success in following the motives of madness even one stage further into their ramifications, but because an inner condition, an experience of strangeness and of not-being-able-to-overcome with the resulting feeling of being destroyed and hollowed out are depicted through the langue and form of the presentation in such a way as to be made clear to the general reader and not just to the psychiatrist" (p. 82).

8. References are to Werner R. Lehmann's edition: *Georg Büchner. Sämtliche Werke und Briefe. Historisch-kritische Ausgabe mit Kommentar,* vol. 1: *Dichtungen und Übersetzungen mit Dokumentation zur Stoffgeschichte* (Hamburg: Christian Wegner Verlag, [1967]). The translations are my own.

9. See Hermann Pongs, "Dämonie der Leere — Büchners 'Lenz,'" in *Das Bild in der Dichtung,* vol. 2: *Voruntersuchungen zum Symbol* (Marburg: Elwert, 1963), p. 255.

10. Walter Moos considers this sentence to be the beginning of modern European prose (p. 111).

11. *The Divided Self: An Existential Study in Sanity and Madness* (Harmondsworth, Middlesex: Pelican Books, 1965), p. 17.

12. Karl Viëtor, " 'Lenz', eine Erzählung von Georg Büchner," *Germanisch-Romanische Monatsschrift* 25 (1937): 13.

13. See Laing, especially pp. 52-53, 91-92, 111-113.

14. Laing cites a similar example of a patient who "lost her autonomous identity" or "her self" when "alone in the gathering dusk in an empty expanse." At such moments this patient would, in her own words, "get frightened and repeat my name over and over again to bring me back to life, so to speak" (pp. 110-111).

15. According to Laing, the schizophrenic may attempt to acquire reality by "1. Touching, 2. Copying, imitating, 3. Magical forms of stealing it. . . . A further attempt to experience real live feelings may be made by subjecting oneself to intense pain or terror" (p. 145).

16. "The child who cries when its mother disappears from the room is threatened with the disappearance of his own being, since for him also [as for the schizophrenic] *percipi = esse*" (Laing, p. 118).

17. The break-up of Lenz's thought patterns and his inability to concentrate are frequently indicated by his use of short, simple sentences and by the elliptical style used to describe his constantly fluctuating behavior: "He ate little; nights half in prayer and feverish dreams. A powerful surging and then thrown back exhausted" (I.91). In the extreme he pauses frequently and is unable to complete thoughts or sentences: "Oh, she is dead! Is she still alive? You angel, she loved me—I loved her. She deserved it, oh you angel. Cursed jealousy! I sacrificed her—she still loved someone else—I loved her, she deserved it—oh good mother, she too loved me. I am a murderer" (I.94-95). Together, these stylistic peculiarities create a hasty, staccato effect and an eerie feeling of deterioration and madness.

18. Karl Freye and Wolfgang Stammler, eds., *Briefe von und an J.M.R. Lenz* (Leipzig: Wolff, 1918), 1:103.

19. The intimate mixture of pain and pleasure is prominent in the writing of mystics and in eroto-mystical poetry. An especially terse statement of the connection of pleasure and pain is contained in the poem "Astralis," which introduces the second part of Novalis's *Heinrich von Ofterdingen,* a novel Büchner may have read: "And as the flames of ecstasy [*Wollust*] burned in me, / I was also penetrated by the highest pain. / . . . / Sadness and ecstasy, death and life / Are here in closest sympathy."

20. According to the "fundamental law of nature" that Büchner postulates in his scientific writing, there must be harmony in and between all things and actions (Cf. II.292 and p. 32 above). The aesthetic implications of this idea will be discussed in connection with Lenz's remarks on art.

21. See Laing, p. 88.

22. Kaufmann does not mention Lenz's mother although she was still alive at this time. Perhaps Büchner does not want to discount the possibility that Lenz's premonition about her is correct. We can be sure, on the other hand, that he wanted to emphasize the conflict that actually did exist between Lenz and his father, since this conflict is a major factor in preventing him from going home. It may be noted in this context that Büchner's own father still refused to communicate with Büchner at this time. And Büchner could not return to his "fatherland," where a warrant for his arrest was still in effect.

23. See above, p. 117.

24. Herbert Fellmann believes that Oberlin never did have a healing in-

fluence on Lenz and that Lenz would have been better off had he never visited him. He also considers the improvement Lenz makes with Oberlin's help to be illusory. "Georg Büchners 'Lenz,'" *Jahrbuch der Wittheit zu Bremen* 7 (1963), 47-50. It seems unlikely, however, that Büchner would have portrayed a man so highly respected by his friends and prospective father-in-law in a derogatory fashion. Nor does the text itself justify such an interpretation. Oberlin helped Lenz to make some real improvement and succeeded in delaying his eventual breakdown, but he was incapable of preventing it altogether. Oberlin's attitude changed while he was away, but Kaufmann and the others who caused the change bear the main responsibility for that. Then, too, Oberlin confronts a new problem when he returns: since Lenz has completely lost his faith in God and religion, the Pastor's religious influence and counseling lose their effectiveness and relevance.

25. "The final seal on the self-enclosure of the self is applied by its own guilt. In the schizoid individual guilt has the same paradoxical quality about it that was encountered in his omnipotence and impotence, his freedom and his slavery, his self being anyone in phantasy and nothing in reality. There would seem to be various sources of guilt within the individual's being. In a being that is split into different 'selves' one has to know which self is feeling guilty about what. In other words, in a schizoid individual there is not and cannot be a non-contradictory unified sense of guilt. On general principles, one might suppose that one sense of guilt might have its source in the false self, and another source of guilt might arise in the inner self. If, however, we call any guilt that the false-self system might be capable of having, false guilt, one will have to be careful to avoid regarding the inner self as the source of 'genuine' or true guilt." "If there is anything the schizoid individual is likely to believe in, it is his own destructiveness. He is unable to believe that he can fill his own emptiness without reducing what is there to nothing. He regards his own love and that of others as being as destructive as hatred. To be loved threatens his self; but his love is equally dangerous to anyone else. His isolation is not entirely for his own self's sake. It is also out of concern for others." (Laing, pp. 92-93.)

26. The last and most important line of this strophe receives special emphasis in the original because of its long vowels and heavy accents and because it counterbalances the statement of the first three lines. It corresponds rhythmically with a poem by Lenz which Büchner quotes in a letter to his fiancée. (See II.428.)

27. Fellman interprets Lenz's remark differently. He believes that Lenz considers his condition to be a "consistent" product of his situation and of the human situation in general. Consequently, he considers those who do not recognize this or who have not undergone a similar development to be inconsistent (p. 70). Fellman's explanation is interesting, but it probably presupposes a greater degree of rationality and logical thinking than Lenz is capable of. It also appears to overlook the tenacity with which Lenz tries to remain like other people.

28. *The Sickness unto Death* (Garden City, New York: Doubleday, 1954), pp. 146-154. See Gustav Beckers, *Georg Büchners 'Leonce and Lena'. Ein Lustspiel der Langeweile* (Heidelberg: Carl Winter, 1961) for a detailed comparison of Büchner and Kierkegaard.

29. The use of the word *"Ruhe"* to denote a desirable state of calm and tranquility, on the one hand, and to connote the catalepsy *(Starrheit)* of schizophrenia on the other is clearly illustrated in the passage just quoted. "It was not so much the desire for death—for him there was no rest [*Ruhe*] or hope in death. Rather, in moments of the most dreadful anxiety or of the dull rest [*Ruhe*] that borders on nonbeing. . . ." In its first occurrence, "rest" has a positive value. Like "hope," with which it stands, it represents something Lenz would like to achieve. The "rest bordering on nonbeing," on the contrary, like the "most dreadful anxiety" with which it is equated, represents precisely that state Lenz wants to avoid, namely, the numbness and rigidity of madness. Later in the same paragraph, "rest" is used with still another connotation. It refers there to the moments in which his mind is occupied with some mad idea. Such "rest" is obviously not as desirable as that experienced in moments of complete sanity and self-composure, but it is still "not so horrible as the fear which longs for salvation and as the eternal torment of restlessness [*Unruhe*]!" It could be pointed out that "torment of restlessness" is equated here with "anxiety which longs for salvation," whereas "anxiety" was equated earlier with "rest bordering on nonbeing." By completing the syllogism, we find that "torment of restlessness" is thus equated with "rest bordering on nonbeing."

30. *Aspects of the Novel* (Middlesex, England: Pelican Books, 1962), pp. 52-53, 70.

31. The rejection of idealism in art is quite in harmony with the aesthetic ideas of the historical Lenz, who wrote in "Anmerkungen übers Theater": "in accordance with my sensibility I value the characteristic, even the caricaturist, ten times more than the idealistic, hyperbolically speaking, for it is ten times more difficult to represent a figure with precisely that exactitude and truth with which the genius recognizes it, than to work for ten years on an ideal of beauty that ultimately exists as such only in the mind of the artist who created it" (Heinz Kindermann, ed., *Von deutscher Art und Kunst*, vol. 6: *Irrationalismus* [Leipzig: Reclam, 1935], p. 251).

32. See especially the beginning of Büchner's lecture "Über Schädelnerven" (II.291-293).

33. Since failure to make normal linkages in language is symptomatic of schizophrenics, Büchner's use of asyndeton and parataxis is well-suited to his subject. See Joseph Church, *Language and the Discovery of Reality* (New York: Vintage Books, 1961), p. 160. Büchner often uses sentence fragments, ambiguity, and ellipsis to gain concentration and power of expression: he requires the reader to fill in the gaps and to supply the connections himself. In the following sentence, for example: "He continued on indifferently, he was not concerned with the path, upward then downward" (I.79), the "upward-then downward" may be read as the completion of the clause, "He continued on indifferently." Through its syntactical position, however, it appears to function as a relative clause to "path," but with the relative pronoun and verb missing, i.e., "he was not concerned with the path which led upward then downward." Since it can be considered as complementing both preceding clauses, the "upward then downward" is doubly functional. More complex and expressive is the following example: "He often hesitated in conversa-

tion, an indescribable anxiety befell him, he had lost the end of his sentence; then he thought he should retain and repeatedly say the last word he had spoken, only with great effort did he suppress this desire" (I.98) The first half of this complex sentence consists of three independent clauses joined only by commas, i.e., without being related to each other by connectives. The pluperfect tense of the third clause would seem to indicate that it precedes the other two in time and is therefore the cause of the stuttering and the fear mentioned in those clauses, but there is no syntactical indication that this is so. The second half of the sentence adds a conclusion consonant with each of the three first clauses, as if each one had been introduced by "when." The final clause is not parallel with the other clause in its group in the way the first three clauses are in theirs. (The relationships discussed here are generally lost in translation. This type of construction does not work as well in English as it does in German with its more flexible syntax.)

34. Cf. Ronald Hauser's detailed discussion of the structure of this narrative: *Georg Büchner,* Twayne World Authors Series (New York: Twayne Publishers, 1974), pp. 51-60.

35. Fellmann considers Lenz's description of these paintings to be incompatible with his own and with Büchner's ideas about art. In describing the girls, he transforms a series of observed scenes into a "description of a momentary situation [*momentanes Zustandsbild*]," Fellmann writes, whereas in describing the Dutch paintings he breaks up a painted picture into a rather extended "course of action [*Handlungsablauf*]." In the former he is concerned with the picture, in the latter, the event. He is presumably more interested in confronting transcendence than with describing a picture. Fellmann assumes that Büchner no longer speaks for himself in this passage, but only for Lenz (pp. 96-98). It is unlikely, however, that Büchner would have obscured and weakened this exposition of his ideas on art by including incompatible material. In my opinion, Fellmann interprets Büchner's concept of the *Bild* too narrowly. Just as the scenes or episodes in Büchner's works often begin and end *medias in res*, so his tableaux or frozen moments include within themselves the suggestion of what preceded and what will follow. Lenz's explication of the paintings serves to elucidate and illustrate his theoretical remarks.

36. *Poetics,* sec. 8.

37. J[oseph] P[eter] Stern, "A World of Suffering: Georg Büchner," in *Re-interpretations: Seven Studies in Nineteenth-Century German Literature* (New York: Basic Books, 1964), p. 127.

V. *Woyzeck*

1. Berg's statement originally appeared in the *Neue Musik-Zeitung,* vol. 49, no. 9 (Stuttgart, 1928). It is reprinted in Hans Mayer's edition of *Woyzeck, Dichtung und Wirklichkeit* (Frankfurt am Main: Ullstein, 1963), pp. 159-161. For a slightly abbreviated translation into English see Henry J. Schmidt, *Georg Büchner: Woyzeck* (New York: Avon, 1969), pp. 117-119.

2. *Textkritische Noten. Prolegomena zur Hamburger Büchner-Ausgabe* (Hamburg: Christian Wegner Verlag, 1967), pp. 41-42.

3. *Georg Büchner. Woyzeck: Texte und Dokumente* (Frankfurt am Main: Insel-Verlag, 1969), pp. 25-27. Krause believes that the second manuscript (H2) is much more closely connected with the final one (H4) than has generally been assumed, but this hypothesis does not affect the sequence of manuscripts or scenes.

In his *Kritische Lese- und Arbeitsausgabe* of *Woyzeck* (Suttgart: Reclam, 1972), Lothar Bornscheuer argues with Wilfried Buch (*Woyzeck. Fassungen und Wandlungen* [Dortmund, 1970], pp. 12ff.) that the first manuscript (H1) actually consists of two separate manuscripts (Ha and Hb) and that the last ten scenes of H1 should precede the first ten, thus Ha = H1, 11-20 and Hb = H1, 1-10 plus 21 (pp. 8-10, 76-82). This argument is based upon a comparison of three sets of parallel scenes: H1, 5-7; H1, 11-13; and H4, 11-13. From the similarity of the two triads in H1, Buch and Bornscheuer conclude that H1 must consist of two separate compositional stages, and from the fact that H1, 5-7 is generally closer to H4, 11-13 than H1, 11-13 is, they conclude that the latter precedes the former. While it is true that the scenes H4, 11-13 are based on H1, 5-7, there is no evidence to support the assumption that the two groups H1, 11-13 and H1, 5-7 represent two stages in the treatment of the same material so that one supersedes the other. On the contrary, H1, 11-13 obviously follows H1, 5-7 chronologically: in the earlier sequence (H1, 5-7) Woyzeck receives the command to kill Marie and he envisions a knife without yet having one. In the later sequence (H1, 11-13) he has the knife, but is trying to resist using it. The important discovery of H1, 5 and the command of H1, 6 are presupposed in H1, 11-13.

Bornscheuer himself provides the refutation for the second argument he advances in favor of rearranging the scenes. To begin with, he concludes that H1, 11-20 must precede H1, 1-10 because the changes in the stroke of Büchner's handwriting and the numerous corrections indicate an earlier, more uncertain stage of composition when compared with the greater uniformity of the script of H1, 1-10 (p. 78). The validity of such an argument is questionable in any event, but Bornscheuer goes on to contradict it by stating that the seven scenes of the "murder-complex" (H1, 14-20) constitute the only whole group of scenes which does not undergo a revision or a deletion (pp. 78-79). In maintaining that these were the most mature of the scenes that were not crossed out (p. 81), Bornscheuer contradicts his earlier claim that H1, 11-20 is a "groping rough draft" (p. 78). Since the handwriting already begins to become less certain in H1, 10, this scene rather than H1, 11 must be seen as the first of the series of sloppily written scenes. Furthermore, H1, 21, clearly follows the murder and belongs at the end of the sequence ending with H1, 20 and not after H1, 10, where Buch and Bornscheuer place it. And finally, the fact that H4 uses material from the first group of ten scenes indicates that these come chronologically before the last ten, which must provide the play's conclusion and which would no doubt have been crossed out once Büchner had incorporated them.

4. *Woyzeck. Eine Tragödie von Georg Büchner* (Leipzig [1924/25]).

5. "Of course H [=H4] too is only a fragment. A fragment which is not only without a conclusion but which also lacks the final dramatic structure. Its sequence of scenes was given up long ago and from all sides as impossible.

And so in our text, too, a rearrangement has been undertaken, one that departs from H and that is to be derived from the wording and content of the event itself." Fritz Bergemann, ed., *Sämtliche Werke und Briefe,* 9th ed. (Frankfurt am Main: Insel-Verlag, 1962), p. 484.

6. Bergemann's text has been translated into English by Theodore Hoffmann, *Woyzeck,* in *The Modern Theatre,* edited by Eric Bentley, vol. 1 (Garden City, New York: Doubleday, 1955), and Carl Richard Mueller, *Woyzeck,* in *Georg Büchner: Complete Plays and Prose* (New York: Hill & Wang, 1963), but in both cases additional unauthorized material has been included: Hoffmann adds two extra scenes, and Mueller, five. Mueller also contaminates within individual scenes. For example, he weakens and distorts the inn scene in which Woyzeck discovers Marie's infidelity by filling it out with material from an earlier draft of the same scene—one which Büchner had crossed out. He then completely destroys the effect of his conglomerate scene—one of the most important in the play—by tacking on a scene from H1 which has no connection whatsoever with the action of the inn scene. Also included in Mueller's translation is the scene from H1 in which a Barber discourses at length about courage, nature, and man. This scene was crossed out in the manuscript after most of its content had been incorporated into the speeches of the Journeymen, the Carnival Barker, and the Drum Major. And although the Barber's character is diametrically opposed to Woyzeck's, Mueller places his speeches in Woyzeck's mouth, thus severely confusing and distorting his character. Finally, by ending his construction with the scenic fragment "Court Clerk. Barber. Doctor. Judge," by again identifying Woyzeck with the Barber, who is at the scene of the murder in an official capacity (see Wolfgang Martens, "Der Barbier in Büchners 'Woyzeck' [Zugleich ein Beitrag zur Motivgeschichte der Barbiersfigur]," *Zeitschrift für deutsche Philologie* 79 [1960]: 361-383), and by inventing the stage direction: "WOYZECK stands in their midst, dumbly looking at the body of Marie; he is bound, the dogmatic atheist, tall, haggard, timid, good-natured, scientific," Mueller imposes a conclusion on the play which is not suggested by any of Büchner's manuscripts, and he reveals what meaningless nonsense can result from the indiscriminate mixture of material. It is ridiculous to assume that the author would include stage directions characterizing his hero in the last scene of the play and then do so in terms which contradict the presentation of the play itself.

Without explaining why he does not use Lehmann's text and without addressing himself to the criticism of Bergemann's text put forth by Ursula Paulus, Walter Müller-Seidel, and others, Michael Hamburger chooses to use Bergemann's construction for his recent translation (*Georg Büchner: Leonce and Lena, Lenz, Woyzeck* [Chicago: University of Chicago Press, 1972]). For a translation of Lehmann's construction see Henry J. Schmidt, *Georg Büchner: Woyzeck* (New York: Avon, 1969).

7. Georg Büchner. *Sämtliche Werke und Briefe. Historisch-kritische Ausgabe mit Kommentar,* vol. 1: *Dichtungen und Übersetzungen mit Dokumentationen zur Stoffgeschichte* (Hamburg: Christian Wegner Verlag, [1967]).

8. *Georg Büchners 'Woyzeck'* (Greifswald: Ratsbuchhandlung L. Bamberg, 1925), p. 55.

9. Büchner's friend Wilhelm Schulz, who was with Büchner when he died, wrote in an obituary notice for the *Züricher Zeitung* that "a nearly completed play and the fragment of a novella were among Büchner's papers" (Bergemann, p. 585). Considering the complete lack of any trace of a drama about Pietro Aretino that Büchner is said to have written (see following note), it is safe to assume that the play referred to by Schulz was *Woyzeck*, which Büchner had been working on before his death.

10. Büchner's reference to "two other plays," a comment from Ludwig Büchner (see Bergemann, p. 613), and a reference by Gutzkow to Büchner's "obscene plays" (II. 491) provide the only evidence upon which the existence of a play about Pietro Aretino is postulated.

11. Lehmann, *Textkritische Noten*, p. 59.

12. The following discussion combines my published criticism of Lehmann's construction: "Zur Textgestaltung von Georg Büchners 'Woyzeck'. Anmerkungen zur Hamburger Büchner-Ausgabe, den 'Woyzeck' betreffend," *Euphorion* 65 (1971): 49-57, with a rebuttal of the reasons and arguments advanced by Lehmann in his reply: "Repliken: Beiträge zu einem Streitgespräch über den 'Woyzeck,'" *Euphorion* 65 (1971): 58-83.

13. See H2, 7 and H1, 21. Cf. also the speech of the Barber in H1, 10.

14. Lehmann takes the first part of the Barker's speech from H1, 1 and places it before a similar statement already contained in H2, 3:

H1,1   Gentlemen! Gentlemen! Look at the creature as God made it. Nothing, nothing at all! Now look at art: walks upright, wears coat and pants, has a saber! Ho! Pay your respects! Thus you are a baron. Give a kiss! (*He trumpets.*) The fellow is musical.

H2, 3   Ladies and Gentlemen. Here you can see the astronomical horse and the little cannybird. . . . (I.411)

Likewise, he adds to the following statement in H2, 3: "It will now take place, the representation. The commencement of the commencement will immediately begin," the similar statement from H1, 1: "The representation begin! We're beginning the beginning. It will immediately be the commencement of the commencement" (I.411).

15. "Repliken," p. 75.

16. Ibid.

17. For his edition, Bornscheuer reduces the number of editorial decisions to the minimum required for constructing a playable text: the only addition he makes to H4 is the complex of murder scenes H1, 14-20. With this minimal text he wants simply to provide a "basic framework" and the parts from which the reader, exercising his "right to interpret," can make his own construction or adaptation (p. 3). Implied in such an invitation is the unfortunate suggestion that an author's text can be manipulated to suit the personal tastes and ideological inclinations of individual readers and that there are no objective criteria for judging the validity of texts or interpretations. Bornscheuer makes further suggestions for building on the framework he provides, but since they are incorporated in a complicated discussion of manuscripts and scenes, they will be of little use to the general reader.

To solve the major problem, the space left for the carnival scene, Bornscheuer advocates the simplest possible solution, which is to include only H2, 3 or part of H2, 3, since the latter part of that scene is obviously fragmentary and should be excluded. Bornscheuer favors this scene "because its core, the Barker's text, represents a visible concentration and maturation of the main role, which is divided in Hb [=H1, 1-10] between two scenes" (p. 83). While the role of the Barker (*Ausrufer*) is indeed somewhat expanded in H2, 3, it seems doubtful that it was intended to subsume the role of the showman (*Marktschreier*) presented in H1,2. As originally conceived, this scenic complex included action outside and inside the booth. It is possible that the presentation of the action inside the booth (H1,2) was not revised because Büchner was satisfied with it as it stands. The lack of corrections, the regular script, and the finished nature of this scene might be seen as an indication of the certainty with which it was written. The fact that Büchner rewrote the first part (H1,1) would seem to indicate that this is the part of the scenic complex with which he was not satisfied; and from the fact that this revision (H2,3) was not included in H4 and that the last part of this scene is fragmentary, it can be concluded that Büchner was not yet satisfied with it. Thus, while Bornscheuer's suggestion represents an editorially defensible solution to this problem, it strikes me as being less desirable and less effective than a construction which also includes H1,2.

18. See Krause, p. 96. This scene with its space comprises the last two pages of the quarto. Realizing that this scene would require more than one page, Büchner may have left all of page 8 free to allow himself plenty of space. Spaces after scenes are not uncommon in the final manuscript. Büchner left the last quarter of the page following scene 7 blank, for example, in order to begin a new scene on a new page.

19. "Georg Büchners 'Woyzeck'. Eine kritische Betrachtung zu der Edition Fritz Bergemanns," *Jahrbuch der deutschen Schiller-Gesellschaft* 8 (1964): 237.

20. "Repliken," p. 77.

21. *Georg Büchner: Politik, Dichtung, Wissenschaft* (Berne: Francke Verlag, 1949), p. 193. Viëtor quotes Bergemann's reading, which differs slightly from Lehmann's.

22. "Repliken," p. 77.

23. Krause, pp. 26-28.

24. Lehmann, *Textkritische Noten*, p. 54.

25. "Repliken," p. 78. It is scarcely conceivable that Büchner would not have revealed the significance of Woyzeck's diet in the Doctor scene in H4 if it were really of such central importance. If the play's social criticism is as inextricably bound to Woyzeck's diet as Lehmann suggests, the conclusion to be drawn from the fact that the diet becomes less important in each successive draft is detrimental to Lehmann's argument.

26. Even this emphasis on Woyzeck's various activities is reduced in the final manuscript. In H2, 2, for example, Marie receives an affirmative reply when she asks Woyzeck, who has just returned from the field, whether he has been cutting sticks for the Captain. Because this question is omitted in H4, 2, Woyzeck's activity in the field is not explained. In H1, 8 Woyzeck has to fetch wine for his officer, an activity that is not mentioned in H4. And in H2, 6 the

Doctor asks Woyzeck if he has no spider's eggs or frogs, thus alluding to another of Woyzeck's activities not mentioned in H4.

27. Winkler already recognized that the Professor is a preliminary study for the Doctor (p. 55). He also noted the development which procedes from H3, 1 over H2, 6 to H4, 8. Winkler concludes that, since these scenes are all episodic and parallel to each other, and since only one of them can be included, the earlier ones must give way to the latest. Krause is of the same opinion (p. 88).

28. See Lothar Bornscheuer, *Erläuterungen und Dokumente. Georg Büchner: Woyzeck* (Stuttgart: Reclam, 1972), pp. 11-15, and note 54 below.

29. Viëtor, *Politik, Dichtung, Wissenschaft,* p. 197.

30. Ursula Paulus rightly states that the action involving the Doctor (and the Captain) is concluded in H4, 9 (p. 240 and n. 49). Bornscheuer, on the other hand, agrees with Lehmann's placement of this scene, which he considers to be a thematic intensification of H4, 8 (*Kritische Lese- und Arbeitsausgabe,* p. 86). In his review of new editions and the controversy centering on the construction of a playable text, Klaus Kanzog agrees with my view that the scene H3, 1 belongs to the exposition. See "Wozzeck, Woyzeck und kein Ende. Zur Standortbestimmung der Editionsphilologie," *Deutsche Vierteljahrsschrift* 47 (1973): 439-440 and n. 57. (Kanzog maintains that there is "no Woyzeck-text, but only a score (*Text*-Partitur)" and that all additions to H4 belong in the province of the theater director. I prefer to distinguish between the problems involved in editing a playable text and those pertaining to its performance: the director's work begins where the editor's ends.)

31. Cf. Wolfgang Martens: "Even though the work remained unfinished, nothing more compels us to call it a torso, on which decisive parts, which would open up new areas (such as the postulated trial scenes), are missing. The existing scenes and sketches appear to us, rather, to demonstrate quite adequately the planned course of the action up to the end, Woyzeck's end in the water. When the possible conclusions involving arrest and conviction have become invalid, Woyzeck's drowning cannot be designated as inadequately make-shift, but as the only probable conclusion, given the material we have, and the only conclusion which is inherently compatible with the action as a whole." ("Der Barbier in Büchners 'Woyzeck,'" pp. 381-382.) The possibility of Woyzeck's drowning, whether intentional or not, is also compatible with Büchner's source or sources. Concerning the historical Woyzeck, Clarus reports: "In the summer he was living at the Haasens, he said, the thought of suicide always pursued him. Once, when he had gone bathing, he heard the voice say: *Jump in the water, jump in the water!*" (I.514). Two cases similar to Woyzeck's may also have influenced Büchner's play, and the murderer in both cases, Schmolling and Diess, reported having intended or attempted to kill themselves. See Krause, pp. 172-173, 177, 202-203.

32. Cf. above, p. 41.

33. See Hermann van Dam, "Zu Georg Büchners 'Woyzeck,'" *Akzente* 1 (1954): 89; Helmut Krapp, *Der Dialog bei Georg Büchner,* Literatur als Kunst (Darmstadt: Gentner, 1958), pp. 89-90; and Herbert Samuel Lindenberger, *Georg Büchner* (Carbondale: Southern Illinois University Press, 1964), pp. 99-100.

34. Ursula Paulus also argues for the inclusion of H3, 2 after H1, 20, "Woyzeck by a Pond" (p. 241).

35. Cf. Hermann van Dam, p. 89.

36. Bornscheuer also disagrees with Lehmann's placement of H3, 2. He is inclined, on the one hand, to place it after the final inn scene, as does Hans Jürgen Meinerts, *Georg Büchner, Sämtliche Werke nebst Briefen und anderen Dokumenten* (Gütersloh: S. Mohn, 1963). On the other hand, he hesitates to include the scene at all, since it disturbs the inherent rhythm of the complex of murder scenes (*Kritische Lese- und Arbeitsausgabe,* p. 87). This rhythm consists of an alternation between Woyzeck's frantic flight from the murder and his subsequent flight from the inn to the scene of the murder. (The comments by the people [H1, 16] and the children [H1, 18] are oriented toward the corpse.) The interpolation of H3, 2 between H1, 17 and 18 would indeed interrupt the flow of motion, which is toward the corpse: Woyzeck is too obsessed at this point with the necessity of disposing of the murder weapon to stop and talk with his child. There would be no such interruption, however, if H3, 2 is placed before the inn scene. On his way from the scene of the crime to the inn, Woyzeck stops to talk with his child. Perhaps sensing what has happened, the child rejects his attention and runs off, whereupon Woyzeck continues on to the inn. The events of the inn scene bring a reversal in the direction of motion, and Woyzeck returns to the pond. Placed before the inn scene, H3, 2 can add intensification without effecting change. Only then can its inclusion be justified.

37. "Repliken," p. 83.

38. Ibid.

39. "What do you call the *lawful state?*" Büchner asks his parents in a letter dated 5 April 1833: "*A law* that makes the great masses of citizens into toiling cattle, in order to satisfy the unnatural cravings of an insignificant and spoiled minority? And this law, supported by a brutal military force and the foolish cunning of its agents, this law is an *eternal, brutal force* which violates justice and sound reason, and I will fight against it with word and deed wherever I can" (II.416). In *The Hessian Courier* he writes: "The law is the property of an insignificant class of aristocrats and scholars, who bestow the rule upon themselves through their own contrivance. This justice is only a means to keep you in order, so you can be more easily oppressed; it speaks according to laws which you do not understand, according to principles of which you know nothing, judgments you do not comprehend" (II.38).

40. For the remaining part of this chapter the quotations from *Woyzeck* will be identified by scene. The Roman numeral following the quotation indicates the number of the scene in my construction. See pp. 169-170 and Appendix B.

41. Compare the Second Gentleman in *Danton's Death,* who also fears that he might fall through the earth's crust (I.36). Büchner has this motif from his source; the historical Woyzeck actually did feel persecuted and threatened by the Free Masons. He also had a dream in which he saw three fiery faces in the sky which he identified as the Trinity; he believed this to be a revelation of the number which contained the Free Mason's secret (I.510). Another time he saw three fiery streaks in one part of the sky and heard bells, which seemed to be tolling underground. He then saw a single streak in another part of the sky. From this he concluded that the Free Masons had changed their sign from three upraised fingers to one (I.510-511).

42. Büchner recognizes the psychic origin and nature of these forces, but he also seems to suggest that external forces, the laws of nature, may influence the psyche. See above, pp. 70-71.

43. Genesis 19. 27-29: "And Abraham gat up early in the morning to the place where he stood before the LORD: And he looked toward Sodom and Gomorrah, and toward all the land of the plain, and behold, and, lo, the smoke of the country went up as the smoke of a furnace. And it came to pass, when God destroyed the cities of the plain, that God remembered Abraham, and sent Lot out of the midst of the overthrow, when he overthrew the cities in which Lot dwelt." See Krause for a number of passages which have a bearing on Woyzeck's hallucinations and his references to them (pp. 228-233). Krause quotes from an edition of the Bible (Frankfurt, 1756), with which Büchner may have been familiar.

44. Revelations 9.1-2: "And the fifth angel sounded, and I saw a star fall from heaven unto the earth: and to him was given the key of the bottomless pit. And he opened the bottomless pit; and there arose a smoke out of the pit, as the smoke of a great furnace; and the sun and the air were darkened by reason of the smoke of the pit."

45. Cf. Revelations 6.12: "and, lo, there was a great earthquake; and the sun became as sackcloth of hair, and the moon became as blood," and Acts 2.20: "The sun shall be turned into darkness, and the moon into blood, before that great and notable day of the Lord come."

46. Cf. *Danton's Death,* II. iv-v (I.39-41). When Danton is tormented by his conscience because of the role he played in the September massacre, he calms himself with talk of his passive role as the puppet of forces which used him, as they do all men, as an instrument for accomplishing their own purposes. On the other hand, he knows that only the complete loss of his memory and conscience can bring him the full measure of peace and tranquility he desires. It is difficult to determine whether Woyzeck's conscience torments him, i.e., whether he feels inner guilt, or whether he is only aware of his legal guilt. The fact that he considers himself an instrument of divine retribution seems to suggest that he feels his action was justified.

47. Immanuel Kant, "Idee zu einer allgemeinen Geschichte in weltbürgerlicher Absicht," *Kant's Werke,* vol. 8: *Abhandlungen nach 1781* (Berlin: De Gruyter, 1923), p. 19.

48. Besides the indirect disparagement of man's reason contained in Büchner's letters and works, the following direct remarks may be cited: "Reason, moreover, is only a very insignificant side of our mental being, and education only an accidental form of the same" (II.422); "I'm becoming quite dumb with the study of philosophy; I am becoming acquainted with the poverty of the human mind from yet another perspective" (II.450); "**Camille.** . . . The common fixed ideas that one calls sound reason are intolerably boring. The happiest person was the one who could imagine that he was God the Father, the Son, and the Holy Ghost" (I.70); "**Valerio.** . . . Who will trade me his madness for my sound reason?" (I.107). In the margin of a notebook the schoolboy already protested: "Oh, Herr Doctor! What are intellect, sagacity, sound reason? Empty names! — A dung heap of scholarship, the only worthy goal of human striving!" Fritz Bergemann, ed., *Sämtliche Werke und Briefe* (Leipzig: Insel-Verlag, 1922), p. 762.

49. When Danton and his friends attempt to make death easier by exaggerating and idealizing their heroic roles, Camille urges them to rip off their masks in order to reveal and face the beast that is their true essence. He also reduces man to the biological functions that are characteristic of all animals: "Sleeping, digesting, making children—all do that. The other things are only variations in different keys on the same theme" (I.70-71).

50. Like the "double nature" Woyzeck speaks of in connection with his visions (I.417-418), "double reason" may refer to *"das zweite Gesicht,"* i.e., second sight or clairvoyance. Cf. Bornscheuer, *Erläuterungen und Dokumente*, p. 15. The supposedly clairvoyant horse knows that a jackass is present in the audience.

51. It has become common among those writing in English to translate this as a "mounting up," and to use it in a sexually oriented interpretation. Since only one horse is mentioned, however, it is more than likely that it urinates or defecates. This is parallel to Woyzeck's similar action, which angers the Doctor and refutes his idealized view of man.

52. Büchner is reported to have made a similar statement on his deathbed: "We are death, dust, ashes. How can we complain?" (Bergemann, *Werke,* 1922 edition, p. 580).

53. In the earlier manuscript the idealistic content of the Journeyman's parodistic sermon was contrasted with the realistic content of the carnival scene (cf. H2, 3-4). In its later position the contrast is even more effective. Since the spectator has become emotionally committed to Woyzeck, he must recognize and feel that Woyzeck's conclusion about God and man is much closer to the truth than are the optimistic teleological assumptions parodied by the Journeyman.

54. The Doctor is based upon two professors at the University of Giessen, J. B. Wilbrand and Justus von Liebig. Büchner no doubt took a course from Wilbrand, a medical doctor and anatomist. Like the Doctor in *Woyzeck,* Wilbrand was a proponent of the Romantic, idealistic *Naturphilosophie.* The following quotation from his *Handbuch der Naturgeschichte des Thierreichs* (Giessen, 1829) is interesting for its reflection of Kant's statement on free will as well as for the suggestion that animals are somehow striving to become more like man: "It is obvious that man stands at the peak of the entire animal kingdon . . . because in him the intellectual life developed into reason and intellectual freedom, whereas everywhere in the animals only a striving upward to man can be recognized" (quoted in Winkler, p. 120). As a fellow student of Büchner's recorded in his memoirs, Wilbrand culminated his lectures on anatomy by having his son move his ears, thus demonstrating the use of muscles that have become obsolete in man but not in monkeys. Karl Vogt, *Aus meinem Leben* (Stuttgart, 1896), p. 55.

The noted chemist Justus Liebig may also have been a model for Büchner's Doctor. Liebig was familiar with published research involving the chemical content of the urine of herbivorous and carnivorous animals. During the time Büchner was still in Giessen, Liebig was conducting nutritional experiments on soldiers. Peas were specifically mentioned as a constituent of the prescribed diet; the average daily consumption was exactly controlled. Liebig later published the results of his analysis of the chemical composition of peas and the chemical content of the urine of herbivorous and carnivorous animals. (This information is contained in an interesting report by Dr. Eckhart Buddecke on the background and possible meaning of Büchner's reference to the chemical content of Woyzeck's urine. See Bornscheuer, *Erläuterungen und Dokumente,* p. 15.)

55. Cf. Mario Carlo Abutille, *Angst und Zynismus bei Georg Büchner,* Basler Studien zur deutschen Sprache und Literatur, no. 40 (Berne: Francke Verlag, 1969), p. 124.

56. "Authentic literature is directed against the established schemes and, in its constant progress, against itself. It is continually forced to change, because everything formulated, every structural pattern, once found, suffers a secret loss of authenticity which is immediately visible in the imitation. That is, there is an anti-Platonic concept of truth at work here that does not understand knowledge as memory of preconceived, unchangeable norms, but as a progressing concretization, as the discovery of new spheres of reality and new perspectives." Dieter Wellershoff, *Literatur und Veränderung* (Munich: Deutscher Taschenbuch Verlag, 1971), p. 21.

57. See Hans Robert Jauss, *Literaturgeschichte als Provokation* (Frankfurt am Main: Suhrkamp Verlag, 1970), pp. 199-203, and Wellershoff, pp. 18-19.

58. Wordsworth had already achieved a similar transvaluation in poetry. When his initial faith in the promise of the French Revolution was shattered, he overcame his despair by giving up his role as a political radical for the role of a poetic radical. He regarded it as his mission, as M. H. Abrams writes, "to employ his originality of vision, which subverts the conventional rank of the objects it perceives, in order to effect a revolution in the poetic sources of pathos and sublimity, and so to 'extend the domain of sensibility for the delight, the honor, and the benefit of human nature.'" As the poetical Jacobin of his generation "he accomplished an egalitarian revolution in poetry, deleting the traditional hierarchy and decorums of literary kinds, subjects, protagonists, and styles, with their built-in class structure and inherent scale of aristocratic values. And by an ultimate subversion, Wordsworth did not merely level the Neoclassic order, but turned it upside down, by preferring in his subjects the last over the first and by transforming the humble and the passive into the heroic, the low into the sublime, and the petty into the numinous." *Natural Supernaturalism: Tradition and Revolution in Romantic Literature* (New York: Norton, 1971), pp. 395-396. On Lillo, see Alardyce Nicoll, *The Theory of Drama* (New York: Benjamin Blom, 1966), p. 105.

59. Winkler counted 348 simple sentences in the final manuscript (H4) as compared to only 69 complex sentences. Most of the latter involve coordinate conjunctions, including 17 with "and," and occur mostly in the speeches of the Doctor and the Captain. (Winkler, p. 224.)

60. Krapp, p. 103.

61. Cf. Krapp, pp. 103-105.

62. Cf. Franz H. Mautner, "Wortgewebe, Sinngefüge und 'Idee' in Büchners 'Woyzeck,'" *Deutsche Vierteljahrsschrift* 35 (1961): 548. The performance of *Woyzeck* by the Berliner Ensemble of East Berlin sacrifices this effect by having Woyzeck come for Marie before the Grandmother begins

her tale. In general this staging provides a strong argument against contaminating and distorting the text. Its stated intention is to emphasize "through the montage of fragmentary material the disillusioning analysis of society for which Büchner strove." By including various scenes from earlier manuscripts, the adapters constructed a play consisting of 29 scenes, many of which detract from and weaken its effectiveness. Their construction actually works against their own intention by making Woyzeck somewhat ridiculous and comic rather than pathetic and tragic. At the performance I attended the audience laughed after Woyzeck slit Marie's throat and asked "Are you dead?"

63. See Gonthier-Louis Fink, "Volkslied und Verseinlage in den Dramen Büchners," *Deutsche Vierteljahrsschrift* 35 (1961): 558-593, for a detailed discussion of the function of the songs in *Woyzeck* and in Büchner's other works.

64. It makes no more sense to claim that the sequence of scenes in this type of play can be arbitrarily altered, as do Schmidt and Schechner *(Georg Büchner: Woyzeck,* trans. H. J. Schmidt with intro. and notes by R. Schechner [New York: Avon, 1969], pp. 11, 79) and Richard Gilman (*The Making of the Modern Drama* [New York: Farrar, Straus & Giroux, 1974], p. 41), than it would to make the same claim for the speeches in a scene, the sentences in a speech, or the words in a sentence. The choice and arrangement of material is constitutive of meaning, and alterations cannot be made in the one without changing the meaning of the other.

65. See Nicoll, pp. 56-57.

66. Mautner, p. 527.

67. Mautner considers Woyzeck's vocabulary to be concentrated around three emotional complexes: eroticism and fear—both of which are often overlapped by jealousy—and, following the certain discovery of Marie's infidelity, murder; and four rational themes: nature, the world, man, and fateful compulsion, which is represented for Woyzeck in the words "poor" and "must" (p. 528). Not only is there considerable overlap between the categories defined by Mautner, but the motifs and themes associated with Woyzeck also overlap with those associated with other figures: the abundance of interconnections results in a tightly woven fabric.

68. The transformation in Woyzeck's mind of Marie's "go on" into the rhythmically similar "stab dead" or "stab, stab" is indicated by his statement to Andres in scene 13: "when I close my eyes, it keeps spinning and I hear the fiddles: go on, go on—and then it speaks from the wall. Don't you hear anything. . . . It keeps saying: Stab! Stab! And it slices between my eyes like a knife." The words "knife" and "stab" also recur in the play as motifs. When Marie is disturbed by her bad conscience at the end of the first jealousy scene, she says: "I really am a whore. I could stab myself" (IV). In the scene following his discovery of Marie's infidelity, the motifs of knife and stabbing enter Woyzeck's mind and continue to torment him until the deed is accomplished. What begins as hallucination in scene 12, ends in reality when Woyzeck buys a knife and uses it to stab Marie. But the commission of that deed does not free him from the knife's influence or spell, as it were. The frantic desire to get rid of the incriminating weapon lures Woyzeck back to

the scene of the crime and may become responsible for his own death.

69. See Mautner, pp. 532-533, and Volker Klotz, *Geschlossene und offene Form im Drama* (Munich: Hanser, 1960), p. 107 and nn. 180-184.

70. Winkler rightly states that many passages in *Woyzeck* are incomprehensible without gesture and without modulations of tone and tempo (pp. 206-208).

71. The Innkeeper's "Uuh" sound connects with the same sound made twice by the First Person in the preceding scene, where it also expresses an uncertain horror, caused in that instance by the peculiar sounds which may be coming from the dying Marie: "Uuh! Now! What a sound. . . . Uuh, there it is again. Like a person dying" (XX).

Appendix A

1. Ingeborg Strudthoff, *Die Rezeption Georg Büchners durch das deutsche Theater,* Theater und Drama, vol. 19 (Berlin-Dahlem: Colloquium Verlag, 1957), p. 45. My discussion of the German performances of Büchner's plays is based upon Strudthoff's exemplary full-length study.

2. The theater in Darmstadt where Büchner grew up was of poor quality and performed mostly inferior comedies and operas. During his stay in Strasbourg Büchner would have had better opportunities, but nothing in his letters or other documents indicates that he found time in his busy life to attend theater performances. Strudthoff points out that one "scarcely finds passages in his plays which, as is the case with pronouncedly dramatic writers, directly address the public or the director," i.e., he includes no direct descriptions of characters or settings and only a few indications of gesture and manner of speaking. See Strudthoff, pp. 12-17.

3. Strudthoff, p. 45.

4. Ibid., p. 49. Strudthoff retells the anecdote of the young lady who claimed that Büchner was the brother of the Expressionist Kasimir Edschmid. Her proof consisted of a collection of Edschmid's novellas which carried the dedication: "*Meinem grösseren Bruder Georg Büchner* (To my greater brother Georg Büchner)" (p. 56).

5. Ibid., p. 53.

6. Ibid., pp. 55-56.

7. Ibid., p. 63.

8. Ibid.

9. Ibid., p. 64.

10. Later the same year Klöpfer directed and acted in a production of *Woyzeck* in Vienna. Through a quicker tempo he achieved greater concentration than Reinhardt. However, by overemphasizing the expressionistic elements of the play, this performance lost the sense of reality which is an essential part of Büchner's art. See Strudthoff, pp. 61-73.

11. Ibid., p. 79.

12. Ibid., pp. 82-83.

13. Ibid., p. 87.

14. Ibid., p. 120.

15. Ibid., p. 121.

16. Ibid., p. 125.

17. Ralph P. Rosenberg, "Georg Büchner's Early Reception in America," *Journal of English and Germanic Philology* 44 (1945): 273.

18. See Rosenberg, pp. 270-273.

19. John Mason Brown, "The Laughter of the Gods. Broadway in Review," *Theatre Arts Monthly* 12 (February 1928):89.

20. See John Houseman, "Orson Welles and *Danton's Death*," *Yale/ Theatre*, vol. 3, no. 3 (1972): 56-67, for an interesting behind-the-scene account of the background of this performance. The Mercury Theatre depended for support on "the organized, left-wing semi-intellectual audiences" which "consisted predominantly of the Communist Party, its adherents and sympathizers." However, the Cultural Bureau of the Party objected to the performance of *Danton* on the grounds that it would suggest an "inescapable and dangerous parallel" to the recent Moscow trials and the split in the Party: "To the politically uneducated and even to some of the younger emotional members of the Party, Danton, the hero of the Revolution, who had raised and commanded the armies of the young republic, would inevitably suggest Trotsky, while his prosecutor, the incorruptible, ruthless Robespierre would, equally inevitably, be equated with Joseph Stalin" (pp. 62-63). To escape a Communist boycott, Houseman and Welles had to remove some of the more obvious Trotsky-Stalin parallels. But since the Party still withheld its support, *Danton* closed after only twenty-one poorly attended performances. The financial failure of this expensive production broke the Mercury Theatre and caused its collapse.

21. Cf. Ronald Hauser, *Georg Büchner,* Twayne's World Authors Series (New York: Twayne Publishers, 1974), pp. 127-129. For a survey of Büchner's influence on modern writers see Hauser, pp. 129-138, and Herbert S. Lindenberger, *Georg Büchner* (Carbondale: Southern Illinois University Press, 1964), pp. 124-136.

Johnathan Miller's idiosyncratic staging of *Danton's Death* at the National Theatre in London (1971) was marred in the same general way the American productions are, namely, by overdirecting. In his attempt to convey the impression that the dramatic characters are marionettes masquerading as men and by almost eliminating the People, Miller lost the sense of throbbing life and historical reality which Büchner considered to be the goal and essence of his art. See Jonathan Marks, "Jonathan Miller's *Danton's Death*," *Yale/Theatre*, vol. 3, no. 3 (1972): 99-105.

SELECTED BIBLIOGRAPHY

Bibliographies

Schlick, Werner. *Das Georg Büchner-Schrifttum bis 1965.* Hildesheim: Georg Olms, 1968 [A complete international bibliography of editions and secondary literature up to 1965.]

Drucker, Judith. "A Büchner Bibliography," *Yale/Theatre*, vol. 3, no. 3 (1972): 106-108. [Major translations and secondary literature in English.]

Major Editions

Bergemann, Fitz, ed. *Sämtliche Werke und Briefe.* Leipzig: Insel, 1922; 9th ed., Frankfurt am Main: Insel 1962; Munich: Deutscher Taschenbuch Verlag, 1968.

Bornscheuer, Lothar, ed. *Georg Büchner. Woyzeck: Kritische Lese- und Arbeitsausgabe.* Stuttgart: Reclam, 1972.

Büchner, Ludwig, ed. *Nachgelassene Schriften.* Frankfurt am Main: J. D. Sauerländer, 1850.

Enzensberger, Hans Magnus, ed. *Georg Büchner. Ludwig Weidig. Der Hessiche Landbote: Texte, Briefe, Prozessakten.* Frankfurt am Main: Insel, 1965; also in paperback by the same publisher, Insel Taschenbuch, 1974.

Franzos, Karl Emil, ed. *Sämtliche Werke und handschriftlicher Nachlass.* Frankfurt am Main: J. D. Sauerländer, 1879.

Hausenstein, Wilhelm, ed. *Gesammelte Werke.* Leipzig: Insel, 1916.

Jacobs, Margaret, ed. *"Dantons Tod" and "Woyzeck."* German Text Series. 3rd ed. revised. Manchester: Manchester University Press, 1971.

Krause, Egon, ed. *Georg Büchner. Woyzeck: Texte und Dokumente.* Frankfurt am Main: Insel, 1969.

Landau, Paul, ed. *Georg Büchners Gesammelte Schriften.* 2 vols. Berlin: Paul Cassirer, 1909.

Lehmann, Werner R., ed. *Georg Büchner. Sämtliche Werke und Briefe: Historisch-kritische Ausgabe.* Vol. 1: *Dichtungen und Übersetzungen, mit Dokumentationen zur Stoffgeschichte.* Hamburg: Christian Wegner, [1967]. Vol. 2: *Vermischte Schriften und Briefe.* Hamburg: Christian Wegner, 1971. Vols. 3 and 4 announced.

Meinerts, Hans Jürgen, ed. *Sämtliche Werke nebst Briefen und anderen Dokumenten.* Gütersloh: S. Mohn, 1963.
Müller-Seidel, Walter, ed. *Woyzeck* and *Leonce und Lena.* In *Klassische Deutsche Dichtung.* Edited by Fritz Martini and Walter Müller-Seidel. Vol. 15: *Bürgerliches Trauerspiel und soziales Drama,* pp. 270-315; Vol. 17: *Lustspiele,* pp. 507-539. Freiburg i. Br.: Herder, 1964.
Witkowski, Georg, ed. *Georg Büchner. Woyzeck: Nach den Handschriften des Dichters.* Leipzig: Insel, 1920.

Selected Translations

Hamburger, Michael. *Georg Büchner: Leonce and Lena, Lenz, Woyzeck.* Chicago: University of Chicago Press, 1972.
Hoffmann, Theodore. *Woyzeck.* Vol. 1: *The Modern Theatre.* Edited by Eric Bentley. Garden City, New York: Doubleday, 1955.
Mueller, Carl Richard. *Georg Büchner: Complete Plays and Prose.* New York: Hill & Wang, 1963.
Price, Victor. *The Plays of Georg Büchner.* London: Oxford University Press, 1971.
Schmidt, Henry J. *Georg Büchner: Woyzeck.* New York: Avon, 1969.
— — —. *Georg Büchner: Danton's Death.* New York: Avon, 1971.

Books and Articles

While far from complete, the following list contains most of the important contributions to Büchner scholarship and all books and articles referred to in the text.

Abel, Lionel, ed. *Moderns on Tragedy.* New York: Fawcett, 1967.
Abrams, M. H. *The Mirror and the Lamp: Romantic Theory and the Critical Tradition.* 1953. Rpt. New York: Norton, 1958.
— — —. *Natural Supernaturalism: Tradition and Revolution in Romantic Literature.* New York: Norton, 1971.
Abutille, Mario Carlo. *Angst und Zynismus bei Georg Büchner.* Basler Studien zur deutschen Sprache und Literatur, no. 40. Berne: Francke Verlag, 1969.
Anton, Herbert. "Die 'mimische Manier' in Büchners *Leonce und Lena.*" In *Das deutsche Lustspiel,* 1:225-242. Edited by Hans Steffens. Göttingen: Vandenhoeck und Ruprecht, 1968.
Aristotle. *Poetics.*
Artaud, Antonin. *The Theater and Its Double.* New York: Grove Press, 1958.
Auger-Duvignaud, Jean. *Georg Büchner: Dramaturge.* Paris: L'Arche, 1954.
Bach, Anneliese. "Das dramatische Bild in Georg Büchners Tragödie 'Dantons Tod.' " In *Untersuchung und Bewahrung: Festschrift für Hermann Kunisch,* pp. 1-11. Edited by K. Lazarowics and W. Kron. Berlin: De Gruyter, 1961.
— — —. "Verantwortlichkeit und Fatalismus in Georg Büchners Drama 'Dantons Tod.' " *Wirkendes Wort* 6 (1955-1956): 217-229.
Baumann, Gerhart. *Georg Büchner: Die dramatische Ausdruckswelt.* Göttingen: Vandenhoeck und Ruprecht, 1961.

———. "Georg Büchner: 'Lenz'. Seine Struktur und der Reflex des Dramatischen." *Euphorion* 52 (1958): 153-173.

Baxandall, Lee. "Georg Büchner's 'Dantons Death.' " *Tulane Drama Review* 6 (1961-1962): 136-149.

Beacham, Richard. "Büchner's Use of Sources in *Danton's Death*." *Yale/Theatre,* vol. 3, no. 3 (1972): 45-55.

Beck, Adolf. "Unbekannte französische Quellen für 'Dantons Tod' von Georg Büchner." *Jahrbuch des Freien Deutschen Hochstifts* 23 (1963): 489-538.

Becker, Carl L. *The Heavenly City of the Eighteenth-Century Philosophers.* New Haven: Yale University Press, 1932.

Beckers, Gustav. *Georg Büchners 'Leonce und Lena'. Ein Lustspiel der Langeweile.* Heidelberg: Carl Winter, 1961.

Benn, M. B. "Anti-Pygmalion: An Apologia for Georg Büchner's Aesthetics." *Modern Language Review* 64 (1969): 597-604.

Bentley, Eric. *The Life of the Drama.* New York: Atheneum, 1965.

Bergemann, Fritz. "Der Fall Woyzeck in Wahrheit und Dichtung." *Inselschiff* 1 (1920): 242-249.

———. "Entwicklung und Stand der Georg Büchner-Forschung." *Geistige Arbeit* 4 (1937): 5-7.

———. "Georg Büchner-Schrifttum seit 1937." *Deutsche Vierteljahrsschrift* 25 (1951): 112-121.

Bergson, Henri. "Laughter." In *Comedy*, pp. 61-190. Edited by Wylie Sypher. New York: Doubleday & Co., 1956.

Blackall, Eric A. "Büchner and Alban Berg. Some Thoughts on 'Wozzeck.' " *German Quarterly* 34 (1961): 431-438.

Bornscheuer, Lothar. *Erläuterungen und Dokumente. Georg Büchner: Woyzeck.* Stuttgart: Reclam, 1972.

Buch, Wilfried. *Woyzeck. Fassungen und Wandlungen.* Dortmund, 1970.

Brunn, Walter L. von. "Georg Büchner." *Deutsche medizinische Wochenschrift,* 10 July 1964, pp. 1356-1360.

Brustein, Robert. "Büchner: Artist and Visionary." *Yale/Theatre,* vol. 3, no. 3 (1972): 4-7.

Büchner, Anton. *Die Familie Büchner. Georg Büchners Vorfahren, Eltern und Geschwister.* Darmstadt: Roether, 1963.

Büchner-Preis-Reden 1951-1971. Forward by Ernst Johann. Stuttgart: Reclam, 1972. [Contains speeches by Gottfried Benn, Ernst Kreuder, Martin Kessel, Marie Luise Kaschnitz, Karl Krolow, Erich Kästner, Max Frisch, Günther Eich, Paul Celan, Hans Erich Nossack, Wolfgang Koeppen, Hans Magnus Enzensberger, Ingeborg Bachmann, Günther Grass, Wolfgang Hildesheimer, Heinrich Böll, Golo Mann, Helmut Heissenbüttel, Thomas Bernhard, and Uwe Johnson.]

Büttner, Ludwig. *Büchners Bild vom Menschen.* Nuremberg: Verlag Hans Carl, 1967.

———. *Georg Büchner, Revolutionär und Pessimist. Ein Beitrag zur Geistesgeschichte des 19. Jahrhunderts.* Nuremberg: Verlag Hans Carl, 1948.

Burke, Kenneth. *A Grammar of Motives.* Berkeley: University of California Press, 1969.

Calderwood, James L. and Harold E. Toliver. "Introduction to Comedy." In *Perspectives on Drama*, pp. 163-176. Edited by James L. Calderwood and Harold E. Toliver. New York: Oxford University Press, 1968.

Church, Joseph. *Language and the Discovery of Reality*. New York: Vintage Books, 1966.

Cowen, Roy C. "Grabbe's *Don Juan und Faust* and Büchner's *Dantons Tod:* Epicureanism and Weltschmerz." *PMLA* 82 (1967): 342-351.

―――. "Grabbe's Napoleon, Büchner's Danton, and the Masses." *Symposium* 221 (1967): 316-323.

―――. "Identity and Conscience in Büchner's Works." *Germanic Review* 43 (1968): 258-66.

Curtis, Ernst Robert. *European Literature and the Latin Middle Ages*. New York: Harper Torchbooks, 1953.

Dam, Hermann van. "Zu Georg Büchners 'Woyzeck.' " *Akzente* 1 (1954): 82-99. (Also in Martens, ed., *Georg Büchner*, pp. 305-322.)

David, Claude. "Danton vu par Büchner." *Revue du Nord* 36 (1954): 285-290. (Also in German in Martens, ed., *Georg Büchner*, pp. 323-333.)

Diem, Eugen. *Georg Büchners Leben und Werk*. Heidelberg: Meister, 1946.

Dosenheimer, Elise. "Georg Büchner.―'Woyzeck.' " In *Das deutsche soziale Drama von Lessing bis Sternheim*, pp. 64-81. Constance: Südverlag, 1949.

Edschmid, Kasimir. "Georg Büchner. Rede zum hunderfünfzigsten Geburtstag." In *Deutsche Akademic für Sprache und Dichtung*, Jahrbuch 1963, pp. 140-149. Heidelberg: Lambert Schneider, 1964.

Elema, J. "Der verstümmelte 'Woyzeck.' " *Neophilologus* 49 (1965): 131-156.

Emrich, Wilhelm. "Georg Büchner und die moderne Literatur." In *Polemik*, pp. 131-172. Frankfurt am Main: Athenäum, 1968.

Esslin, Martin. "Naturalism in Context." *The Drama Review* 42 (1968): 67-76.

―――. *The Theatre of the Absurd*. Garden City, New York: Anchor Books, 1961.

Fechner, Jörg-Ulrich. *Der Antipetrarkismus: Studien zur Liebessatire in barocker Lyrik*. Heidelberg: C. Winter, 1966.

Fellmann, Herbert. "Georg Büchners 'Lenz.' " *Jahrbuch der Wittheit zu Bremen*, no. 7 (1963): 7-124.

Fink, Gonthier-Louis. "Léonce et Léna. Comédie et réalisme chez Büchner." *Etudes Germaniques* 16 (1961): 223-234. (Also in German in Martens, ed. *Gerog Büchner*, pp. 488-506.)

―――. "Volkslied und Verseinlage in den Dramen Georg Büchners." *Deutsche Vierteljahrsschrift* 35 (1961): 558-593. (Also in Martens, ed. *Georg Büchner*, pp. 443-487).

Fischer, Heinz. *Georg Büchner: Untersuchungen und Marginalien*. Studien zur Germanistik, Anglistik und Komparatistik, no. 14. Bonn: H. Bouvier Verlag, 1972.

Fleissner, E. M. "Revolution as Theatre: *Danton's Death* and *Marat/Sade*." *Massachusetts Review* 7 (1966): 543-556.

Forster, E. M. *Aspects of the Novel*. Middlesex, England: Pelican Books, 1962.

Frenzel, Elisabeth. "Mussets 'Lorenzaccio' ein mögliches Vorbild für 'Dantons Tod.' " *Euphorion* 58 (1964): 59-68.

Friedrich, Eva. *Georg Büchner und die französische Revolution.* Winterthur: Sailer, 1956.

Freye, Karl and Wolfgang Stammler, eds. *Briefe von und an J. M. R. Lenz.* Leipzig: Wolff, 1918.

Gilman, Richard. "Georg Büchner: History Redeemed." *Yale/ Theatre*, vol. 3, no. 3 (1972): 8-34.

— — —. *The Making of the Modern Drama: A Study of Büchner, Chekhov, Pirandello, Brecht, Beckett, Handke.* New York: Farrar, Straus & Giroux, 1974.

Gravier, Maurice. "Georg Büchner et Alfred de Musset." *Orbis Litterarum* 9 (1954): 29-44.

Greiner, Martin. "Christian Dietrich Grabbe und Georg Büchner." In *Zwischen Biedermeier und Bourgeoisie*, pp. 181-218. Leipzig: Koehler & Amelang, 1954.

Grotjahn, Martin. *Beyond Laughter: Humor and the Subconscious.* New York: McGraw-Hill, 1966.

Gundolf, Friedrich. "Georg Büchner. Ein Vortrag." In *Romantiker*, 1:375-395. Berlin-Wilmersdorf: H. Keller, 1930. (Also in Martens, ed., *Georg Büchner*, pp. 82-97.)

Guthke, Karl S. *Geschichte und Poetik der deutschen Tragikomödie.* Göttingen: Vandenhoeck und Ruprecht, 1961.

Haas, Tom. "A Director's Notes After a Performance of *Woyzeck*." *Yale/ Theatre*, vol. 3, no. 3 (1972): 91-93.

Hamburger, Michael. "Büchner." In *Reason and Energy: Studies in German Literature*, pp. 179-208. London: Routledge & Paul, 1957; New York: Grove Press, 1957.

Hardt, Ernst. *Woyzeck. Eine Tragödie von Georg Büchner.* Leipzig, |1924-1925|.

Hartwig, Gilbert F. "Georg Büchner: Nineteenth Century Avant-Garde." *The Southern Quarterly* 1 (1963): 98-128.

Hasubek, Peter. " 'Ruhe' und 'Bewegung'. Versuch einer Stilanalyse von Georg Büchners 'Lenz.' " *Germanisch-Romanische Monatsschrift* 19 (1969): 33-59.

Hauch, Eduard F. "The Reviviscence of Georg Büchner." *PMLA* 44 (1929): 892-900.

Hausenstein, Wilhelm. Introduction to *Gesammelte Werke*, by Georg Büchner. Leipzig: Insel, 1916.

Hauser, Ronald. *Georg Büchner.* Twayne World Authors Series. New York: Twayne Publishers, 1974.

— — —. "Georg Büchner's *Leonce und Lena*." *Monatshefte* 53 (1961), 338-346.

Helbig, Louis Ferdinand. *Das Geschichtsdrama Georg Büchners: Zitatprobleme und historische Wahrheit in "Dantons Tod."* Kanadische Studien zur deutschen Sprache und Literatur. Berne: Herbert Lang, 1973.

Henze, Eberhard. "Mensch oder Marionette? Gedanken zu Kleist und Büchner." *Merkur* 21 (1967): 1144-1154.

Herrmann, Hans Peter. " 'Den 20. Jänner ging Lenz durchs Gebirg'. Zur Textgestaltung von Georg Büchners nachgelassener Erzählung." *Zeitschrift für deutsche Philologie* 85 (1966): 251-267.

Heselhaus, Clemens. "Die Nemesis-Tragödie: Fiesko-Wallenstein-Demetrius." *Der Deutschunterricht* 4 (1952): 44-59.

Hildesheimer, Wolfgang. "Über Georg Büchner: Eine Rede," In *Interpretationen: James Joyce, Georg Büchner, Zwei Frankfurter Vorlesungen,* pp. 31-51. Frankfurt am Main: Insel, 1969.

Hinck, Walter. "Georg Büchner." In *Deutsche Dichter des 19. Jahrhunderts: Ihr Leben und Werk,* pp. 200-222. Edited by Benno von Wiese. Berlin: E. Schmidt Verlag, 1969.

Hirsch, E.D. *Validity in Interpretation.* New Haven: Yale University Press, 1967.

Höllerer, Walter. "Büchner. 'Dantons Tod.'" In *Das deutsche Drama vom Barock bis zur Gegenwart: Interpretationen,* 2:65-88. Edited by Benno von Wiese. Düsseldorf: August Bagel Verlag, 1958.

― ― ―. "Georg Büchner." In *Zwischen Klassik und Moderne. Lachen und Weinen in der Dichtung einer Übergangszeit,* pp. 100-142. Stuttgart: Ernst Klett Verlag, 1958.

Houseman, John. "Orsen Welles and *Danton's Death.*" *Yale/Theatre*, vol. 3, no. 3 (1972): 56-67.

Huizinga, Johan. *Homo Ludens: A Study of the Play Element in Culture.* Boston: Beacon, 1966.

Ionesco, Eugene. "Discovering the Theatre." In *Theatre in the Twentieth Century,* pp. 77-93. Edited by Robert W. Corrigan. New York: Grove Press, 1963.

Irle, Gerhard. "Büchners Lenz. Eine frühe Schizophreniestudie." In *Der psychiatrische Roman,* pp. 73-83. Stuttgart: Hippokrates, 1965.

Jansen, Josef. *Erläuterungen und Dokumente, Georg Büchner: Dantons Tod.* Stuttgart: Reclam, 1970.

Jauss, Hans Robert. *Literaturgeschichte als Provokation.* Frankfurt am Main: Suhrkamp Verlag, 1970.

Jens, Walter. "Poesie und Medizin: Gedenkrede für Georg Büchner." *Neue Rundschau* 75 (1964): 266-277.

Johann, Ernst. *Georg Büchner in Selbstzeugnissen und Bilddokumenten.* Rowohlt Monographien, no. 18. Hamburg: Rowohlt, 1958.

Kant, Immanuel. "Idee zu einer allgemeinen Geschichte in weltbürgerlicher Absicht." In *Kant's Werke,* vol. 8, pp. 15-31. Berlin: De Gruyter, 1923.

Kanzog, Klaus. "Wozzeck, Woyzeck und kein Ende: Zur Standortbestimmung der Editionsphilologie." *Deutsche Vierteljahrsschrift* 47 (1973): 420-442.

Kayser, Wolfgang. "'Grotesk! grotesk!'—Büchners Woyzeck." In *Das Groteske: Seine Darstellung in Malerei und Dichtung,* pp. 70-74. Hamburg: Rowohlt, 1960.

Kerr, Walter. *Tragedy and Comedy.* New York: Simon and Schuster, 1967.

Kierkegaard, Soren. *Fear and Trembling and The Sickness unto Death.* Garden City, New York: Doubleday, 1954.

Klotz, Volker. *Geschlossene und offene Form im Drama,* Literatur als Kunst. Munich: Hanser, 1960.

Knight, Arthur H.J. *Georg Büchner.* Oxford: Basil Blackwell, 1951.

Kobel, Erwin. *Georg Büchner. Das dichterische Werk.* Berlin: Walter de Gruyter, 1974.

Koopmann, Helmut. "'Dantons Tod' und die antike Welt. Zur Geschichts-philosophie Georg Büchners." *Zeitschrift für deutsche Philologie* 84 (1965): 22-41.

Krapp, Helmut. *Der Dialog bei Georg Büchner*, Literatur als Kunst. Darmstadt: Gentner, 1958. (Since 1959: Munich: Hanser.)

Krauss, Ingrid. "Die Erbschaft des Schopenhauer-, Büchner- und Heineschen Pessismus." In *Studien über Schopenhauer und den Pessimismus in der deutschen Literatur des 19, Jahrhunderts,* pp. 96-104. Berne: Verlag Paul Haupt, 1931.

Laing, R.D. *The Divided Self: An Existential Study in Sanity and Madness.* Harmondsworth, Middlesex: Pelican Books, 1965.

Langen, August. "Zur Geschichte des Spiegelsymbols in der deutschen Dichtung." *Germanisch-Romanische Monatsschrift* 28 (1940): 269-280.

Lehmann, Werner R. "Prolegomena zu einer historisch-kritischen Büchner Ausgabe." In *Gratulatio. Festschrift für Christian Wegner zum 70. Geburtstag,* pp. 190-225. Hamburg: Christian Wegner, 1963.

———. "Repliken: Beiträge zu einem Streitgespräch über den *Woyzeck.*" *Euphorion* 65 (1971): 58-83.

———. "Robespierre—'ein impotenter Mahomet'? Geistes- und wirkungsgeschichtliche Beglaubigung einer neuen textkritischen Lesung [in 'Dantons Tod']." *Euphorion* 57 (1963): 210-217.

———. *Textkritische Noten. Prolegomena zur Hamburger Büchner-Ausgabe.* Hamburg: Christian Wegner Verlag, 1967.

Lenz, J.M.R. "Anmerkungen übers Theater." In *Von deutscher Art und Kunst.* Vol. 6: *Irrationalismus.* Edited by Heinz Kindermann. Leipzig: Reclam, 1935.

Lindenberger, Herbert Samuel. "'Danton's Death' and the Considerations of Historical Drama." *Comparative Drama* 3 (1969): 99-109.

———. *Georg Büchner.* Carbondale: Southern Illinois University Press, 1964.

Lipmann, Heinz. *Georg Büchner und die Romantik.* Munich: Hueber Verlag, 1923.

Lukacs, Georg. "Der faschistisch verfälschte und der wirkliche Georg Büchner. Zu seinem Todestag am 19. Februar 1937." In *Deutsche Literatur in zwei Jahrhunderten,* pp. 66-88. Berlin-Spandau: Hermann Luchterhand Verlag, 1961. (Also in Martens, ed., *Georg Büchner*, pp. 197-224.)

Mackay, Barbara. "*Leonce and Lena.*" *Yale/Theatre*, vol. 3, no. 3 (1972): 68-82.

Majut, Rudolf. "Aufriss und Probleme der modernen Büchner-Forschung." *Germanisch-Romanische Monatsschrift* 17 (1929): 356-372.

———. *Lebensbühne und Marionette. Ein Beitrag zur seelengeschichtlichen Entwicklung von der Genie-Zeit bis zum Biedermeier.* Berlin: Emil Ebering, 1931.

———. *Studien um Büchner: Untersuchungen zur Geschichte der problematischen Natur.* Berlin: Emil Ebering, 1932.

Marks, Jonathan. "Jonathan Miller's *Danton's Death.*" *Yale/Theatre,* vol. 3, no. 3 (1972): 99-105.

Martens, Wolfgang. "Der Barbier in Büchners 'Woyzeck'. (Zugleich ein

Beitrag zur Motivgeschichte der Barbiersfigur)." *Zeitschrift für deutsche Philologie* 79 (1960): 361-383.

———. ed. *Georg Büchner*. Darmstadt: Wissenschaftliche Buchgesellschaft, 1965. [A collection of some of the best writings on Büchner.]

———. "Ideologie und Verzweiflung. Religiöse Motive in Büchners Revolutionsdrama." *Euphorion* 54 (1960): 83-108. (Also in Martens, ed. *Georg Büchner*, pp. 406-442.)

———. Review of *Georg Büchners 'Leonce und Lena.' Ein Lustspiel der Langeweile*, by Gustav Beckers. *Euphorion* 58 (1964), 326-334.

———. "Zum Menschenbild Georg Büchners. 'Woyzeck' und die Marionszene in 'Dantons Tod.' " *Wirkendes Wort* 8 (1957-1958): 13-20. (Also in Martens, ed., *Georg Büchner*, pp. 373-385.)

———. "Zur Karikatur in der Dichtung Büchners. (Woyzecks Hauptmann)." *Germanisch-Romanische Monatsschrift* 39, Neue Folge 8 (1958): 64-71.

Mautner, Franz Heinrich. "Wortgewebe, Sinngefüge und 'Idee' in Büchners 'Woyzeck.' " *Deutsche Vierteljahrsschrift* 35 (1961): 521-557. (Also in Martens, ed., *Georg Büchner*, pp. 507-554.)

May, Kurt. "Büchner. 'Woyzeck.' " In *Das deutsche Drama vom Barock bis zur Gegenwart: Interpretationen*, 2:89-100. Edited by Benno von Wiese. 2nd ed. Düsseldorf: August Bagel Verlag, 1962. (Also in Martens, ed., *Georg Büchner*, pp. 241-251.

Mayer, Hans. *Georg Büchner und seine Zeit*. 2nd ed. Wiesbaden: Limes Verlag, 1960.

———. *Georg Büchner, Woyzeck, Dichtung und Wirklichkeit*. Frankfurt am Main: Ullstein Bücher, 1963.

———. "Prinz Leonce und Doktor Faust. Büchners Lustspiel und die deutsche Klassik." In *Zur deutschen Klassik und Romantik*, pp. 306-314. Pfullingen: Neske, 1963.

Mayer, W. "Zum Problem des Dichters Lenz." *Archiv für Psychiatrie* 62 (1921): 889-890.

Moos, Walter. "Büchner's 'Lenz.' " *Archiv für Neurologie und und Psychiatrie* 42 (1938): 97-114.

Mühlher, Robert. "Georg Büchner und die Mythologie des Nihilismus." In *Dichtung der Krise: Mythos und Psychologie in der Dichtung des 19. und 20. Jahrhunderts*, pp. 97-145. Vienna: Verlag Herold, 1951. (Also in Martens, ed., *Georg Büchner*, pp. 252-288.)

Müller-Seidel, Walter. "Natur und Naturwissenschaft im Werk Georg Büchners." In *Festschrift für Klaus Zeigler*, pp. 205-232. Edited by E. Catholy and Winifried Hellmann. Tübingen: Niemeyer, 1968.

Neuse, Erna Kritsch. "Büchners *Lenz*. Zur Struktur der Novelle." *German Quarterly* 43 (1970): 199-209.

Nicoll, Allardyce. *The Theory of Drama*. New York: Benjamin Blom, 1966.

Novalis (Friedrich von Hardenberg). *Heinrich von Ofterdingen*. Rowohlts Klassiker der Literatur und der Wissenschaft: Deutsche Literatur, vol. 12. Munich: Rowohlt, 1963.

Olson, Elder. *The Theory of Comedy*. Bloomington: Indiana University Press, 1968.

Oppel, Horst. *Die tragische Dichtung Geog Büchners*. Stuttgart: Hempe, 1951.

————. "Stand und Aufgaben der Büchner-Forschung." *Euphorion* 49 (1955): 91-109.

Parker, John J. "Some Reflections on Georg Büchner's *Lenz* and its Principal Source, the Oberlin Record." *German Life and Letters* 21 (1967-1968): 103-111.

Paulus, Ursula. "Georg Büchners 'Woyzeck'. Eine kritische Betrachtung zu der Edition Fritz Bergemanns." *Jahrbuch der deutschen Schiller-Gesellschaft* 8 (1964): 226-246.

Peacock, Ronald. "A Note on Georg Büchner's Plays." In *The Poet in the Theatre*, pp. 181-193. New York: Hill & Wang, 1960. (Also in German in Martens, ed., *Georg Büchner*, pp. 360-372.)

Penzoldt, Günther. *Georg Büchner*. Friedrichs Dramatiker des Welttheaters, vol. 9. Velber bei Hannover: Erhard Friedrich, 1965.

Plard, Henri. "A propos de 'Leonce und Lena'. Musset et Büchner." *Etudes Germaniques* 15 (1954): 26-36. (Also in German in Martens, ed., *Georg Büchner*, pp. 289-304.)

————. "L'ennui dans 'Leonce und Lena.' " *Etudes Germanique* 17 (1962): 175-177.

————. "Soif de justice et goût de néant dans les drames de Georg Büchner." *Revue de l'Université de Bruxelles* 5 (1952-1953): 290-309.

Pongs, Hermann. "Dämonie der Leere—Büchners 'Lenz.' " In *Das Bild in der Dichtung*. Vol. 2: *Voruntersuchungen zum Symbol*, pp. 254-265. Marburg: Elwert, 1963. (Also in Martens, ed., *Georg Büchner*, pp. 138-150.)

Pütz, Heinz Peter. "Büchners 'Lenz' und seine Quelle. Bericht und Erzählung." *Zeitschrift für deutsche Philologie* 84 (1965): 1-22.

Rabe, Helmut. "Büchners 'Woyzeck'. Versuch einer Analyse der Szenenfolge." *Theater der Zeit* 15 (1960): 38-47.

Reich, Willi. *Alban Berg*. Translated by Cornelius Cardeu. Harcourt, Brace & World: New York, 1965.

Renker, Armin. *Georg Büchner und das Lustspiel der Romantik: Eine Studie über 'Leonce und Lena.'* Germanische Studien, vol. 34. Berlin: Emil Ebering, 1924.

Richards, David G. *Georg Büchners Woyzeck: Textgestaltung und Interpretation*. Bonn: H. Bouvier Verlag, 1975.

————. "Zur Textgestaltung von Georg Büchners *Woyzeck*: Anmerkungen zur Hamburger Büchner-Ausgabe, den *Woyzeck* betreffend." *Euphorion* 65 (1971): 49-57.

Roche, Reinhard. "Stilus demagogicus. Beobachtungen an Robespierres Rede im Jakobinerklub. (Georg Büchners 'Dantons Tod')." *Wirkendes Wort* 14 (1964): 244-254.

Rössing-Hager, Monika. *Wortindex zu Georg Büchner, Dichtungen und Übersetzungen*. Deutsche Wortindices, vol. 1. Berlin: De Gruyter, 1970.

Rosenthal, Erwin Theodore. "Büchners Grundgedanke: Sehnsucht nach Liebe." *Revista de Letras* 3 (1962): 201-217.

Scheuer, Erwin. *Akt und Szene in der offenen Form des Dramas, dargestellt an den Dramen Georg Büchners*. Berlin: Emil Ebering, 1929.

Schiller, Friedrich. *Sämtliche Werke: Säkular-Ausgabe*. Vol. 12. Stuttgart: J. C. Cotta'sche Buchhandlung Nachfolger, 1904.

Schlegel, Friedrich. *Prosaische Jugendschriften*. Ed. J. Minor. Vol. 2. Vienna: 1882.

Schmid, Peter. *Georg Büchner: Versuch über die tragische Existenz*. Berne: Verlag Paul Haupt, 1940.

Schmidt, Henry J. *Satire, Caricature and Perspective in the Works of Georg Büchner*. Stanford Studies in Germanics and Slavics, no. 8. The Hague: Mouton, 1970.

Schonauer, Franz. "Das Drama und die Geschichte. Versuch über Georg Büchner." *Deutsche Rundschau* 87 (1961): 533-550.

Schröder, Jürgen. *Georg Büchners 'Leonce und Lena'. Eine verkehrte Komödie*. Munich-Allach: Wilhelm Fink Verlag. 1966.

Schwarz, Egon. "Tod und Witz im Werk Büchners." *Monatshefte* 46 (1954): 213-136.

Shaw, Leroy Robert. "Symbolism of Time in Georg Büchner's 'Leonce und Lena.'" *Monatshefte* 48 (1956): 221-230.

Simon, John. "On *Danton's Death*." *Yale/Theatre*, vol. 3, no. 3 (1972): 35-44.

Spalter, Max. *Brecht's Tradition*. Baltimore: Johns Hopkins Press, 1967.

Steiner, George. *The Death of Tragedy*. New York: Hill & Wang, 1963.

Stern, Joseph Peter. "A World of Suffering: Georg Büchner." In *Re-interpretations: Seven studies in nineteenth-century German literature*, pp. 78-155. New York: Basic Books, 1964.

Strohl, Jean. *Lorenz Oken und Georg Büchner. Zwei Gestalten aus der Übergangszeit von Naturphilosophie zu Naturwissenschaft*. Zurich: Verlag der Corona, 1936.

Strudthoff, Ingeborg. *Die Rezeption Georg Büchners durch das deutsche Theater*. Theater und Drama, vol. 19. Berlin-Dahlem: Colloquium Verlag, 1957.

Szondi, Peter. "Büchner: 'Dantons Tod.'" In *Versuch über das Tragische*, pp. 103-109. Frankfurt am Main: Insel, 1961.

Thieberger, Richard. *La mort de Danton de Georg Büchner et ses sources*. Paris: Presses universitaires de France, 1953.

― ― ― . "Situation de la Büchner-Forschung (1)." *Etudes Germaniques* 23 (1968): 255-260.

― ― ― . "Situation de la Büchner-Forschung (II)." *Etudes Germaniques* 23 (1968): 405-413.

― ― ― . "Zur Eliminierung des wortes 'Masonet' in Büchners 'Danton.'" *Neophilologus* 45 (1961): 221-224.

Ullman, Bo. *Die sozialkritische Thematik im Werk Georg Büchners und ihre Entfaltung im "Woyzeck" mit einigen Bemerkungen zu der Oper Alban Bergs*. Stockholm: Almqvist und Wiksell, 1972.

― ― ― . "Georg Büchner. Textkritische Probleme." *Moderna Sprak* 64 (1970): 257-65.

Viehweg, Wolfram. *Georg Büchners "Dantons Tod" auf dem deutschen Theater*. Munich: Laokoon-Verlag, 1964.

Viëtor, Karl. "Die Quellen von Büchners Drama 'Dantons Tod.'" *Euphorion* 34 (1933): 357-379.

― ― ― . "Die Tragödie des heldischen Pessimismus. Über Büchners Drama

'Dantons Tod.' " *Deutsche Vierteljahrsschrift* 12 (1934): 173-209. (Also in Martens, ed., *Georg Büchner*, pp. 98-137.)

— — —. *Georg Büchner: Politik, Dichtung, Wissenschaft.* Berne: Francke Verlag, 1949.

— — —. *Georg Büchner als Politiker*, 2nd edition. Berne: Francke Verlag, 1950.

Völker, Ludwig. "Woyzeck und die Natur." *Revue des langues vivantes* 32 (1966): 611-632.

Waldmann, Günther. "Georg Büchners Lustspiel 'Leonce und Lena' als realistische Selbstreductio ad absurdum des Romantisch-Idealistischen." *Pädagogische Provinz* 13 (1959): 339-349.

Weiss, Walter. "Georg Büchner." In *Enttäuschter Pantheismus: Zur Weltgestaltung der Dichtung in der Restaurationszeit*, pp. 247-301. Dornbirn: Vorarlberger Verlagsanstalt, 1962.

Wellershoff, Dieter. *Literatur und Veränderung.* Munich: Deutscher Taschenbuch Verlag, 1971.

Werner, Fritz. "Georg Büchners Drama 'Dantons Tod' und das Problem der Revolution." *Die Welt als Geschichte* 12 (1952): 167-176.

Westra, Pier. *Georg Büchner dan ses rapports avec ses contemporains.* Rotterdam: Gravendyk, 1946.

White, John S. "Georg Büchner or the Suffering through the Father." *The American Imago* 9 (1952), 365-427.

Wiese, Benno von. "Georg Büchner. Die Tragödie des Nihilismus." In *Die deutsche Tragödie von Lessing bis Hebbel*, pp. 513-534. 5th ed. Hamburg: Hoffman & Campe, 1961.

— — —. "Georg Büchner, 'Lenz.' " In *Die deutsche Novelle von Goethe bis Kafka: Interpretationen*, 2: 104-126. Düsseldorf: August Bagel Verlag, 1965.

Wiles, Timothy. "*Woyzeck*, immer zu." *Yale/Theatre*, vol. 3, no. 3 (1972): 83-90.

Winkler, Hans. *Georg Büchners 'Woyzeck.'* Greifswald: Ratsbuchhandlung L. Bamberg, 1925.

INDEX

Except for the major works, Büchner's writings are listed under his name. Characters from the works are listed alphabetically at the end of the entry for the work in which they appear.